Conversations with Erica Jong

Literary Conversations Series

Peggy Whitman Prenshaw
General Editor

Conversations
with Erica Jong

Edited by
Charlotte Templin

University Press of Mississippi
Jackson

www.upress.state.ms.us

10   09   08   07   06   05   04   03   02   4   3   2   1
∞

Library of Congress Cataloging-in-Publication Data

Jong, Erica
    Conversations with Erica Jong / edited by Charlotte Templin.
        p.   cm.—(Literary conversations series)
    Includes index.
    ISBN 1-57806-509-7 (alk. paper)—ISBN 1-57806-510-0 (pbk. :
alk. paper)
    1. Jong, Erica—Interviews.   2. Authors, American—20th
century—Interviews.   I. Templin, Charlotte.   II. Title.   III.
Series.

PS3560.O56 Z63   2002
818'.5409—dc21   2002022984

British Library Cataloging-in-Publication Data available

Books by Erica Jong

Fruits & Vegetables. New York: Holt, Rinehart and Winston, 1971.

Fear of Flying. New York: Holt, Rinehart and Winston, 1973.

Half-Lives. New York: Holt, Rinehart and Winston, 1973.

Here Comes and Other Poems. New York: New American Library (Signet), 1975.

Loveroot. New York: Holt, Rinehart and Winston, 1975.

How to Save Your Own Life. New York: Holt, Rinehart and Winston, 1977.

At the Edge of the Body. New York: Holt, Rinehart and Winston, 1979.

Fanny: Being the True History of the Adventures of Fanny Hackabout-Jones. New York: New American Library (Plume), 1980.

Witches. Illus. Joseph A. Smith. New York: Harry N. Abrams, 1981.

Ordinary Miracles. New York: New American Library (Plume), 1983.

Parachutes & Kisses. New York: New American Library, 1984.

Megan's Book of Divorce: A Kid's Book for Adults as Told to Erica Jong. Illus. Freya Tanz. New York: New American Library, 1984. Republished as *Megan's Two Houses: A Story of Adjustment.* New York: Dove Kids, 1996.

Serenissima: A Novel of Venice. Boston: Houghton Mifflin, 1987. Republished as *Shylock's Daughter: A Novel of Love in Venice.* New York: HarperCollins, 1995.

Any Woman's Blues. New York: Harper & Row, 1990.

Becoming Light: New and Selected Poems. New York: HarperCollins, 1991.

Fear of Fifty: A Midlife Memoir. New York: HarperCollins, 1994.

The Devil at Large: Erica Jong on Henry Miller. New York: Random House (Turtle Bay), 1993. New York: Grove Press, 1994.

Inventing Memory: A Novel of Mothers and Daughters. New York: HarperCollins, 1997.

What Do Women Want? Bread, Roses, Sex, Power. New York: HarperCollins, 1998.

Contents

Introduction

Ever since Erica Jong burst on the literary scene in 1973 with *Fear of Flying,* she has been a lively and important voice in American letters. Cast into the role of spokesperson for her generation of women in the 1970s, she has continued to address the concerns of the American woman through the decades, while also taking on other subjects, such as Jewish identity. She has published six volumes of poetry and seven novels, as well as nonfiction works.

This collection, which contains interviews from 1973 to 2001, offers the reader the opportunity to hear the author's voice on issues raised by all these works. The voice in these interviews is a passionate voice, a witty voice, and a voice of authority on matters of literary history, the publishing industry, the patriarchal establishment, and the creative process. Each interview is reprinted in its entirety to enhance scholarly value, even though this editorial decision necessitates occasional repetitions.

Jong started her writing career as a poet, and, appropriately, this collection begins with a conversation in the *New York Quarterly* about her poetry. Her early poetry and her first novels present a woman's voice of her time—frankly sexual, more than a little rebellious but also beset by a woman's fears. Her most recent novel, *Inventing Memory: A Novel of Mothers and Daughters* focuses more explicitly on her Jewish heritage, while her most recent publication, *What Do Women Want? Bread, Roses, Sex, Power,* highlights her role as essayist and cultural critic. She made her appearance as a memoirist with *The Devil at Large,* about her friendship with Henry Miller, and *Fear of Fifty: A Midlife Memoir.*

In *Fear of Flying* Jong published a literary novel but soon found herself to be a media icon with a huge popular success on her hands. The novel sold over three million copies in the first year (and went on to sell over twelve million worldwide). The novel became one of the top ten best-selling novels of the seventies. The story of the extraordinary moment of the publication of *Fear of Flying* and its effect on the author is told in feature articles in newspapers of the time. In a *Los Angeles Times* feature story in 1974, Jong describes being pursued by magazine editors with requests for brief articles about optimism in marriage, lists of her favorite books, and other subjects.¹ Numerous other articles appeared capitalizing on Jong's celebrity. A sought-after talk show guest, Jong gained a media celebrity that became a stumbling block for many arbiters of literary reputation, who tended to think that a celebrity writer could not be a literary writer. It made no difference that in Jong's case celebrity was thrust on a writer who had embarked on a literary career. The interest in Jong as a sexual icon in the early days of her career is clear in the interview with *Playboy* magazine, where the emphasis is divided between her personal sexual life and her role as author.

Jong's fans were demanding, and she commented that she spent the first six months after the publication of *Fear of Flying* answering letters. Her disillusionment with fame is evident in a comment to Elaine Showalter and Carol Smith: "People say they love your work, but what they mean is that they want to have you, in the blood, body, and flesh." Fame is a handicap, not an asset: "As a writer I can hardly stand it. Men calling in the middle of the night with sexual propositions, people who want an hour of your time to learn to write, people who call with all kinds of rumors about how much money you're making. The envy, the hatred, the constant bullets." Jong was jarred by the problems of fame, and the topic recurs in conversations with John L. Kern and with me, but she turned to the writerly solution of using the problem of celebrity in her work. Her second novel, *How to Save Your Own Life,* deals with the situation of the celebrity-writer, and *Serenissima* (later retitled *Shylock's Daughter*) also features a celebrity protagonist. In the interview with Kern, Jong admits that "I was caught up in the confusion created by my own celebrity for about a year or so after the publication of *Fear of Flying.*"

Jong's fame was deeply marked by the notoriety associated with sex. Her experience is part of the centuries-long history of the vilification of women writing about sex and provides a modern-day example of the phenomenon. Janet Todd explains in *The Sign of Angelica: Women, Writing, and Fiction* that the writing woman was from the beginning seen as guilty of a specifically sexual impropriety.² In a conversation with Karen Burke in *Interview* magazine, Jong laments, "Our books are often criticized as if *they* were women."³ One of the issues Jong returns to a number of times is the criticism she experienced because she directly addressed sexual issues and created sexually explicit descriptions. She comments in the Showalter/Smith interview that "To a lot of men, a woman who writes about sex is basically a whore." She says to Diana Cooper-Clark: "I fear the retribution that falls on a woman who writes about sex. I fear the retribution which falls from the literary establishment. I fear the Bible-thumping Puritans who want to silence women who write about passion."

While celebrity provided visibility for Jong's work, it also had a down side. For many, Jong's depiction of female sexuality was seen as flagrantly transgressive. She was accused of deliberately writing sensational material to get readers, as she mentions to Diana Cooper-Clark. One of the most interesting issues in Jong scholarship is the tension between a popular success and a literary reputation. Jong's example suggests that the writer who has a popular success is in danger of having her work denigrated as mass culture. Received almost exclusively as a novel about women's sexuality, *Fear of Flying* came to be seen as vulgar by many reviewers. Jong was attacked, even vilified, by the literary press for her sexual fiction, and her reputation was permanently marked by the early reception of her work. In the interview with Wendy Martin, we find Jong in the position of defending her success with readers, as if such success might signal a lack of quality.

The trajectory of Jong's reputation raises interesting issues. When *Fear of Flying* appeared in hardcover, it garnered some enviable reviews from literary reviewers, including John Updike and Henry Miller, who clearly placed the novel in the category, "literature." When the paperback appeared and the novel became a huge popular success some months later, the attacks began. Reviewers such as Paul Theroux and Alfred Kazin thought Jong entirely undeserving of the attention paid to her and denounced her novel as vulgar and unliterary. Theroux wrote the review that galled Jong for decades, as we know from her references to the review that have popped in interviews and articles, including her conversation with Susie Bright in 1993. Characterizing Jong as a vulgar exhibitionist, Theroux writes in the *New Statesman,* "Erica Jong's witless heroine looms like a mammoth pudenda, as roomy as Carlsbad Caverns, luring amorous spelunkers to confusion in her plunging grottoes." Kazin, writing for *New York,* characterizes Jong as "as commonplace a mind as ever appeared on the best-seller lists, but a woman novelist who obviously speaks for all the oppressed women writers in the country."[4]

A group of conservative female reviewers also came down on Jong very sharply, accusing her of "self-pity and self-display," of writing fiction of the school of the "New Bawd," openly lewd, but also claiming to be "superior in intellect, sensitivity and perception."[5] Such treatment could well have given the aspiring woman writer pause in the 1970s, at least if she espoused the liberation movements of her time. (A woman who wrote in a more traditional way was safe from such attacks, as Jong comments several times in these interviews.) Jong's reception reveals the perils of being cast in the role of representative of cultural change. Many of Jong's early reviews project a deep uneasiness with changes that have characterized modern life, and in their indictment of modern culture they associate feminism (or what they perceive as feminism) with what they view as degenerative changes. For a number of the reviewers aggressive female sexuality and aggressive female authors are associated with a modernity that deconstructs fundamental verities: the natural "roles" of men and women and the "natural" institutions of a mythic past. They align Jong with narcissism, moral decline and the disintegration of the self.

But not all the early reviewers (and certainly not all the early readers!) were so negative. In particular women who shared Jong's values and life experience were ecstatic about the novel. Those reviewers who praise *Fear of Flying* see more artistic complexity. They see irony, comedy, and wit and make distinctions between the narrator and the author. Above all, they see the novel as addressing issues they face in their own lives: the need for sexual freedom and, importantly, the confining nature for women of the romance plot. Molly Haskell, for example, sees Jong's protagonist, Isadora, as "caught, like most of us, between the need for a mate and the need to be free."[6] Jong's famous "zipless fuck" is seen by these women as a fantasy escape from women's gendered sexual roles, not as gratuitous vulgarity. The deep interest feminists of the time had in Jong is reflected in the interview with Elaine Showalter and Carol Smith, which appeared in the *Columbia Forum,* and the interview with Rozsika Parker and Eleanor Stephens in the British feminist journal, *Spare Rib.* In the Showalter/Smith interview, there is a very serious discussion of the issues for women raised by the book, but the interview is also noteworthy for the emphasis on formal characteristics of Jong's art, including her humor, a subject ignored or not noticed by those whose main reaction was horror and dismay.

Jong's reputation has continued to be shadowed by the spectres raised by her association with huge popularity and sexual fiction. Although her books have been praised in reviews of prestigious reviewers and publications, she has gotten more than her share of vituperative, vitriolic reviews. She comments extensively in the interviews I did with her on this matter. Over the years, her work also found admirers in the academic and literary communities.[7] However, in recent years Jong's work has not as often been the subject of scholarly attention as some other contemporary writers. Among those who take a positive view of Jong's literary achievements is Lisa Maria Hogeland, who identifies Jong as one of the most significant writers of the women's novel in the 1970s. In *Feminism and Its Fictions: The Consciousness-Raising Novel and the Women's Liberation Movement,* Hogeland praises Jong for her astuteness in analyzing female sexuality within the constraints of gendered social roles. Considering *Fear of Flying* in the company of novels by such writers as Fay Weldon, Alix Kates Shulman, E. M. Broner, Margaret Atwood, Joan Didion and Mary Gordon, Hogeland praises Jong for the complexity of her literary feminism.[8]

The polarization of the responses to Jong's work is revealing, and it is to that polarization that critics and scholars should look for knowledge not only about Jong's career but also about the constitution of literary reputation and the complexities of the categories of high and low culture, especially as these relate to gender. Jong's reputation can only be understood as framed by the decades of controversy over her work. As a highly interested observer of the reception of her work, Jong provides valuable commentary on the complex dynamics of literary reputation.

It is not surprising that the interviews reprinted here often deal with Jong's role as a pioneer in writing about sex. *Fear of Flying* was not only the first novel that brought issues of female sexuality to a mass audience; it was also, according to Hogeland, "one of the most important novels about women's sexuality in the decade."[9] Jong comments to Jean W. Ross that the novel opened doors for men as well as women writers, much as Henry Miller predicted it would. Jong told Diana Cooper-Clark that the strong criticism directed against her for *Fear of Flying* was because "on a mythological level what I had said was that women can live, *women can have sex and live, by God!*" In a number of interviews, she staunchly maintains her point that women should not be silenced.

Throughout her career, Jong has continued to write about sex in a way that seems a gesture of defiance toward the cultural attitudes that denigrated her. Although she got support from impressive sources, e.g., Henry Miller, she had to draw on her own courage in her refusal to be silenced. Her response to the rampant criticism was to continue writing about sex and to talk about writing about sex—and about sex. Most recently Jong has identified herself with what is called the "pro-sex" movement, which has arisen in response to the "anti-porn" movement. In the interview with Susie Bright, Jong identifies current feminism with an anti-sex position, and dissociates herself from it.

Jong and Bright agree with what Jong has long said—that women are not so different from men.

But Jong has always wanted to be free to write about topics other than sex. She began to comment early in her career that she wanted to write about more than sex, that there are other subjects besides sexuality, as we see in the earliest interviews collected here. The association of Jong with sexual writing has as much to do with the reception of her work as with the substance of the work.

While Jong's message has often been simplified as "Sex is good," her real focus, as far as gender critique is concerned, is far more complicated. One of Jong's enduring subjects is the destructiveness of romanticism for women (obscured for many readers in their focusing on the woman's search for love and for sexual partners). Though Jong's early reviewers and interviewers may not have always recognized the importance of this theme, Jong has called it to people's attention from the earliest interviews. With the publication of her second novel, *How to Save Your Own Life,* Jong was sometimes put on the defensive by her feminist interviewers, who saw that novel as endorsing the heterosexual romance plot. Jong insisted in her comments to Rozsika Parker and Eleanor Stephens that it is possible to write about the joy of romantic relationships without saying that if "[women] are unhappy, it's because they have not found the right man."

As Jong sought to escape the category of woman-who-writes-only-about-sex, she experimented with the novel form. In her third novel, *Fanny: Being the True History of the Adventures of Fanny Hackabout-Jones,* Jong undertook the task of recreating the eighteenth-century, down to its very language, and imagining a woman counterpart to Tom Jones. A critical success from the moment of publication, *Fanny* gave a welcome boost to Jong's literary reputation. In this collection, Jong talks to Ralph Gardner and to Diana Cooper-Clark about the novel, citing Fanny as her favorite character, as well as her most radical. Jong's third novel, *Parachutes & Kisses,* featured the Isadora protagonist once again, but her fifth novel, *Serenissima,* involved extensive research on sixteenth-century Venice and introduced the innovation of time travel. Jong describes a concept of time to Jean W. Ross that is similar to the layers of time Margaret Atwood used in *Cat's Eye* in 1988: "I believe that time does not exist in the unconscious. I believe that Einsteinian physics proves that time is circular and that we can drop into it an any moment. . . . I have tried as a novelist to mirror in *Serenissima* that doubleness and tripleness of vision with which we see the world."

Any Woman's Blues, while taking up the familiar subject of a woman need-
ing to free herself from various constraints, employs a form influenced by
postmodernism. Jong explains to Steve Kemper of the *Hartford Courant* that
she toned down some of the formal innovation in *Any Woman's Blues* out of
sympathy for her readers. In her most recent novel, *Inventing Memory: A
Novel of Mothers and Daughters,* Jong experiments with a multi-generational
novel that ends in 2006. In several interviews, including the conversation
with Ralph Gardner, Jong defends an aesthetic of clarity: innovation should
be consistent with clarity and remembering the reader.

One subject that comes up in many interviews is confessional writing.
Since those who chose to denigrate Jong often called her writing confessional, Jong has thought deeply about the category "confessional writing."
As early as 1973, she tells the *New York Quarterly* that "There is no such
thing as confessional poetry. Anne Sexton gets loaded with the term and it's
absurd. It has become a put-down for women, a sexist label for women's
poetry. People who use the term are falling into the subject-matter fallacy.
Subject matter doesn't make a poem." In her interview with Wendy Martin,
she insists on the importance of personal writing by women poets that preceded her: "In poetry today, there is no woman writer who has not been
liberated, whose work has not been opened up, by the so called confessional
poets like Lowell and Plath and Sexton."

One constant in Jong's writing is her use of humor, and one of the pleasures of reading these interviews is the abundant wit. Jong explains in the
interview with Showalter and Smith how humor, as well as being her personal survival tool, functions as an important element of the personal style
she has developed. She discusses her love for the eighteenth-century satirists
in the interview with Diana Cooper-Clark, and she at times has to insist that
some of her scenes are satiric, not realistic. It may be the mark of a pioneering
work that some people do not get the humor, she implies. Jong tells Philip
Fleishman (while engaged in writing *Fanny*) that she is deeply drawn to
satire. After remarking that satire is "always a doubleness of vision," she
adds, "One of the things I would like to do even more in my work is to take
the outrageous satirical perspective."[10]

Jong came of age as a writer at the time of the first generation of second-
wave women's liberation, and then came to be identified with the issue of
women's sexual liberation. Because of her visibility, she became an icon of
feminism. From being feminism's symbol, it was a short step to feminism's
scapegoat. While the larger society blamed Jong for feminism, feminists did

not always approve of her. The interviews collected here shed light on Jong's sometimes complicated relationship to feminism. The discussions remind us that feminism is not monolithic: there are important differences between groups and individuals inside the feminist tent.

In *The World Split Open: How the Modern Women's Movement Changed America,* Ruth Rosen explains the phenomenon of "trashing" that disfigured the movement in the seventies and eighties.[11] Some women in the movement came down very hard on other women they saw as ideological "enemies." Women were trashed for many reasons: having married and borne children, having middle-class status, being too concerned with individual development, being intellectual or elitist. Rosen cites Jong as an example in her book: Jong states in *Fear of Fifty* that she was deeply hurt on several occasions by attacks from women, as when she was booed for reading poems on motherhood.

In the interviews collected here we see not trashing but evidence of some differences between feminists. Rozsika Parker and Eleanor Stephens challenge Jong on the issue of heterosexuality, reminding her that "one of the things we have to fight against is the absolute imperative to be heterosexual." Jong defends herself, insisting that the lesbian episode in *How to Save Your Own Life,* the novel under discussion with her interviewers, did not constitute an attack on lesbianism. In a conversation with Philip Fleishman, she defends the lesbian episode, saying that "everything's fair game for satire."[12] In the interview with Wendy Martin, Jong mentions her impatience with feminists who think that the purpose of literature is to provide role models. In conversation with me, she recounts her differences with ideological feminists and lesbian separatists. Jong tells Viveka Vogel that she felt more silenced by the women who attacked her than she ever did by male critics. Nonetheless, Jong speaks consistently in these interviews as a woman seeking liberation from patriarchal control.

Jong is among those writers who have made significant contributions to both poetry and the novel. Her comments on the poet's craft reveal a confident and dedicated poet. Her comments on the strategies for writing poetry are useful for anyone who wants to understand the creation of poetry. In the interview in the *New York Quarterly,* she offers a list of the distinguishing characteristics of a poet: "a gift for language, an ability to see into the heart of things, and an ability to deal with important unconscious material." Of particular interest are her comments on the Muse, in which she says she really believes, at least as a way to talk about the sources of poetry. Her discussion of poetry draws her most deeply into the subject of the origins of creativity. She identifies self-consciousness as the enemy of art several times in these interviews.

In the last interview, conducted in 1999 and 2001, we see Jong looking back on a career of nearly thirty years as a published writer. Jong is still an active imaginative writer and cultural critic and author of non-fiction essays, and her comments on literature and culture are as passionate as they were in the early interviews. The interviews published here offer fascinating glimpses of the person behind the works. They allow the scholar and the general reader to hear Jong tell her own story, and they provide insights that can be brought to the reading of her works.

Notes

1. Jane Wilson, *Los Angeles Times,* 24 November 1974, 1, 8–10.

2. Janet Todd, *The Sign of Angelica: Women, Writing and Fiction, 1660–1800* (New York: Columbia UP, 1989).

3. Karen Burke, "Interview with Erica Jong," *Interview,* June 1987, 95.

4. John Updike, "Jong Love," review of *Fear of Flying,* by Erica Jong, *New Yorker,* 17 December 1973, 149–51; Henry Miller and Erica Jong, "Two Writers in Praise of Rabelais and Each Other," *New York Times,* September 1994, 27; Paul Theroux, "Hapless Organ," review of *Fear of Flying,* by Erica Jong, *New Statesman,* 19 April 1974, 554; Alfred Kazin, "The Writer as Sexual Show-off; or, Making Press Agents Unnecessary," *New York,* 9 June 1975, 36–40. For a more complete discussion of the reception of Jong's work, see Charlotte Templin, *Feminism and the Politics of Literary Reputation: The Example of Erica Jong* (Lawrence: University of Kansas Press, 1995).

5. Patricia Meyer Spacks, "Fiction Chronicle," review of *Fear of Flying,* by Erica Jong, *Hudson Review,* Summer 1974, 285. Millicent Dillon, "Literature and the New Bawd," review of *Fear of Flying,* by Erica Jong, *Nation,* 22 February 1975, 219.

6. Molly Haskell, rev. of *Fear of Flying,* by Erica Jong, *Village Voice Literary Supplement,* 22 November 1973, 27.

7. See Anthony Burgess, *99 Novels: The Best in English Since 1939, A Personal Choice* (New York: Summit, 1984); Mary Anne Ferguson, "The Female Novel of Development and the Myth of Psyche," *Denver Quarterly* 17.1 (Winter 1983): 58–74; Emily Toth, "Dorothy Parker, Erica Jong, and the New Feminist Humor," *Regionalism and the Feminist Imagination* 3.2,3 (1977–78): 70–85; Nancy A. Walker, *A Very Serious Thing: Women's Humor and American Culture* (Minneapolis: University of Minnesota Press, 1988).

8. Lisa Maria Hogeland, *Feminism and Its Fictions: The Consciousness-Raising*

Novel and the Women's Liberation Movement (Philadelphia: University of Pennsylvania Press, 1998).

   9. Ibid., 61.

   10. Philip Fleishman, "Interview with Erica Jong," *Maclean's,* 21 August 1978, 4.

   11. Ruth Rosen, *The World Split Open: How the Modern Women's Movement Changed America* (New York: Viking, 2000).

   12. Fleishman, "Interview," 6.

Chronology

1942   Erica Mann, the second daughter of four daughters of Eda (née Mirsky) and Seymour Mann (formerly Weissman), is born on March 26 in New York City. Her mother is a painter, and her father is a musician/songwriter and later a businessman. The Manns live on the Upper West Side while Erica is growing up.

1947–52   EM attends Public School 87 on Seventy-seventh Street and Amsterdam Avenue in a program for gifted students.

1952–55   EM attends the Birch-Wathen School.

1955–59   EM attends the High School of Music and Art in Manhattan as an art major. She paints, writes, and edits the school paper and yearbook.

1959–63   EM attends Barnard College, majoring in writing and English literature, with a minor in Italian literature. She studies poetry with Robert Pack and literature with James Clifford. While at Barnard, she edits the college literary magazine and produces poetry programs for the Columbia campus radio station. In 1961 she studies Italian literature and language at the Sarah Lawrence College Summer Program in Florence, Italy. In 1963 she is granted the B.A. degree, *magna cum laude* and Phi Beta Kappa.

1963   EM married Michael Werthman. They live near Columbia University.

1964   Werthman suffers a mental breakdown and is hospitalized at Mt. Sinai Hospital. He eventually returns home to California. An annulment of the marriage follows.

1964–65   EM does graduate work at Columbia University, where she is a Woodrow Wilson Fellow. She teaches English at the City University of New York, including a survey of English literature from Chaucer to Pope, writing, and freshman English. She lives on the Upper West Side.

1965   EM does a master's thesis on "Women in the Poems of Alexander

Pope" and is awarded the M.A. degree. She begins work on the
Ph.D. in eighteenth-century English literature.

1966   EM marries Allan Jong, Chinese American Freudian psychiatrist.

1966–69   The Jongs go to Heidelberg, Germany, when Allan is drafted.
            They live near the 130ᵗʰ Station Hospital of the U.S. Army. Erica
            writes poems and stories; reads the work of Anne Sexton, Sylvia
            Plath and other poets; visits sites connected with the Holocaust;
            undergoes Freudian analysis in Heidelberg with Dr. Alexander
            Mitscherlich; teaches in the University of Maryland's Overseas
            Division in Hiedelberg; attempts a Nabokovian novel entitled *The
            Man Who Murdered Poets.* Her poems are published under the
            name Erica Mann in various literary magazines in the U.S.

1969–70   EJ returns to Columbia to study poetry in the School of the Arts
            with Stanley Kunitz and Mark Strand. She leaves halfway through
            the Ph.D. program in eighteenth-century literature. She teaches at
            Manhattan Community College. The Jongs live on 77th Street,
            where EJ grew up.

1970–72   EJ receives poetry awards from the American Academy of Poets,
            Poetry Magazine (Bess Hokin Prize), the Poetry Society of
            America (Alice Faye di Castagnolia Award), the Borestone Moun-
            tain Poetry Anthology, and the *New York Quarterly* (Madeline
            Sadin Award).

1971   EJ is awarded a CAPS (Creative Artists Public Service) Grant,
            given on the basis on poems and bits of *Fear of Flying,* for poetry,
            and gives poetry readings all over New York City and the state of
            New York. *Fruits & Vegetables* is published by Holt, Rhinehart
            and Winston under the name Erica Jong. EJ meets editor Aaron
            Asher.

1971–74   EJ teaches poetry workshops at the 92ⁿᵈ Street Y in Manhattan.

1973   EJ is awarded a fellowship from the National Endowment of the
            Arts for her fiction and poetry. *Fear of Flying* is published by
            Holt. *Half-Lives* is published by Holt.

1974   EJ separates from Allan Jong. She goes to California to work on
            the film script of *Fear of Flying* and options the film rights to
            Julia Phillips and Columbia Pictures. Phillips decides to direct the
            film herself. EJ loses a lawsuit to get back the rights. (The film is

not made.) She lives in Malibu with Jonathan Fast, science fiction writer. She meets Henry Miller.

1975   EJ divorces Allan Jong. She purchases her home in Weston, Connecticut.
            Loveroot is published by Holt.

1975–76   *Fear of Flying* is number one on the *New York Times* bestseller list.

1977   *How to Save Your Own Life* is published by Holt. EJ marries Jonathan Fast.

1978   Molly Jong-Fast is born on August 19.

1979   *At the Edge of the Body* is published by Holt.

1980   *Fanny: Being the True History of the Adventures of Fanny Hackabout-Jones* is published by New American Library.

1981   *Witches* is published by Abrams.

1983   *Ordinary Miracles* is published by Holt. EJ teaches at Breadloaf.

1984   *Parachutes & Kisses* and *Megan's Book of Divorce* (later retitled *Megan's Two Houses*) are published by Holt. EJ is divorced from Jonathan Fast. Fast sues EJ for custody of Molly and loses the lawsuit.

1984–88   EJ purchases a brownstone row house at Ninety-fourth Street, between Lexington and Park Avenues, in New York, where she lives with Clayton Wheat, her daughter Molly, and Molly's nanny, Margaret Kiley.

1987   *Serenissima: A Novel of Venice* is published by HarperCollins. (The novel is later retitled *Shylock's Daughter*).

1988   Signet publishes the fifteenth anniversary edition of *Fear of Flying*.

1989   EJ marries Ken Burrows, an attorney. She and Burrows purchase an apartment in Manhattan.

1990   *Any Woman's Blues* is published by HarperCollins.

1991   *Becoming Light: New and Selected Poems* is published by HarperCollins.

1991–93   EJ serves as president of the Authors Guild during the affair of

Salman Rushdie and increasing conglomeration of the book industry.

1993   *The Devil at Large: Erica Jong on Henry Miller* is published by
        Random House (and republished by Grove Press in 1994).

1994   *Fear of Fifty: A Midlife Memoir* is published by HarperCollins.

1997   *Inventing Memory: A Novel of Mothers and Daughters* is pub-
        lished by HarperCollins.

1998   *What Do Women Want? Power, Sex, Bread & Roses* is published
        by HarperCollins.

Conversations with Erica Jong

Craft Interview with Erica Jong

Mary Jane Fortunato / 1973

From the *New York Quarterly* (No. 16. 1974), 23–48. Reprinted with
permission of the *New York Quarterly.* The interview was conducted
in June 1973.

NYQ: How do you start a poem?

Erica Jong: That's a very difficult question. My way of writing has
changed considerably in the part few years. At this point, I usually get a first
line. I don't know where that first lines comes from and I don't know who
says it to me. It may be the Muse. (I really believe in the Muse, by the way.)
But the process seems to be that I get a line and write it down as quickly as
I can and generally from that I allow things to build. I follow the images one
after the other seemingly automatically. That doesn't mean that my poems
are not revised or edited, but they come in a very mysterious way. Almost by
dictation.

I didn't always write this way, however. When I was in college I wrote in
a much more premeditated manner. I would struggle from one line to the
next, poring over a rhyming dictionary, counting out the meter on my fingers.
Although I now write very freely, I'm conscious of the oral qualities of the
poetry and of the rhythm. Also, I don't let everything stand. The second draft
is written extremely critically. Most of the process consists of striking out
the crap—the bad lines.

But I can't tell you where my first line comes from. I do know that I
recognize Osip Mandelstam's description of the kind of foretrembling which
precedes writing a poem. It's a weird kind of excitement which feels somewhat like sexual tension and somewhat like anxiety. It's as if an aura exists
around you—and you know you're going to write a poem that day. The real
question of beginning is when you get the hook into the poem, and that hook
is the first line. It may not always remain the first line. It may become the last
line, or it may drop out of the poem altogether, but it's the line that starts
your imagination going.

NYQ: Do you usually finish the poem in one day or work on it for a while?

EJ: It depends. Some poems are finished in one day. Others take years.
Sometimes the process is merely a question of refining, and sometimes you

have to grow into a poem. I have a poem which is just beginning now, and I haven't the faintest idea when I'll finish it. There are two lines that really live. Two images. But they haven't grown into a poem yet.

NYQ: It's working?

EJ: It's there working, yes. I'm reminded of the motto Kafka had over his writing desk—"Wait." And it's true. You're not always conscious of working on a poem. And then it happens. It erupts like a volcano. Your imagination is working all the time in a subterranean way. And when it comes time for you to write the poem, the whole thing explodes.

NYQ: What about ideas for a novel—is it a whole section, a chapter . . . ?

EJ: *Fear of Flying* was written in such a funny way that it's difficult to describe the process. I had been working for years on sections of it and I had attempted two earlier novels that I didn't finish. I had been collecting autobiographical fragments, fantasies, character sketches, ideas. When the framing device for this book—the trip across Europe—occurred to me, I suddenly found a way to make a coherent story out of materials which had been obsessing me for quite some time.

NYQ: One of the questions we were going to ask you was about the Muse. Because you do mention her in a very specific person way sometimes.

EJ: How do you mean?

NYQ: You talk about her in a very familiar way as if you met her and she's right there beside you. Could you talk about it?

EJ: Well, I used to think that all this talk about the Muse was a lot of bullshit. But I was wrong. I'm convinced that there are powers we cannot find names for. Maybe the Muse is really the same as the collective unconscious. I don't think it matters. Maybe the Muse is one's own unconscious which connects with the collective unconscious. Or maybe the Muse is a supernatural being. But I think there are forces we have no way of scientifically codifying, and inspiration is one of them. Why is it that at a given moment in your life certain elements come together and fuse in a way that makes a poem or that allows you to write a novel you've been dreaming of for years?

NYQ: So you call it the Muse?

EJ: Yes, but that's just one of many possible terms. That quality of inspiration, that sudden chill, the thing that makes your hair stand on end . . . I don't know what else to call it. You see, I think part of being a poet is learning how to tap that secret part of yourself which connects with the communal unconscious. So you spend a lot of time imitating other people's poems. Writing on subjects that, let's say, aren't of interest to you but were of interest to the poets you admire. You're learning your craft. But what you're really learning during those years of apprenticeship is how to explore yourself. And when that happens—I've said this in the poetry seminar about a million times—when craft and the exploration of self come together, that's when you become a poet. All the stuff you produced before that was derivative apprenticeship work. And you usually know it when that point arrives.

NYQ: One of the quotations you had in your article "The Artist as Housewife" was "Everyone has talent, what is rare is the courage to follow the talent to the dark place where it leads." What has helped you the most to go into those dark places?

EJ: I had to learn to trust myself. I had to learn to trust that part of my mind which had the potential of being original. I think lots of things helped. Getting older and having more confidence in my own voice. The other thing (unfashionable as it's become) was psychoanalysis. Artists tend to be afraid of it. They think they'll lose their creativity. But what analysis teaches you is how to surrender yourself to your fantasies. How to dive down into those fantasies. If you can do it on the couch—and not all the people can do it on the couch either—then, you may learn to trust the unconscious. To follow its meandering course. Not to look for a goal. As in an analytic session where you begin meandering. "Oh, this doesn't make any sense at all. I'm saying X. I'm saying Y." And then at the end of the session you discover that it does quite make sense. It makes more sense than most "rational" discourse. There are a lot of dreadful analysts around—just as there are a lot of incompetents in any other profession. But about 2 per cent of them are artists and understand artists. I was also lucky to have a couple of teachers who knew where I was going. And who encouraged me when my poetry began to take the inner direction. Mark Strand, for example, said at one point, when I showed him my early poems, "You haven't really been fucked by poetry yet." I don't know if he would remember having used that phrase, but I've never forgotten it. Then, when I showed him the first draft of *Fruits & Vegetables,* he said, "Now you're into something! Keep with it." He recognized that I was dealing with sexuality in a way that was more daring for me and that I had begun to allow my imagination free rein. His encouragement was vital at that time.

NYQ: You mention voice in that same article. You say that the poet's main problem is to "raise a voice." How did you find your voice and how do you suggest a poet find his voice? Going into himself?

EJ: Well, I remember my gradual realization that the person I was in life and the person I was in my poems were not the same. When I wrote poetry I assumed a kind of poet role. It probably came out of some old grade school notion of what a poet is. We all have that and it somehow stands in our way. I realized that in life I was a clown, alternately very solemn and serious—and at other times, kidding around wildly. But I never had allowed that range in my work. I had always been attracted to satire, and even in my high school and college poems, I had tried to write satire. But it was a kind of formal satire. It wasn't really open and spontaneous. I had to learn how to let spontaneity into my poems.

NYQ: You speak frequently of the need for authenticity. Is the need for authenticity the need for trusting yourself?

EJ: Yes, because all you have to write out of is your own kinkiness, the idiosyncrasies of your personality, the special spectacles through which you view the world. If you censor those things out in deference to some fear of exposure, fear of what your family, your husband, your lover or your friends may think, then you're going to lose authenticity. When you write, you're not writing for an outer social world that approves or does not approve. Writing is for that inner place, that inner place in other people, too. That's what I mean by authenticity. And it's very hard to get past this obsession with trying to please. It's especially hard for women. Men are afraid, too, of course, but in women that fear of self-exposure is even more cultivated.

NYQ: Many of your poems refer to specific people who seem to be in your life. There is a poem called "Chinese Food," for example, where there are specific people by name. And in some of your recent poems you mention your mother. Do you deal with these poems that are maybe biographical in one way, maybe nonliteral in other ways—how do you deal with this issue of speaking from your voice and also other people?

EJ: I don't think that any of the people in my poems are real people in a strict biographical sense. Obviously, they are people frozen at certain moments in time. My real biographical mother is not merely like the mother in that poem. And she would be the first to say so.

I don't think that biographical question is a fair criterion by which to measure a poem. There's a wonderful quote from Jerzy Kosinski which I

used in my novel. He says that you can't have such a thing as straight autobiography or confessional writing because even if you try to write down literally what you remember, memory itself fictionalizes and orders an structures.
Even if you make a film or a tape, you have to edit it, and so doing, you put
a controlling intelligence around it. It ceases to be the same as biography.

What you're talking about in my poems is that they refer to—yes, I have
a mother—everybody has a mother—I could have written twelve other poems
about my mother in different incarnations, and I probably will as time goes
on. But I don't see the people in those poems as real people. The Chinese
food poem mentions people who were present at a given dinner. But those
people aren't really depicted. And I don't see my poems as confessional at
all. I see them as "structures made to accommodate certain feelings." (The
phrase Kosinski uses.) Obviously they come out of my life. But then all
poets' poems come out of their lives.

If the people in the poems were just people in my own life and hadn't any
universal meaning, nobody else could connect with those poems. They would
be so personal that they would mean nothing to anybody but me. That's why
I think the term "confessional poetry" is an absolute misnomer. I don't think
there is such a thing as confessional poetry.

NYQ: One term you do use is "author" in the sense of authority. What
would you say is the author's particular responsibility as an author writing
today?

EJ: When I talk about authority, what I mean is: You are the person where
the buck stops. You are responsible for what you write. You cannot write a
book in committee, nor with a certain editor, publisher or reviewer in mind.
Writing is one of the few professions left where you take all the responsibility
for what you do. It's really dangerous and ultimately destroys you as a writer
if you start thinking about responses to your work or what your audience
needs. That's what I mean by authority. And that's why I say again and again
to my poetry seminar: "Don't even listen to me. We're offering criticisms of
your poems and we're saying—'O.K., that line works, that line doesn't work.'
But if you want to ignore it, go ahead and ignore it because learning to be a
writer means learning to ignore people's advice when it's bad." You have to
reach that place in yourself where you know your own sound, your own
rhythm, your own voice. That's what it's all about. You'll find that with many
great authors of the past, their strengths and weaknesses are so intertwined
that one can't unravel them. A contemporary author like Doris Lessing is a

good example of this. She can be incredibly hard to read, even boring at times. And yet she's a great writer. It's the very heaviness of her writing, the way she works out a detailed portrait of society that makes her so good. How could an editor sit down with *The Golden Notebook* and excise passages? God knows there are sections of it that are heavy going. Yet the strengths of the book and the faults are so interwoven that editing it would be impossible. You can't make *The Golden Notebook* into an E. M. Forster or Elizabeth Bowen novel. It's a different animal. You try to refine your work as much as you can. But ultimately you have to say: "I am I. I am the author." That's what I want everyone in my seminar to learn eventually.

NYQ: You mentioned earlier some of the problems of being a woman poet. In your article "The Artist as Housewife" you said, "Being an artist of any sex is such a difficult business that it seems almost ungenerous and naive to speak of the special problems of the woman artist. . . ." What are those special problems?

EJ: There are many. Despite the fact that we've had Sappho, Emily Dickinson, Jane Austen, the Brontës, Colette, Virginia Woolf, etc., etc., etc., there is still the feeling that women's writing is a lesser class of writing, that to write about what goes on in the nursery or the bedroom is not as important as what goes on in the battlefield, that to write about relationships between men and women is not as important as writing about a moon shot. Somehow there's a feeling that what women know about is a lesser category of knowledge. It's women's fiction, women's poetry or something like that. Women are more than half the human race, and yet since the culture has always been male dominated, the things men are interested in are thought to be of greater importance than the things women are interested in. Also, there is still a tremendous condescension toward women in reviewing. Whenever people tote up the lists of the greatest writers now writing, you get the same male names over and over. Roth, Malamud, Singer, Updike . . . the same old litany. . . . You don't get Eudora, Welty, Doris Lessing, Mary McCarthy, Adrienne Rich, Anne Sexton. Why? There is a kind of patriarchal prejudice which infuses our whole culture. I think it is not always malicious on the part of men—it's often purely unconscious. The psychological reasons behind this are many. Probably womb envy—that most unrecognized phenomenon— plays a significant part. Since the majority of psychologists and anthropologists have been male, they've been reluctant to recognize it. Men have the feeling that women can create life in their bodies, therefore how dare they create art? A book I'm very interested in is *The First Sex* by Elizabeth Gould Davis. It deals with male envy of the female and its manifestations throughout different cultures.

NYQ: Do you think women writers have more difficulty getting published because of this?

EJ: It's hard to generalize because women are being published now for faddish reasons. Let's just say women don't have difficulty being published. But they do have difficulty being taken seriously as writers. Certain kinds of commercial writing are almost exclusively done by women—Gothic romances, children's books. Yet being published is quite a different thing from being accorded respect as an artist. Secondhand bookstores are strewn with books which were published and forgotten.

NYQ: You mentioned women writers. Do you find it more often that women are reviewed as women than as writers?

EJ: I've never seen a review of a woman writer in which her sex was not mentioned in some way. And frequently reviewers do things like comment on appearance. Carolyn Kizer was reviewed (I think in *Time* or *Newsweek*) as "the Mae West of the poetry world" or some crap like that. There are many good looking male poets, and people don't go around saying, "Isn't W. S. Merwin a cutie?" I mean, he's very handsome. Richard Wilbur is very handsome. Mark Strand is very handsome. I hope I haven't left anybody out. But people don't talk about that in reviews of men. With women they always talk about it. And if a woman's ugly, they harp on that too. Did you see that reference to Gertrude Stein's "fat ankles" in the *Times* a few weeks ago? It's as if you're a piece of meat. Besides condescension and not being taken seriously, there's that awful category of "woman poet." Women's conflicts—as if they weren't applicable to all of us.

NYQ: Now when you go into your workroom and begin to work, and you're a poet and also a woman, what special kind of traps to you have to look out for because of this scene in terms of your craft? In terms of your voice?

EJ: As I said in the "Artist as Housewife" article, I went for a long time not dealing with my feelings about being a woman, because I had never really seen it done before. In college I read Auden, Yeats and Eliot, and imitated a male voice. I didn't think of it as a male voice, I thought of it as a poet's voice, but it didn't deal with the things that I wanted to deal with. Perhaps the reason Sylvia Plath as so important to my generation of young women was that she wrote about being a woman and she wrote about its negative side. She dealt with birth, menstruation—all the things that male poets don't deal with. So she liberated us. Now I think we can go on beyond that. We don't always have to write about female rage.

NYQ: Do you have any work habits? In *Fear of Flying,* Isadora writes in the nude. Do you have work habits like this?

EJ: I don't always write in the nude. Anyway, that's not a work habit.

NYQ: Do you have any—certain papers—in longhand?

EJ: I write in longhand and I write very fast. I like to have a pen that flows rapidly because when the words start coming they come so fast that my handwriting is virtually illegible. I can't compose on a typewriter, although my second draft is typed. It gets pasted into my notebook side by side with the scrawled first draft and I refine it from there.

NYQ: Do you keep a journal?

EJ: I don't really have time, though I would love to. I've kept journals at many times in my life, starting from when I was about thirteen or fourteen. But it's boring and contrived to keep a journal every day. Better to write as the mood strikes. But I don't even have time to do that except on rare occasions. Writing a novel, writing poems, writing letters to many correspondents, trying to keep notes on poems that come to mind—there just isn't time to keep a journal. Also you use up the energy that might go into poems.

NYQ: Do you write every day—your poems, your novel. Do you write at a set time?

EJ: Writing a novel is a very tough discipline. Poems can be written in spurts, irregularly. I sometimes write ten poems at once. But of those ten, perhaps one third will eventually be published. With a novel it's a whole different thing. You sit down every morning and push that pen across the page, and you have to get from one point to another. You know that you have to move your character to a certain city and out again and you must do it that day whether you feel like it or not. You don't always start out inspired, but you work your way into the scene, things start happening. You begin pushing that pen along, and then maybe after two hours you're really going. Things you hadn't expected are happening on the page. There's such a hell of a lot of sheer plugging. Sometimes you write chapters and chapters and wind up discarding them. But you plod along day after day. You have to get up every morning at eight (or whenever) and sit down for at least three or four hours.

By the way, I think that you can be a writer with four hours a day to write. Although you may need two hours of warm-up time before, and two hours of wind-down time afterward.

NYQ: We were talking about serving your apprenticeship as a poet and becoming a poet.

EJ: There was something I wanted to add about that. You have to find that place in yourself where you have great control, yet great freedom. Control over your craft so it's almost automatic. And at the same time great freedom to deal with unconscious material. That's the point at which you become a poet. Both things are not always operating at optimum pitch, however. You may sit down in the morning and feel you're going to write a poem, but the poem you produce may be just a warm-up for some other unwritten poem.

NYQ: Do you see special exercises like free association exercises or games to get you going?

EJ: No, I don't, but sometimes I read.

NYQ: Which poets?

EJ: Lately I've been reading a lot of Neruda. God help me for saying that. Every time you mention a name in an interview, you get haunted by that name from then on. Critics will clobber me with "influenced by Neruda"— but the reason I read him is that he shows me the possibilities of the imagination. I love the way he associates from one image to the next. It gets my mind going. But when I write, I write poems very different from the ones I've been reading. I may read a poem by Neruda that deals with death. But that doesn't mean I'm going to write a poem about death.

NYQ: What do you do when you are plunging under water and you hit a block, when you can't write any more; when the poem doesn't mesh and when you sense it's a block rather than just being finished for that day?

EJ: You leave the poem in your notebook and come back to it eventually. Months or years later you may see it very clearly. I save all my notebooks, and from time to time when I don't know what I'm going to write, I read them over and find the first line of a poem which I started but couldn't finish and sometimes I'm able to finish it. Nothing you write is ever lost to you. At some other level your mind is working on it.

NYQ: Are there times when you can't write anything? How do you get around them?

EJ: One of the happy things about writing both prose and poetry is that you always have something to do. We have a funny idea in this country about overspecialization. Lately I've been writing poems, articles and prose fiction, and it's been a good combination for me. Obviously you're not going to be at the peak of inspiration every day. And if you're not writing poems, why should it be dishonorable to write an article?

NYQ: Then you don't have problems with blocks?

EJ: Not at the moment. God knows lots of them in the past, and may have again in the future. Knock on wood.

NYQ: In your article "The Artist as Housewife" you wrote about the willingness to finish things being a good measure as to whether one was adult or not. Could you talk about this willingness to finish work as a special problem of the artist?

EJ: I want for years not finishing anything. Because, of course, when you finish something you can be judged. My poems used to go through 360 drafts. I had poems which were rewritten so many times that I suspect it was just a way of avoiding sending them out.

NYQ: You can see it very clearly now.

EJ: When I look at some of those drafts, I realize that beyond a certain point I wasn't improving anything, I was just obsessing. I was afraid to take risks.

NYQ: Is this more of a problem with women, do you think?

EJ: It's hard to generalize, but since women are encouraged not to have responsibility for their own lives, I suppose they do have more of a problem in this respect. Of course throughout history there have always been women who didn't give in to the demand that they remain children. Nevertheless, a woman's time tends to be more fragmented. (I can just hear all the male poets I know who have office jobs screaming and yelling.) But perhaps it's not a problem of sheer time; perhaps it has more to do with not trusting yourself. Also women want to find men they admire and look up to. That's very dangerous.

NYQ: What started you writing?

EJ: I don't remember a time when I didn't write. As a kid I used to keep journals and notebooks. I wrote stories and illustrated them. I never said I wanted to be a writer, but I always wrote. Still, it was hard to make the step of saying, "I'm a writer" before I had published. I would shuffle my feet and look down at the floor. After my first book was accepted for publication, I began to think, "Gee, I'm a poet." Talk about being other-directed.

NYQ: You mentioned once that your early poems were in traditional verse form and that you came rather late to free writing. What would you say about that kind of classical training for a poet?

EJ: I think it's tremendously important. You get letters from people saying: "I love to write poetry and I have twenty-six books of poetry in my desk drawer but I never read poetry." The country is full of "poets" who have never bought a book of poetry. If every person who sends poems to magazines would just buy one slim volume of verse, poets would not be starving. I've spent years reading poetry. I went to graduate school and read ancient and modern poetry, imitated Keats, imitated Pope, imitated Browning. . . . Learning is good for a poet as long as she doesn't become a professional scholar.

NYQ: Can you write prose and poetry simultaneously?

EJ: For the first six months when I was writing my novel, I wrote poems simultaneously. But then when I got very deep into *Fear of Flying* (when I got past the 200-page point) it really took over and from that point on I couldn't write poetry. Many of the poems in *Half-Lives* were written the year before *Fruits & Vegetables* was published, and many of them were written the following year. Some of them were written during the time I was beginning the novel. But fiction takes over your life. The final section in *Fear of Flying* (the chapter where Isadora is alone in Paris, abandoned in the hotel room) nearly did me in. I felt that I was Isadora and was abandoned in that hotel room. It was ghastly. Then I spent months writing chapters which never found their way into the book at all. The ending was finally rewritten about seven times. The last chapter, which is now about six pages long, was rewritten so many times you wouldn't believe it. And I finally wound up with a minimal amount of words but just the right sort of indeterminate feeling I wanted. I had written it every other way imaginable.

NYQ: Other endings?
EJ: Yes. And I won't tell you what they are.

NYQ: Was it coincidence or were you working toward prose poem form that one of the last poems in *Half-Lives* has long prose poem sections in it?
EJ: I think I'm going to do more of that. Prose and poetry intermingled.

It didn't really have to do with my writing the novel, but I'm very interested in mixed forms. Even the novel has a few poems in it.

NYQ: You mentioned that you raised your own consciousness as an artist while your home was in Germany. (Then you mentioned just now that Paris became a locale for you.) Generally speaking, how do you feel your locale affects the way you work as a poet?

EJ: The German experience was complicated because it made me suddenly realize I was Jewish. I had been raised as an atheist by cosmopolitan parents who didn't care about religion, and living in Germany gave me a sense of being Jewish and being potentially a victim. That opened up my poetry. I wrote a whole sequence called "The Heidelberg Poems," some of which were published in the *Beloit Poetry Journal* under my maiden name. They dealt with a kind of primal terror and with being a victim of Nazism. After writing those poems, I was able to explore my own feelings and emotions in a way I hadn't before. The experience wasn't pleasant, but it was a deepening one.

NYQ: How do you find the New York locale as a place for a working poet?

EJ: I must say that I don't give a lot of importance to locale despite what I just said about Germany. At that point in my life it was important to be in touch with those feelings of terror. But I don't thing it matters where the hell you write. You write where you are. You write from your head. You don't write in Paris or London or Heidelberg. But perhaps I'm too harsh about this because I'm not a landscape poet. I write about my own inner geography.

But there are other things in New York that are very distracting. Too many parties. Too many telephone calls. Too many people. Yet when I found myself last summer at Cape Cod sitting alone for hours and listening to the ocean, trees and stuff, I would call long distance to New York because it was too quiet. I couldn't stand it. Still, I do think it's kind of phony when young people say: "I'm going off to Europe with my notebook in hand. I will be inspired by the fountains of Rome or sitting in a café in Paris." What crap. (I did it, too, of course.) You write best in a place where you're familiar and can stack papers on the floor. But beyond that, locale doesn't matter.

NYQ: When you talk about that room of your own, what do you mean particularly?

EJ: I mean a place where you can close the door, make a mess if necessary, and nobody bothers you. My mother, who is a very talented painter, never had a room of her own, had to set up her easel in the living room and put away her paints if people were coming over. That's very destructive, especially for a woman. Staking out your territory is the big definition of identity that you win within your family or with the man you live with. That in itself is a very important struggle. When you can say to the person (or people) you live with: "This is the place where I work," then part of the battle of your identity as an artist has been fought. And in a very tangible way.

NYQ: Could you comment on the question of the selfishness of the artist to demand time and space—the whole question of selfishness as a working condition?

EJ: We all suffer about this. If you want to have human relationships, it's very hard to say, "Now I am closing the door to work." But the people you live with have to be aware that you are not shutting them out and it's not a rejection of them. It's very hard to be a writer because it means taking seriously your own nightmares and daydreams. If you're a young unpublished writer and you're closing yourself in a room, neglecting other people, it seems very selfish. Almost like masturbation. But you have to believe in yourself. It helps a lot if the people you live with respect what you're doing. My husband respected my work at first more than I respected it. He'd say, "You have to work." And I'd say, "Help, let me out!"

NYQ: Like Colette.

EJ: Well, not quite. Willy locked her in a room to turn out these Claudine novels. He was exploiting her financially.

NYQ: You once suggested writing a poem from a dream and dream images. How do you feel about using dream material?

EJ: Again, that has to do with total self-surrender. But I've always found that if you try to use literal dreams in your work they're very boring. It's like waking up in the morning and trying to tell your dreams to somebody at the breakfast table. Fascinating to you, but to the other person, incredibly boring. "There was this floating apple and winged eyeball and blood." It doesn't interest anyone else. So when you use dream images in poems you have to universalize them. Like any other poetic images.

NYQ: How do you feel about the use of drugs to get into a poem?

EJ: I've never been able to do it. With pot, all I want to do is sit around and eat. I don't have any interest in writing whatsoever. Alcohol also makes me incapable of writing. Hashish is like pot—only more so. And I've never tried LSD. I tend to think that drugs are useless to writers. But that may just be because I have not been able to use them. I think when you write you need a combination of great control and great abandonment. What the drug gives you is great abandonment, but the control goes all to hell.

NYQ: What special things to you want to happen, do you think can happen in a workshop?

EJ: The best thing that happened to me when I was in a workshop at the School of the Arts was that I met a lot of other poets. They turned me on to lots of books. Also I got feedback on my work. I met people I could exchange poems with. And from time to time somebody would say something that made me think hard. I don't think a workshop teaches you how to be a writer, but it serves its purpose in indirect ways.

NYQ: What assignments do you find helpful for beginning writers, thinking over your own workshops?

EJ: That's hard. Some students come to you with too much freedom. They cannot censor themselves at all. For those you have to stress craft. Other students come to you so hung up on craft that they have absolutely no freedom. For them you stress freedom. What works for one student doesn't work for another. So to say something in an interview like: "Craft is the most important thing" is misleading.

NYQ: Did the workshops help you in your own writing?

EJ: Yes. But that was because I went around a lot and worked with different poets. It's dangerous to have only one mentor. What you'll do is pick up all that poet's prejudices and imitate them. It's much better to study with a variety of people.

But the most important education you get is on your own. It's like what Rilke said in *Letters to a Young Poet:* "There's only one way—go in to yourself." You learn in solitude from reading other writers. And from writing and writing and writing. A workshop can accelerate that process, but the basic learning you do is alone.

NYQ: You've run workshops for high school students and for adults. What do you find happening in the two age groups when you get started?

EJ: It's really not all that different except that (as you'd expect) a high school student is less sophisticated. I honestly think it's a rare high school student who has her or his own voice. You must have a certain amount of maturity to be a poet. Seldom do sixteen-year-olds know themselves well enough. You can work a lot with students at that level, but it's really preparatory work. I go into shock when I see a South American poet with a first book at the age of nineteen. In North America we tend to have a prolonged adolescence. We're more likely to publish around the age of thirty. I think it was Neruda's *Twenty Poems of Love and a Song of Despair* which was published when he was nineteen or twenty. But in South America they tend to grow up faster than we do. It must be the heat.

NYQ: It may have to do with the competitiveness of the publishing business.

EJ: I don't know anything about publishing in South America. But I do know from my experience with other writers that most North Americans don't come into their maturity until they are at least twenty-five. I hate making generalizations like that because I can see people writing it down and saying—Ah, until I'm twenty-five . . . There are always millions of exceptions.

I used to sit around reading books and comforting myself. Virginia Woolf didn't publish her first book till she was past thirty. Katherine Anne Porter was thirty-three when she published her first short story. I would pore over such facts. If I had known someone in high school or college and saw something published by him before I was published, it threw me into an envious rage. Being unpublished is so painful.

NYQ: How do you feel about publishing? Do you feel it's important for a poet to be published?

EJ: Obviously if you write, you want to communicate with other people. To say that you don't is phony. But I'm not sure that publication always reflects quality. Magazines buy poems for very strange reasons. And for a young poet to determine whether or not his work is successful, dependent on whether or not he gets published, is a very dangerous business. I think the best poems in my first book never got taken by magazines. My name was unknown, so nobody cared. Also, many of them were long, and lots of magazines use poems as fillers.

NYQ: What about sending out?

EJ: Yes, I think it's helpful to send work out depending on what kind of reaction you have when it's rejected. If you take that as a final judgment, it's dangerous. But if you do it in a kind of lighthearted way (who does it in a lighthearted way? Nobody!) it's okay. You must realize that people who ac-cept or reject your poems are not always right.

NYQ: You can be affected by the recognition after publication.

EJ: I was helped by the freedom it gave me. You see, I was one of these people who was very hung up. I had all kinds of blocks and problems and didn't believe I was a poet, so when people began saying to me, "Hey, you really can write," it gave me a lot more confidence and it made writing easier. But this is tremendously individual. I think for somebody else, it might be ruination. I am very self-critical and don't publish everything I write. I some-times get requests from little magazines which say: "Send us anything you have." And my theory is I'm not going to publish anything I have. If I publish a poem I want it to be something I care about.

NYQ: What about poetry readings? How do they affect your own writing?
EJ: They've made me very aware of the rhythms of my poetry.

NYQ: Would you rather have your poetry read on a page or heard as a poem?
EJ: Both. I like people to hear me read because I think that they under-stand the poetry better. When I read, I feel I'm giving life to the poem.

NYQ: Does this desire to have your poetry read influence some of the forms you use like the list poems or the poems where a certain word or phrase is repeated?
EJ: No, it isn't premeditated. I do think my poetry has a kind of sound quality. Very often it uses repetition. But I think that poetry by nature is a form brought alive by the human voice.

NYQ: Could you comment on what you think poetry is?
EJ: It's voice music. Ancient poetry was all produced for that purpose. And that's still a very strong tradition. I don't think it was produced by the "reading scene" of the late sixties and early seventies. This was the ancient function of poetry. We haven't created a tradition—we've just rediscovered it. There was a period in American poetry in the forties and fifties when verse was very difficult, involuted, and meant to be studied and read on the page. That was partly the influence of the New Criticism. Since tight academic verse was being written by a certain segment of American poets, those of us who went to college at the time thought that to be the nature of poetry. On the contrary, that period was actually rather aberrant. Poetry has more often

been a spoken thing than a difficult metaphysical puzzle. When I write, I always hear the voice in my head. I'm baffled that there is even a question about it.

Still, since we're into definitions of poetry, I think I ought to add that condensation is essential. Images are important to me because the image is a kind of emotional shorthand. Poetic language must be rhythmic, fresh, interesting language, but it must also be condensed and pack a lot of meaning into a little space.

NYQ: Are there any contemporary poets that you feel particularly close to?

EJ: I could name them but then the people I hadn't named would wonder why I hadn't named them and it would only be because they hadn't popped into my head. There are so many.

NYQ: Do you think there are many good poets around?

EJ: I think we're living at a time of great renaissance for poets.

NYQ: You mentioned once that when you were a beginning poet it helped to get together with small groups of poets and read work in progress. Do you continue to do that?

EJ: I have a number of friends who are writers and who read my work. There were specific people who were very important to me when I was putting together my first book. I used to get together with Norma Klein and Rosellen Brown and Patricia Goedicke. I think it's very important to find friends whose prejudices you know. And who care about you and your work and will be honest with you. You must share enough values with them so that you can trust each other. Finding such friends might be the most important thing a young poet does. You need a critic, but it can't be just *anybody.* The idea of sending your work to a stranger is perhaps not such a good idea. You need somebody whose prejudices you know.

NYQ: There must be a need for criticism. So many manuscripts came in to the *Quarterly* with requests for criticism.

EJ: Yes, and it's so hard to honor such a request because you don't know the person. And often you don't know what kind of psychological problems are going on behind the request. It's not as simple as it looks. If you write a critical letter to somebody, you may absolutely destroy that person. Or make him furious.

NYQ: Do you get manuscripts from strangers?

EJ: Yes. Everybody does. It's just impossible to deal with. You don't know how this person is going to react to what you say or what you may be stirring up.

NYQ: Do you have a favorite poem?

EJ: How can you have a favorite poem? Your favorite poem is always the one you just wrote. The others are not quite real to you. I read *Half-Lives* now (those poems were finished about a year ago and other people tell me they're enjoying them), but I can't enjoy them. They seem very remote from me now.

NYQ: What will your next book of poems be like?

EJ: It's too early to tell. I think I will do some more combinations of prose and poetry like "From the Country of Regrets." Overlapping of forms. I'm also working on a long poem which looks like it might become a self-portrait in verse. I'm writing on very traditional subjects again and poems that rhyme occasionally. I'm writing a poem to Keats and a poem to the moon and a poem to spring. After all the wild stuff in my first two books, here I am writing poems to Keats and to spring.

NYQ: You've spoken about the frustration of writing from the point of view of a woman. Did you get to the point where you felt trapped by your subject matter?

EJ: It took me a long time to break through to the freedom of writing out of a woman's voice, and then it seemed to be *all* I was writing about. Now I want to go beyond that. Sexuality is an important part of life, and sometimes it seems to be *all* of life. But there *are* other subjects. One tends to become impatient with oneself and doesn't want to repeat the things one has learned.

NYQ: That doesn't mean you won't come back to it.

EJ: I don't know. I don't have any program, I just sit down and write. When I have enough poems, I'll see if they make a book. I didn't realize that *Half-Lives* was a book which dealt with fulfillment and emptiness until I began putting the poems together. Then it became apparent to me that I had subterranean rivers of imagery in those poems. Certain themes repeated themselves and I saw that a lot of the poems dealt with emptiness, wholeness, halfness and so on. And a book began to come together. So I arranged the sections the way they naturally fell. I can't tell you what the third book will be "about" until I see what poems accumulate. But I am quite sure that at certain periods in your life you deal with certain themes; and if you grow, those themes have to change.

NYQ: We wanted to ask you some questions about translation. Have any of your poems been translated into other languages? And then, do you ever do translations? Do you read poetry in foreign languages?

EJ: I don't read poetry in foreign languages. Although I know some foreign languages tolerably in a kind of school way, and used to be able to speak some of them when I lived in the countries where they were spoken, I don't really know any language well enough to translate. I suppose I don't try translation because I write prose when I'm not writing poetry.

NYQ: When you speak of translations as the kind of thing poets can do, what recommendations would you make to a young poet about choosing something in a related field like translations or teaching or something entirely different to be a way of surviving economically while he struggles?

EJ: I think the best thing for a young poet is to grow up in Latin America. And to be made a diplomat.

NYQ: Like a Neruda.

EJ: We don't have ways of rewarding our poets like that. I don't know what a poet can do to survive. Everything you think of has terrible disadvantages. If you're a college teacher you're always up to your neck in bad student writing. If you're an editor you get so weary of books being thrust at you that the printed word almost loses its force. Advertising is not the most joyous profession. (I know poets who do all these things.) Maybe the best "profession" for a poet is to be born very wealthy. When I was in graduate school, I was told to get my Ph.D. in English and to use my summers to write. I found that getting a Ph.D. in English was not conducive to writing at all.

NYQ: How do you feel about confessional poetry?

EJ: Who the hell was it who invented that dumb term? There is no such *thing* as confessional poetry. Anne Sexton gets loaded with the term and it's absurd. It has become a putdown term for women, a sexist label for women's poetry. People who use the term are falling into the subject-matter fallacy. Subject matter doesn't make a poem. And so a critic who uses that term is showing his total ignorance of what poetry is about.

There is this tendency to think that if you could only find the magic way, then you could become a poet. "Tell me how to become a poet. Tell me what to do." Is there a given subject that makes you a poet? Well, that's ridiculous.

What makes you a poet is a gift for language, an ability to see into the heart of things, and an ability to deal with important unconscious material. When all those things come together, you're a poet. But there isn't one little gimmick that makes you a poet. There isn't any formula for it.

NYQ: In general, modern poetry requires (underline one): more vegetables, less vegetables, all of the above, none of the above.
EJ: The answer is: All of the above.

NYQ: That gets into your whole minimal vs. maximal poetry. You want everything.
EJ: I do want to get everything into my poetry. I want to get the whole world in. Colette had a term for it. She said that she wanted the "impure." Life was impure and that was what she wanted in her art—all the junk and jumble of things. Wallace Stevens also uses the image of a man on a dump: the poet—the man sitting on the dump. Life is full of all kinds of wonderful crap. Splendid confusion. Poetry should be able to take it all in.

NYQ: What do you think of interviews?
EJ: You always read them and say, "Oh, no. That's not me." No matter how candid you are, you *hate* the person you seem to be. But I understand the impulse to get a person down on paper. I'm reading my novel in galleys now and thinking: "Who wrote this book? What kind of shit is this?" And I'm thinking that the only way that I'll ever get it all down is to write another book because I don't like this one any more.

NYQ: You made a statement a while ago about writing from your inner landscape. And yet you also talk about writing as a woman poet. At a point when women poets are having a renaissance, how do you see this relationship between writing from this inner landscape and writing as who you are quite apart from where you live and the time you live in? And also being alive in a moment when there are lots of forces—psychoanalysis, the women's movement, moving down to the end of the century, and that kind of thing.
EJ: What should I answer first? One question at a time . . . Actually, I don't think those things conflict. If you're writing about your inner landscape you're writing about that inner landscape as female. It's female first and then beyond that it's human. The two things don't cancel each other out. It's just a question of how you get there. Of course, you're affected by the movements of your time, but not in a direct way. Look—I was not living in the United States between 1966 and 1969—which was the explosion of the hippie sub-

culture, the flower children, the student revolutionaries—and yet there were many people who on reading *Fruits & Vegetables* saw me as a sort of flower child of that generation. If you're a poet, you *do* have your navel plugged in to the *zeitgeist* and you *are* tuned in to the currents of your time. And not in a literal, obvious way. But your antennae are working. You don't plan it.

NYQ: A completely different question that we didn't ask you is if there are any reference works on the craft of poetry for students to read or that you particularly love yourself.

EJ: You know the books I've recommended for my seminar. And some of the other books I find really indispensable are: *The Glass House,* Allan Seager's biography of Theodore Roethke; Rilke's *Letters to a Young Poet:* Keats's letters; Mandelstam's *Hope Against Hope* (which shows you what it's like for a poet in a totalitarian country); books on mythology like *The Golden Bough* or *Women's Mysteries* or *The Great Mother.* I would certainly recommend *The Book of the It,* a book that really loosens up the imagination. I would very much recommend Theodore Roethke's *Straw for the Fire,* Virginia Woolf's *Writer's Notebook,* Collette's *Earthly Paradise.* Those are not books strictly speaking on the craft of writing, but I don't think you're going to learn much about poetry from reading about iambic pentameter, spondees, trochees and things like that. If that's what you're thinking of—a handbook. (There are many good handbooks of poetry. There's Untermeyer's *The Pursuit Of Poetry,* which is very complete and good.) But for the most part you learn to be a poet (as Rilke says) by going into yourself and by reading lots of other writers. I think I once told you that when I began writing free verse, I read and reread Denise Levertov's books. I figured that *she* knew where to break a line. Her white spaces on the page *meant* something. So I reread and reread her books trying to figure out where she broke her lines and why. I might have gone to William Carlos Williams too, because that was where she learned. You learn to write by reading the poets you love over and over and trying to figure out what they're doing and why they're doing it. You read Galway Kinnell's *Book of the Nightmares* and you see the way it interweaves certain images throughout the book. Study the poets you love. Read them again and again. That's how you learn to be a poet. Unfortunately though, talent is something you're born with. And that's not very democratic. A gift for language is essential. So is a feeling for the rhythms of prose and poetry. The other gift is stamina—that willingness to *do* it and *do* it and *do* it. I don't know where you get that. I knew many people in college who had plenty of talent but never became writers. They gave up. A good portion of the struggle is just that willingness to keep on doing it. Ultimately, I would say I write because it gives me a great deal of pleasure to write. I would rather write than do almost anything else. Somebody will say to me, "Oh, you've been very productive," and the implication is that I've been disciplined and plodding. But writing is such an incredible joy and pleasure that at times it scarcely feels like work. There are also bad times, though.

NYQ: Have you ever thought of another career?

EJ: I thought of being a painter, and for years I did paint. There was a time when I wanted very much to be a doctor. At one time I thought I was going to be a college professor. And, of course, I still teach. But I think writing is the only profession which has enough surprises in store to hold me for the rest of my life. If you keep growing and changing, writing is an endless voyage of discovery. The surprises never stop. All that runs out is time.

An Interview with Erica Jong

Elaine Showalter and Carol Smith / 1974

From *The Columbia Forum* (Winter, 1975), 12–17. Conducted in Spring 1974. Reprinted with permission of Elaine Showalter and Carol Smith.

Carol Smith: Did you make significant changes in *Fear of Flying* as you were writing?

Erica Jong: There were a number of chapters, now discarded, in which Isadora had numerous dreams, fantasies, and wrote imaginary letters to people in the past. As I remember, there were about a hundred pages of despair and depression, which I later pared down considerably. I made a conscious decision to limit her depression to fewer pages, and to reassert the comic tone when she got her period and began hobbling around in a diaper. If I had not done this, the book would have been quite different, and, I think, strangely inconsistent with the time. It would have been comedy and farce as far as Paris, and despair and depression to the end, with a very gloomy and hopeless denouement. I wrote it that way, in fact, but it seemed to me not to work. And then I burrowed through a number of other drafts and revisions before I finally came out with this ending.

Elaine Showalter: Why did you call the last part of the book "A Nineteenth-Century Ending"?

Jong: You know, it's very hard to describe the writing process, because you go through all kinds of psychological changes in the writing of a novel. It's not hard to begin a novel, but it's hard to carry it through to the end, because generally it takes you more than a year to finish, and in the process you're growing and changing. You're going through psychological changes yourself, and the book becomes almost a container for all the things that are happening in your head. I'd found this considerable pull in myself to give it a conventional ending, and the various things that I thought about were: Depression—Isadora goes home in defeat. She'll crawl back to her husband, or just get in bed and lie there in the fetal position in despair, waiting passively for something to happen to her. Or she'll get killed in a car crash. I really didn't know where to take this woman who had found her independence. Or she'll get pregnant—have a baby—that would be the solution, the Anne

Roiphe ending. And I really played with all these things, which I think was a measure of where I was at the time.

ES: Did you really think seriously about her having a baby?
Jong: No, I didn't write it. It didn't get that far.

CS: You saw motherhood as a form of defeat?
Jong: I don't think that having a baby is either liberation or lack of liberation. It could be either, depending upon what your view of having a baby is, which could change in the course of your own life. I don't think that any of these things are liberation in and of themselves. But then I was considering several different endings. One is: She leaves her husband and establishes life as a single person, which is our twentieth-century shibboleth about liberation. Splitting is liberation, right? Divorce is liberation.

CS: Did you think of focusing on her work in that part?
Jong: Oh sure, work. Work: no men; identity will not be defined by men— and then I realized that really wasn't the issue at all. The issue was that she had come to depend on herself, and she knew no man was ever going to be everything to her, whether it was Adrian or Bennett. And that no marriage was going to be everything, and that the main thing was to go back to work, and to mother herself. The issue was, where was the center of her self going to be, psychically. I believe that you can be a complete person in marriage, or a complete person outside of marriage. I know any number of "liberated women" who split from their husbands and said, Now, this is it, now I'm a liberated person; but if they're not liberated, divorce doesn't make them so. So they go into a frantic frenzy of screwing everybody in sight, and they feel very independent, and then they go right into exactly the same kind of oppressive relationship with somebody else. A lot of women have objected to this ending, women who after years of conventional marriage have finally split and discovered themselves. After years in Westchester they are now going to the New School, and they say, how could you have Isadora return to her husband? They are very bothered because their sense of themselves is very conflicted.

CS: Was that a meaning of "A Nineteenth-Century Ending," then, that it appeared conventional, but was actually ironic?
Jong: The title "A Nineteenth-Century Ending" was totally ironic. I was really thinking about the nineteenth-century shibboleth that marriage solves everything. The Victorian novel always ends with marriage. In the twentieth-

century novel, divorce is the end-point, the beginning of the new life. The way we plot our novels reveals something about our world view. In the nineteenth century, novels were never written about people in old or middle age or people bearing children or people having careers. Novels were about adolescence, early adulthood, and ended with marriage. *Fear of Flying* is a picaresque novel about a young woman up to the age of 30. I could conceive of many books written about women at other stages of their lives. This is very much an under-30 novel.

ES: You don't have her ending in an airplane.

Jong: Oh, there was another ending on an airplane and many other endings. One man wrote to me and said, How clever of you to end the book in a *mikvah*. It's the bath that Orthodox women take after their period, the cleansing bath, because they've been unclean when they were menstruating. And I had never thought of that, but of course it's the new beginning, and the baptism, and there are a lot of obvious symbols, but it's also a real bath.

ES: Did you have the title first?

Jong: No. Another title was *The Misadventures of Isadora Wing*. It was conceived as a picaresque. And then for a while it was *The Ms. Adventures of Isadora Wing*—much too gimmicky, and discarded as cheap and topical. I didn't want that. And then it was called, in my notebook, *Confessing*. Then *The Confessions of Isadora Wing: The Adventures and Misadventures of Isadora Wing*. I don't remember all the titles.

CS: Did you think of flying as the essence of her independence?

Jong: Flying meant a lot of things to me. It meant sexuality, it meant independence, it meant literal flying, it meant creativity, in the way that the word "fire" was used by poets like Alexander Pope to mean sexual heat, creativity, inspiration, passion.

CS: You discussed in a letter to us the endings of some other novels you'd been reading. You mentioned *The Summer Before the Dark*—the ending, you said, is "terribly depressing and disappointing"; *A Charmed Life* by Mary McCarthy "does the unspeakable thing of bumping off the heroine in the last paragraph"; *Portnoy's Complaint* "ends with a fantasy, which seems integral to the book." You said about Saul Bellow, "Bellow's endings seemed an exception to this unsatisfactoriness and nearly always have to do with some sort of renewal or rebirth."

Jong: Yes. I always feel very fulfilled by his novels. I like the fact that his hero is always reborn at the end in some way. It's very much in accord with my sense of life. Perhaps it's a delusion that we get better and more knowledgeable as we go on through life. Maybe the lovers you have at 30 are not really better than the ones you had at 20. But somehow I have to go on believing that as I get more wrinkles I'm somehow choosing better and demanding more and wanting more out of life. If I don't believe that, then I won't go on living.

ES: Do you think that a novel ought to end with that sense of progress or knowledge gained?

Jong: Oh, I'm not going to say what a novel ought to do.

ES: Do you like novels better when they do?

Jong: Yes, that's an absolutely personal preference. I'm not going to impose my taste on Samuel Beckett if he doesn't want it, if he believes that despair and gloom and depression prevail. Every novelist will find the ending that accords with his world view.

CS: Is the unspeakable thing that Mary McCarthy does at the end of *A Charmed Life* bumping off her heroine in the last paragraph or bumping off her heroine, period?

Jong: What's unspeakable is that she kills her heroine. She doesn't know what to do with her intelligent woman. I think it bespeaks a kind of despair. Most of Doris Lessing's endings also reveal a kind of despair about the condition of women.

CS: In your poems humor sets your writing apart. It seems to be a kind of affirmation, an ability to be resilient, to distance things and to come to terms with them and see them with perspective.

Jong: Humor is my personal survival tool. And it's a survival tool in my writing, I think. You invent a form that is an expression of your own character. As you develop as a writer you try to find whatever originality you have by inventing a form that can contain whatever your spirit is as a person. I think if you can find an objective correlative for that in a writing style, then you can write in an original way. What I did in inventing this style is really to take the extremes of my own character—despair and wild hilarity—and find a form that expressed them.

CS: *Fear of Flying* begins with a comic set of present experiences and then investigates each of them in depth so that they cease to be comic. It seems to me that's a new kind of fictional balancing.

Jong: I think that we live the present through the filter of the past all the time. It was essential to me that the reader know about Isadora's past, her first marriage, her lovers, all those things that make us know her.

ES: In some ways the structure of *Fear of Flying* is like *Portnoy's Complaint.* Do you think that the voice that you use is anything like the one Roth uses? Is this *Isadora's Complaint?*

Jong: Oh, I loved that book. I thought it was Roth's best book. I think I learned something from it: the switching back and forth between past and present. I reread *Portnoy's Complaint* many times and I realized that one need not worry about leaping back and forth, that it could be very readable. His books were proof to me that it could be done.

ES: In John Updike's review for *The New Yorker,* he says *Fear of Flying* is a "lovable, delicious novel (each chapter garnished with epigraphs)." You used epigraphs from Byron, Plath, Colette, Kosinski, Dumas, Sexton, Freud, Auden, Shakespeare, Cole Porter, and Lawrence. How did you choose them?

Jong: As in my poetry books, everything sort of fell into place little by little. It became a mosaic. The quotation from *Don Juan* came to me midway through the book. I was reading Byron. Some of the epigraphs were things I had in notebooks, lines that I loved. I collect epigraphs in a commonplace book, because I like them; I like the aphorism as a literary form. My notebook is very fragmentary. I don't keep a record of every day, though there was a time in my life when I did. I just make notes and jottings, a line here, a line there, a newspaper clipping, a poem.

CS: How has writing a best-selling novel affected your life?

Jong: As a writer, I can hardly stand it. Men calling in the middle of the night with sexual propositions; people who want an hour of your time to learn to write; people who call with all kinds of rumors about how much money you're making. The envy, the hatred, the constant bullets.

ES: When the book first came out you were feeling very positive about success.

Jong: I was feeling very positive about doing something I was afraid of. I had written honestly about things I had to write about, although I was scared to death to do it. The sense of triumph was exhilarating. I felt that I was gaining territory for other women and other writers. And there was a sense of reinforcement when writers I loved-Elizabeth Janeway, John Updike—came through and said, You've done something new. But the other thing is the way people gobble you up, which has nothing to do with your personal triumph. My feeling is that most people see you as a contact, someone to be devoured, not as a person. I started out assuming that everyone was as scared as I was, as desperate and as delicate. It's just not true. Lots of people are brash and hateful and exploitative; they want to jimmy their way into your life, take you over, and eat you up. To a lot of men, a woman who writes about sex is basically a whore. That assumption is not made about men who write about sex. A man is thought to be a lusty lad; a woman who does it is a whore. I would hear rumors about who I was sleeping with. According to these rumors, everybody. At the 92nd Street Y, Anaïs Nin said she didn't want to publish the parts of her diary about sexuality because she had seen what had happened to Violette LeDuc; a woman who writes about sex gets crunched by the critics. She didn't see the point: by self-censorship women perpetuate the stereotypes. Somebody like Elizabeth Hardwick, a male-dominated critic, although brilliant, will say things like, "Women never chronicle the climbing on and the climbing off." Or say, as Helen Vendler does, that a woman's writing is narrow. But these same women never realize that they are imposing those restrictions, narrowing the range of female writing and then complaining that female writing is narrow.

CS: Has the popularity of the novel changed your working patterns?

Jong: You don't realize the extent to which you're dependent on a few hours of peace and quiet until it's taken from you. You think you don't need it. But there were days this fall and winter when the phone rang constantly, and I tried to answer, to be nice to everyone. I tried to be decent and friendly, not aloof. Also, I didn't want to become a member of the Establishment. But you can't help it. I felt eaten up alive, and I began to think about people like Janis Joplin and the astronauts. Writers in our society aren't even really famous, like astronauts or rock stars or athletes. Maybe, though, to writers celebrity is worse. You learn to be a writer by getting your antennae finely attuned, and when there's the deluge, there you are with your antennae, taking it all in.

ES: How are you managing now?

Jong: I don't answer my phone and I've stopped answering my mail. I can't ignore everything. I usually work on a schedule, but it's been interrupted by lectures and trips. But you can't complain about it to everyone, because it's what every woman thinks she wants.

ES: You start out by wanting to be responsive, and you turn into Miss Lonelyhearts.

Jong: That's the title of an article I've just written—"Ms. Lonelyhearts." It's contrary to one's work. I have to find a center within myself, and pull stuff out of it. There were times this year when I felt I might as well have ten children for all the peace and quiet I had. People say they love your work, but what they mean is that they want to have you, in the blood, body, and the flesh. If I were to say to some young writer, "The best of me is on paper. It's there for you anytime. The best thing, the most distilled, is there."—They don't want that. Essentially they're not interested in writing, they're interested in eating.

CS: Before, you felt that while you had been told everyone hated a successful woman, it wasn't true. People were attracted to you.

Jong: Both are true. People are attracted to you, but then you wonder about the system of values by which people are attracted to you. So success builds in disadvantages.

ES: Were you pleased about John Updike's review in *The New Yorker?*

Jong: It gave me a kind of credibility for which I was very grateful. I didn't agree with everything he said, but he's a writer with a moral force I admire. He knows what art is, and he doesn't confuse art with politics or influence. I'm not sure Norman Mailer knows the difference. I think Updike does. He's a writer who wants to grow and have a canon of work.

ES: Do you like his poems?

Jong: I like *Midpoint* very much, and felt a lot of things in common with it. Some of his poems are obviously light verse, and he knows it, and is unpretentious about them. Some of his poems are beautiful. I like the way he tried to use the collage, of visual and verbal effects; I think the collage is one of the major twentieth-century art forms. But basically what was so gratifying about having him praise my book is that he is a writer who sees himself in a continuity with other writers, and also sees his own work as a continuum.

ES: And you do, too? Where do you see yourself? As a poet, a novelist?

Jong: I think one's preoccupations keep coming up again and again in prose, poetry, or articles. A writer's work is joined together by certain patterns of imagery that crisscross the forms. D. H. Lawrence writes about figs in prose or poetry. I don't know where exactly I'm going next. My new poems are rather different from my old poems. I got consciously tired of writing about sexuality, men and women, and I wanted to move on to other subjects. I didn't want every poem to be about eating. I wanted to return to some of the preoccupations of my earlier work, rhyme and meter. When *Fruits & Vegetables* was published, a lot of people saw me as a flower child of the late Sixties. But at Barnard, from 1959 to 1963, I was writing sonnets and sestinas. My junior year I wrote a mock epic with rhymed and stopped couplets. I started out writing Richard Wilbur-type poetry, on all the things that were fashionable: the fountains of Rome, the Protestant graveyard in Rome, the canals in Venice, landscape poems, Villa D'Este poems, poems about Keats' house in Hampstead. For me to get from there to *Fruits & Vegetables* was an enormous leap. When people called *Fruits & Vegetables* undisciplined free verse, I laughed. It had taken me years of work to get to the point where I could write free verse. *Fruits & Vegetables* was my cry of liberation from the classics.

ES: How did you make the change?

Jong: By reading French Symbolist poets and South American surrealists, and by being in psychoanalysis. I had been writing poems about what I thought were poetic subjects, and they didn't engage my deepest feelings. People said poems were supposed to be about Unicorn Tapestries, and I thought when you wrote a poem it had to be about certain things. It was simple-minded. If someone had said, Write a poem about little Hiawatha, I would have done it. We all start out with an unconscious image of what a poem is. For Yeats it was Celtic twilight.

ES: And for you it was Richard Wilbur.

Jong: Sure. At Barnard, Robert Pack had us reading Richard Wilbur, and early May Swenson, Howard Moss, Howard Nemerov. An Allen Ginsberg book in the classroom would have been heresy. We read early Yeats, late Yeats, Eliot. Really good people, but no one would have thought of bringing Neruda, or Yves Bonnefoy. Or even Rimbaud. It was Anglophile, academic, American poetry. Maybe if I had studied with Gary Snyder I would have gotten another tradition. But I don't think it matters where you start. When I got out of college and graduate school, and I was living in Europe alone trying to teach myself how to write, in isolation from this academic world, I deliberately started expanding my education. I started doing all the things I had never done. I was very bemused by tradition. I thought you couldn't write until you could write a mock-epic. I used to read *Paradise Lost* and think I couldn't write like that. I was very intimidated by the past. So I had to go through a period of reading Neruda and French Symbolist poets and trying to make myself a twentieth-century poet. Then I moved beyond the American academic poetry on which I had been trained. I came back to some of those people later; I came back to Wallace Stevens, still loving him. And I still admire Richard Wilbur. But that wasn't the only tradition there was.

ES: Is becoming a twentieth-century poet a change of subject, rather than a change of heart? Is it to become politically engaged?

Jong: No, the way I think of it is trying to bring together the disparate elements of a fragmented universe. A collage. *The Waste Land* is a collage; Ingmar Bergman's films are collage. *Fruits & Vegetables* is a long poem written as a collage. *Country of Regret* is a collage. My new poem about Keats is a collage of Keats' letters and my meditations on them. What makes a poet modern is the attempt to bring together the dissociated sensibility. But of course I'll be writing the same poem for the rest of my life, as all poets do.

ES: What about *Half-Lives?*

Jong: The focus of that book was all the poems about obsessive sexuality. Wholes and halves, and looking for fulfillment, at least in the "Age of Exploration" section, and finding the separation could not be bridged. I can't make a system of my own poems. The whole book was about unfulfillment and emptiness, the woman looking toward merging and fusion, as a way of making up that emptiness.

ES: Who is writing fiction now that you like?

Jong: Jean Rhys. I haven't read anything as moving as *Good Morning, Midnight* for a long time. I think Doris Lessing is a genius although she bores the pants off me at times. She's so weighty and chewy; she's the George Eliot of our generation. She writes a real old-fashioned *Bildungsroman* but she's the only one around trying to do that. There are a lot of very gifted poets around, Muriel Rukeyser, Marge Piercy, Galway Kinnell. Although Marge Piercy's novel *Small Changes* was intolerably polemical. A book like *Good Morning, Midnight* tells you more about the condition of women than *Monster,* or *Small Changes.* Everything is there. In *Small Changes* you had people eating crunchy granola and saying, "If only we could get control of our bodies." Marge is a brilliant writer, but she's gone astray.

ES: What about Adrienne Rich and Anne Sexton?

Jong: Adrienne Rich's art has not been quite so invaded by her politics.

She's a more spare poet, and she very seldom lets politics interfere. Anne Sexton is confronting some scary things—the disintegration of the body, age. I feel at times that Anne Sexton suffers from playing Anne Sexton. It happened to Hemingway, somebody she admires—being stereotyped, and accepting the stereotype. Updike has resisted that—resisted becoming a star, although obviously he could be one if he wanted to be. He's chosen the anonymity he needs to be a writer. As for me, the role people want *me* to play—every male chauvinist wants to fuck a feminist.

CS: How do you see the future of feminist writing?

Jong: I think as long as women are held down economically and are dependent on men, they are going to be very angry. They'll see the limits of their experience as the trip to the gynecologist, how the obstetrician puts them down. And it's real—they are oppressed. But when you get to a state where you are controlling your own destiny, the anger diminishes, and you begin to see into the minds of the other people, and you see how men function. But you have to have freedom to do that. I can understand how women who have been, as Doris Lessing says, "semi-slaves" for centuries haven't got that empathy. They can't afford empathy. When you become a person, you can afford it. If I wrote a novel with a man as my protagonist, I know there would be many feminists who would say, "Sell-out! She has betrayed us!" But I'm now in a situation where I can empathize with men. It's not just a sell-out by the successful women. Truly, when you don't have to ask anyone for anything, you can be kinder. But most people, most women certainly, are never in that position in their lives.

ES: What changes would you like to see for women writers?

Jong: I'd like to see a lot more women in the world of writing, reviewing, teaching, so that those of us who are here aren't turned into tokens. I'd like to see a parity so we wouldn't be freaks, so that the female life-style—which is different—could be represented. *Fear of Flying* was a declaration of independence. It was my way of saying, "Okay, gang, I'm throwing off all these old shackles, and I'm declaring myself. I'm writing a novel in the language I speak inside my head, and I'm going to write about the things that are important to me." It was a counterphobic book. It would have been safer to write a trim, spare little novel. But now I'd like to go on—to write a spare little novel, or a novel with a male protagonist, if I feel I can understand one. This is a beginning. I don't want to be frozen as Isadora Wing. But America makes it hard for writers to grow.

CS: Do you recommend more tolerance from critics, or the author refusing to become a celebrity?

Jong: Both. The enterprise of art is something that is ongoing.

ES: What connections are ongoing for you? The academic?

Jong: I'm a scholar for life; it's internalized.

ES: And analysis?

Jong: I'm really closer to being a Jungian than anything else. I believe in the communal unconscious. I really believe that what motivates human beings are their dreams, their fantasies, and their mythologies. Of course, these crisscross political systems. I don't write my dreams down, because they're very boring; I try to change them. But one of the greatest experiences of my life was psychoanalysis. The crucial period for me was the first two years, in Germany, with an M.D. psychiatrist at the Sigmund Freud Institute in Frankfort, a famous writer and theorist, and a marvelous man. My consciousness became available—sometimes too available. There are certain days when I'm in a heightened state, when I know I'm going to write poetry. On a day like that, I look at the trees against the sky, and I think, the trees are piercing the sky. I feel very anxious, in a state of excitement that's almost sexual but not quite. Every object in the world seems to be animated and slightly threatening. It's like when Francis Bacon was asked about the models for his *abattoir* paintings, and he said, "I don't need models. I look at the lamb chop on my plate." All the things people say analysis won't do for women it did for me. Now, in 1974, the feminist line is that psychoanalysis will make you an oppressed woman who accepts her oppression, adjusts to her husband's bullshit, sits home, has babies, and keeps two sets of dishes. But it made me much more striving, much more independent, and more determined to be an artist.

Playboy Interview

Gretchen McNeese / 1975

From *Playboy* (September 1975), 61–78, 202. Copyright © 1975 by *Playboy*. Reprinted with permission of *Playboy*. All rights reserved.

Less than two years ago, she was known principally as a poet—one with a fondness for ampersands and startling metaphor ("& the hole in the penis/ sings to the cunt") and sassy swipes at male chauvinism ("Beware of the man who praises liberated women; he is planning to quit his job"). Her poetry sold well—for poetry. Then, late in 1973, came the publication of her first novel, *Fear of Flying*, a bawdily adulterous romp across Europe by a young woman frantically searching for sexual and emotional fulfillment, which was greeted by a chorus of rave reviews (and a gaggle of horrified ones, from critics who were turned off by the book's no-holes-barred imagery or threatened by its feminist implications). Novelist John Updike was perhaps most accurate in his prediction: *"Fear of Flying,"* he wrote in *The New Yorker*, "feels like a winner." It was. Last November, *Fear of Flying* was issued in paperback—and immediately took off like one of the jumbo jets that so terrorized its antiheroine, Isadora Wing. At last count, the Signet softcover was in its 28th printing with more than 3,500,000 copies off the presses, had been oscillating between the number-one and number-two spots on the best-seller lists for months and was the topic of heated debates at cocktail parties, consciousness-raising groups, college classrooms—and in locker rooms—throughout the country.

All of which took its author, 33-year-old Erica Jong (the J is pronounced as in John), totally by surprise. She had never expected to see the book published. (One printer, in fact, had refused to set the manuscript in type because of its considerable four-letter-word content.) Suddenly, she found herself alternately consulted as a sexual guru, solicited as a potential bedmate, sought after as a guest speaker, hailed as the most visible star in that new galaxy of liberated women writers described by *Newsweek* as "map makers of the new female consciousness," and, in effect, banned by the Smithsonian Institution. (Actually, it was Jong who, charging censorship, canceled a planned talk at the Smithsonian, after being advised she should avoid discussing sex and

36

politics. It later turned out that Smithsonian secretary S. Dillon Ripley had already directed that her scheduled appearance be quashed.)

Since becoming a public personality, Jong herself has been the subject of conflicting reports: She was in a deep depression; she was bubbling with happiness. Her marriage was on the rocks; it was stronger than ever. She was writing; she wasn't. When the dust began to clear this past spring, the public learned that Erica Jong was alive and well and living in Malibu; that she and her psychiatrist husband were divorcing; that producer Julia Phillips and Columbia pictures were planning a film version of *Fear of Flying* and that she had two books (*Loveroot*, a volume of new poems, and *Here Comes and Other Poems*, a collection of previously published Jong poems and essays, plus a literary-magazine interview) coming out in June. *Loveroot*, in fact, is a Book-of-the Month Club alternate selection this month.

Jong is the first to admit that had it not been for her novel, her poetry wouldn't be on any book-club lists. The overwhelming success of *Fear of Flying* cannot, of course, be traced entirely to the book's raunchiness. One reviewer, intrigued by the *F.O.F.* sales phenomenon, got the names of the book's female borrowers from local libraries and questioned them about its appeal. They answered, in the main, that it was a book they could relate to—often that Isadora Wing was expressing thoughts and feelings they had previously believed were theirs alone. Surprisingly enough, many male readers agreed. As Christopher Lehmann-Haupt of *The New York Times* wrote: "I can't remember ever before feeling quite so free to identify my own feelings with those of a female protagonist—which would suggest that Isadora Wing, with her unfettered yearnings for sexual satisfaction and her touching struggle for identity and self-confidence, is really more of a person than a woman."

There were minority opinions, some expressed stridently. Novelist Bill Brashler called it "a thoroughly obnoxious book. I read about 60 pages and then threw it against the wall." Militant feminists have damned Isadora for the fact that despite all her struggles toward self-assertion, she still depends on men to give her self-assurance. They call the ending of the book—when a confused Isadora returns, albeit rather tentatively, to her husband—a cop out. Its author has an answer for that one; the book was intended, she says, to be a "saga of unfulfillment."

To find out what all of the fuss is about, *Playboy* sent Senior Editor Gretchen McNeese to California to determine whether Jong is, as she herself once worried aloud, the "matron saint of adulteresses," or whether she is, as her pen-and-pun pal Louis Untermeyer, the poet, claims, "just a nice Jewish girl." McNeese's report:

"When I arrived in California, I found my subject in a dither. The concrete floor of the Malibu beach house in which she lives with writer Jonathan Fast was at the moment being jackhammered into shards, the better to afford access to an odoriferously leaking sewage-disposal pipe underneath. Writer Henry Miller, with whom Erica shares a sort of mutual-admiration society, had taken her and Jon into his home in nearby Pacific Palisades to await plumbing repairs.

"Despite it all, Erica welcomed me when I called at Miller's to pick her up. Everybody describes her as plump; I thought her round-faced and shapely. Her nearsighted, blue eyes are partly hidden by enormous, pink-tinted glasses that she pushes up into her thick shock of tawny blonde hair when she's having her picture taken. I found her soft-spoken and articulate; she talks with vitality, in well-constructed paragraphs, scarcely interrupted by the 'y' knows' and 'uhs' that clutter most people's speech.

"Our first session took place in my motel room, but by the following day, the beach house was sufficiently restored for us to meet there. It sits high on a bluff overlooking the Pacific and one wall is a wide expanse of glass; the effect is something like that of being in a wheel house of an enormous ocean-going vessel, setting sail for the Orient. In the living area, there's a jungle of philodendrons, rubber plants and other vegetation, illuminated by skylights. To one side is a kitchenette in which Erica brewed pot after pot of coffee to fuel our conversation. On the counter, awaiting a pickup game, lay a Frisbee. On the other side of the house is the bedroom, dominated by a king-size waterbed; outdoors, there is a small Jacuzzi bath.

"As we talked, we could hear the rapid tattoo of Jon's typewriter; he was completing a draft of his first novel. (He recently sold a story for a made-for-TV movie, *Everybody's Watching,* to—coincidentally—Playboy Productions.) Occasionally, he'd take a break, joining us for a joke or a sandwich or serenading us with a few strums on his banjo.

"Erica seems to attract devoted, not to say fiercely loyal, friends. One such, writer Alice Bach—whose stories for 'young adults' are as different from *Fear of Flying* as is *Little Women*—was asked by a women's magazine (which she declines to identify) to do an expose on Jong. She refused, reporting that there was nothing to expose. Another New York friend, Grace Darling—*Foreign Affairs* advertising director and the person who first brought Erica's work to the attention of publisher Holt Rinehart, & Winston—

observes: 'We all miss her terribly. It's as if the light went out when she left New York. But then, everyone who meets Erica loves her.'

"Which may well be true. It's certainly true that everyone who *hasn't* met Erica but who *has* read *Fear of Flying* wonders about the odd coincidences, if, indeed, they are coincidences, between the author and her novel's principal character, Isadora Wing. Both grew up in artistic, relatively affluent, Manhattan families. Both are Phi Beta Kappa graduates of Barnard who went on, almost, to earn doctorates in literature at Columbia. Both are blonde poets; they write, in fact, the same poetry. Both have been married twice: first to a college sweetheart who had a nervous breakdown, then to a Chinese-American child psychiatrist with a mono-syllabic surname. Just how autobiographic *is Fear of Flying*? I decided I'd ask."

Playboy: This is the question everybody's asking, so let's get it over with: How much of *Fear of Flying*'s Isadora Wing is really Erica Jong?

Jong: You mean will the real Isadora Wing stand up? Or lie down—preferably on the analyst's couch? Sure, there's a lot of me in Isadora, but a lot of characters and events in the book are totally invented. I didn't set out to write autobiography; I set out to write a satirical novel about a woman in search of her own identity, and I did not stick to the facts very closely—frequently not at all. There never was an actual odyssey across Europe, for example.

Playboy: Isadora's Chinese-American psychiatrist husband, Bennett Wing, seems to have been modeled on your own husband.

Jong: You said it, I didn't.

Playboy: But was there really an English analyst like the one with whom Isadora ran off?

Jong: Hmmmm. Well, there are any number of impotent Englishmen to choose from. The one I chose was lucky—though I don't suppose you could call him a lucky stiff. At any rate, I doubt that this character would recognize himself.

Playboy: Are the people who *did* recognize themselves in your book still speaking to you?

Jong: More than ever. People love any kind of immortality, from scratching their names on a wall to being depicted in a novel, even satirically. The friends who have been most incensed with me are those who can't hallucinate themselves into the book at all. They've complained to me, "Didn't I make *any* impression? I wasn't in that book." I've heard many guesses at each character in *Fear of Flying*, and most of them were completely wrong. They were people I'd never even met or even heard of. So I'm constantly explaining to people that what I write is an admixture of reality and fantasy, and that I mix it up as I please—to elevate it to myth, hopefully. Sometimes when I finish writing, I can't even remember what actually happened and what didn't. But I guess there are people who can't make the distinction between writing and life or between autobiography and myth.

Playboy: We've heard that you've been annoyed with people who can't make that distinction—who expect the real Erica to be an easy lay because the fictional Isadora is so openly sexual. Is that true?

Jong: Oh, yes; I found that very unnerving at first; having men sort of sidle up to me and proposition me, thinking that because I put myself on paper in a certain kind of way, I'm available to anyone who asks. I remember one night before I went to the American Booksellers convention. I asked Anne Sexton, who was a good friend, "What do I do when men come up to me on the convention floor and start saying, 'Hey, baby, I want a zipless fuck'?" And Anne said, "Thank them. Thank them and say, 'Zip up your fuck until I ask for it.'"

Playboy: The zipless fuck—a quickie with a total stranger, without even having to unzip—is Isadora's most notorious fantasy. Is it one you share?

Jong: I don't happen to be searching for ziplessness at this point in my life. I certainly *had* those fantasies, at 23 or 24 years old, of wanting anonymous sex. Or thinking I wanted it. But, of course, whenever it was offered to me, or when I would wake up in bed with someone who was unspeakably idiotic, I would think, *who needs it?* Probably the zipless fuck is better as a fantasy than as a reality.

Playboy: Fantasy or reality, the zipless fuck is a phrase you're likely to be stuck with the rest of your life.

Jong: Well, zippers are always getting stuck.

Playboy: There's even a zipper on the cover of *Fear of Flying*'s paperback edition. And a navel, which is also on the cover of your first book of poetry, *Fruits & Vegetables*. Do you have a belly-button fixation?

Jong: Do you think the publishers think of me as a navelist rather than a novelist? You should have seen the original design for the softcover edition of *Fear of Flying*. It showed a Happy Hooker-type lady sitting in the crack formed by the parted zipper, wearing a flimsy sort of Erskine Caldwell blouse and sucking her finger. She looked like a very tacky version of the *Cosmopolitan* girl, actually. The cover that was used seemed tasteful by comparison.

Playboy: But that kind of cover sells books. So does sex inside. What do you say to people who accuse you of having put sex into your novel just to sensationalize it, to boost sales?

Jong: That's the kind of easy, top-of-the-head response I get from not very thoughtful people. It is *not* the response that I get from my mail. What I get from readers very often is, "Why did they put this sexy, lurid cover on your book? Why is your book sold as a sex book? Your book is really about identity, about a woman finding herself. The sex is incidental; the sex is *part* of identity." When I was writing *Fear of Flying*, I didn't think that it would ever be published. To me, the important thing about this book was that it be honest about everything—about being Jewish in Germany, about wetting your pants when you get sexually excited, about all areas of life. That's the theme that runs all through my work, and sex is just one tiny part of that. It isn't all of life, but it *is* a part of life, and I always find it astounding when people concentrate only on the sex in my work.

Playboy: But it *has* been promoted as sexy, hasn't it?

Jong: Oh, the logistics of mass-market publishing are such that a paperback publisher, like a movie company, needs a handle to advertise something by. New American Library saw my book as the first breakthrough novel about female sexual fantasies. Publishing is a faddish business, and after the publication of Nancy Friday's book *My Secret Garden*, sexual fantasies were, excuse the expression, hot. So that's the handle N.A.L. used for its sales force. After all, *every* product needs a handle in our consumer culture. I mean, no one says *Playboy* is the magazine that publishes John Cheever or John Updike, though I know that every time I turn to *Playboy*, I can find a new short story I'll want to read. *Playboy* is known as the magazine with the nude centerfold.

Playboy: How do you feel about the nude centerfold? Some outspoken liberationists have complained that it exploits women.

Jong: No, I don't think they're being exploited, but they're not really *women* to me, they're almost figments of the imagination, sort of the apotheosis of the male mammary dream. I think they have a kind of fantasy value.

Playboy: Could you fantasize *being* one?

Jong: Never—but then, I've always found my distinction in another area. If all I had to recommend me was the decorative value of my body, perhaps I would want that form of recognition. But I must say, I'm glad I don't have to get what I want in the world through my looks, because that's such an ephemeral kind of success, the kind that makes you fear your 30th birthday. But about the centerfold, I have no real objections to it. I recently learned, by reading between the lines of your Mel Brooks interview, that men all over America jerk off into it, and now that I know this, I think it serves a useful social function. "Redeeming social value," as they say.

Playboy: We don't have any research to substantiate that finding, so we'll change the subject. There seems to be little doubt that the ways men and women deal with each other are changing. What do you see as the most important changes in relations between the sexes?

Jong: Is that like asking, "What relations between men and women would I take to a desert island?" I *do* see certain definite trends: one of them is that women are becoming increasingly independent economically. So they are in a position to choose men not out of a desperate need for a social rudder or an economic supporter but out of their own desire for companionship, for friendship, for love, for sex. That time has come for only a fraction of women, self-supporting professional women. It has come for me. But when it comes for *most* women, we'll see great changes, because women will not put up with the stuff they've put up with for centuries.

Playboy: What kind of stuff?

Jong: Being nursemaids to their men; taking what is dished out to them; being chief cook and bottle washer, baby sitter, nanny; entertaining the husband's guests, the whole servant-master relationship.

Playboy: What about women who are content with that conventional husband-is-boss relationship? Would you criticize them for that?

Jong: No, but I would hazard a guess from the mail I've gotten that many women who are *in* that situation don't *want* to be, that they are chafing in it. And, in that sense, the men who fear women's revolution are right. The women's movement *is* going to take something away from them—the right to be masters in a master-slave relationship. If you can conceive of relations between people only in that way, certainly you would much rather be the master than the slave. It's very tempting for me, too, at times. I mean, there have been times in my life when I've thought, God, wouldn't it be great to have a man at home who would be faithful, be there all the time, and I could run around and do what I wanted and still come back to this person?

Playboy: Every woman should have a wife?

Jong: Yes. At times, I've fantasized having the kind of relationship with a man that men have always had with women. But if you really stop and think about what that implies about your view of the other person, it's not so terrific. I frankly think that, for all the difficulties inherent in it, it's much better to have a relationship between two equals. So if men are losing some of their old prerogatives, I think they're gaining something better. But it's hard to convince them, sometimes.

Playboy: Some psychologists speculate that some men are so threatened by these changes that they've become impotent. Have you run into many guys who can't get it up?

Jong: Isadora experiences that in the novel, but I haven't. I have had men say, "I'm *afraid* I would be impotent with you, because you are who you are." But it doesn't happen. In fact, one of the things that men often tell me is, "I'm so surprised that you're unthreatening. I'm so surprised that you're feminine. That you're warm. That you're funny. That you're cuddly." I don't know *why* they're surprised. I guess they make the assumption that a woman who is successful is going to be a ball breaker. It's not my fault that they have that crazy response. That's what the culture feeds them, that a woman must have become successful by being a ball breaker. This assumption does not exist about men. It's considered perfectly natural for a man to be businesslike, efficient, competent at what he does without that going against his masculinity. But if a *woman* is good at what she does, and is strong-minded and determined, then it's assumed that in some way she must be unfeminine.

Playboy: Have you, like Isadora, found yourself using your sexual wiles to get something you want out of a man?

Jong: I've never slept with an editor in order to get my work published or anything like that. But I've *thought* of it. And I'm sure I've done a lot of eyelash-batting and handholding and kissing people on the cheek rather more warmly than I have meant it; everyone has. I was told, for example, that one woman writer, when she was on a publicity tour, slept with all the book salesmen, and that they'd never had it so good. I have no particular moral objections to that, but I would be incapable of doing it.

Playboy: Germaine Greer, in her *Playboy* interview, says that coercion of women for sexual purposes, even if it isn't violent, is rape. "If a man takes you out on a motorway and stops the car and says, 'Now you can walk or fuck,' and you fuck, you have been raped," she claims.

Jong: She's right. I think women frequently feel they have to give sexual favors to get ahead. Women still have to take crumbs of power from men, so what do they do? A lot of things they wouldn't normally do, and sometimes those things imply a certain kind of sexual submission—pleasing, Uncle Tomming, niggering it up pretending to ideas they don't really hold. Maybe Germaine Greer would call that mental rape, and maybe she would be right. Example of mental rape: Women who will not sign a petition for fear their husbands might not agree with it. There are such women. I was shocked to discover that there were.

Playboy: Are you politically oriented yourself? We recall that Isadora refuses to bed with boys who like Ike.

Jong: I *care* about politics, but I don't do enough about it. As for Isadora and Ike, that was true in my own life, only with me it was Nixon. I made it Ike in the book because it sounded more euphonious. I remember once back around 1955, when a prep school boy took me out in his car, and we went up to a secluded street in Riverdale and started necking. Then he said something about how Nixon was his ideal, and I said, *"Take me home."* I was completely turned off.

Playboy: You rejected him, then. Gay Talese, who has been studying modern sexual lifestyles for a proposed book, has stated that women don't fear rejection as men do. Do you agree?

Jong: I like Gay, but I disagree with that statement completely. Women are very afraid of rejection. I think what Gay means is he thinks a woman can always get laid, whereas a man can't. I was at a party once where he asserted, "Any woman in this room could go out onto any street corner and get laid in half an hour, whereas I don't believe any man in this room could." And the men in that room were all very attractive. But if what he said is true; so what? Who wants to get laid in just half an hour? And who wants it on the street?

Women are *very* afraid of rejection. The rejection of not getting the telephone call, not being asked out, is just as bad as the rejection of being turned down for sex. But, you know, men are afraid of loneliness, too. I've seen men who fall apart more after a divorce than women do; men who have absolutely gone bananas when they've been left. I don't see vast psychological differences between the sexes. I'm not saying there *are* no differences. I believe there are. But I think it would be healthier for us all to stress the similarities.

Playboy: What are some of the differences you do believe in?

Jong: Well, I think men are truly afraid of castration, in a way that is symbolic and also affects their daily lives. I believe women are stronger, more resilient both emotionally and physically, partly because they are not coddled in the way that men are. They have to take care of everybody, and I think that makes for incredible toughness.

Playboy: Another male fear, you claim in your novel, is that women are talking about them. You wrote: "Men have always detested women's gossip because they suspect the truth: Their measurements are being taken and compared." Is that really true?

Jong: My friends tend to be very explicit—at least with me. We talk endlessly about men in bed and their dimensions and how they fuck. I think if men ever heard the things we say to one another, they'd wilt.

Playboy: Like what?

Jong: Oh, I've had long conversations with women about the anatomies and techniques of various lovers: What shape was his penis? How long did it take him to come? I know that women aren't *supposed* to talk like that, but to my knowledge, they do it much more than men. A lot of very sensitive men have complained to me, as a matter of fact, that they don't have as close relationships with their men friends as I do with my women friends.

Playboy: Is that because of the old homosexuality bugaboo?

Jong: Buggery-boo, you should say. Yes, I think it is. I think it's also that they're very afraid of showing weakness in front of one another. Men construe intimacy as weakness. That's part of the sexist brainwashing our society subjects men to.

Playboy: How about some of the other things our society lays on men? We hear a lot of talk that a woman should be free to choose between a career outside the home and a life as a housewife. Very few men have such a choice; they are expected to support at least themselves, if not a family.

Jong: I know lots of women who have absolutely no qualms about supporting a man, who do it and feel no conflict. I will tell you that I do not know very many men who could take it.

Playboy: Why not?

Jong: It's not because women won't let them but because a man's identity in this culture depends so much on his profession, his monetary status, the plastic credit cards in his wallet, that most men cannot do without these props.

Playboy: You've said that a great deal of your own identity comes from your professional accomplishments. If you had to identify yourself— introduce yourself to a stranger, say—without reference to your work, how would you do it?

Jong: That's really a very interesting question. Almost impossible, isn't it? Hmmmm. I would probably say that I like to laugh a lot, that I'm a clown, which I tend to be; that I'm prone to put on weight, that I'm quite horny—

Playboy: Does it surprise people when you admit to them that you're quite horny?

Jong: It surprises *me* to discover it about myself. I don't know if I'm hornier than other people, but I think I may be more in touch with my sexual feelings. My life seems kind of incomplete if there isn't a sort of sexuality in it. I don't mean random, promiscuous sexuality. I'm not interested in that. What I mean is that unless there is a person to whom I am attached, feel warmly with and have good sex with, I feel that my life is really truncated. It's an important component in my life that I don't like having to do without.

Playboy: Linda Lovelace prescribes daily orgasms for everybody. Other- wise, she says, people get very uptight. Do you buy that?

Jong: I don't know whether you have to have an orgasm everyday, al- though it would be, certainly, very nice. I hate to quantify because people who read this are going to say, "Oh, my God, I didn't have one today!" Sort of like taking your vitamins. Or those marriage manuals you used to see that said no orgasm is a good orgasm unless it's simultaneous with your partner's. That has fucked up more people than anything. That is the biggest, silliest myth. I mean, sometimes they are simultaneous, they just happen to be, and that's fine. But if you're thinking about it, it won't happen.

I do think one's feelings about orgasm are completely variable. Certainly there are times when, if you really love somebody, you can get totally into the idea of giving pleasure. This may sound like something that goes against all kinds of feminist beliefs, but a man can do it as well as a woman; I mean, there are times when you just want to give the other person pleasure. If it's *consistently* like that, then there's something wrong with the relationship. The fun in fucking is the variety.

Playboy: Any particular variations you enjoy?

Jong: No, all kinds, I think. I like gentle sex, but I also like tough sex sometimes. I can get enormously turned on by being dominated in bed, although I would hate being raped. Sometimes I like to be the one who's active, absolutely driving the man wild, while he is relatively passive. Or you can both be equally active. I think it's nice to do it in all different positions, different ways, including hanging from the chandelier.

Playboy: Have you ever tried it hanging from the chandelier?

Jong: No. And this house *has* no chandeliers. But I can heartily recommend sunken bathtubs, Jacuzzis, water beds.

Playboy: Do you ever fuck outdoors?

Jong: A lifelong New Yorker? Fucking outdoors? Where? In Central Park?

Playboy: Maybe you'll have more opportunity here in California. Speaking of fucking, what's your opinion of the diagnosis often made by men that all some women need is a good fuck?

Jong: A lot of *men* need a good fuck, but they're incapable of getting it because they regard their penises as sort of detached from the rest of their bodies. I think there are very few people who know how to get a good fuck, getting on that subject.

Playboy: OK, how does one get a good fuck?

Jong: I think probably the essence of it is understanding that your body and head are connected. The trouble with most people is that they're too focused on their genitals. I really think that's what makes some men bad lovers. There are certain men who will always grab for the clitoris, you know, massage it then thrust home and that's it. And there are other men who—this is terrible—never take off their pajama tops while screwing. There are others who never take off their socks. There are others who never take off their glasses. Now, this *bespeaks* fragmentation. These men think that sex is all in the genitals. There are other men who, immediately after having made you come, zing out, withdraw, roll over and go to sleep. For good sex, you should take time with it; treat it as something that's important, that you're not ashamed of, that is fun. Rolling around on the floor, licking apple butter off each other, if that's what you dig.

Playboy: There's a lot of licking in your poems, isn't there?
Jong: Yes. Well, I'm a very oral person. I like licking a lot.

Playboy: Licking or being licked?
Jong: Both. I also like barking.

Playboy: Barking?
Jong: Arf! Arf! What I mean by barking is a certain kind of playfulness. Bed should be a place where you can to some extent regress and become childlike and funny and totally relaxed, and that relaxation can take any form, from making jokes to crawling around on all fours and barking like a dog. I think if adults don't have certain areas in their lives in which they can be playful, they crack after a while. And one of those areas, to me, is sex.

Playboy: Have you always felt that way?
Jong: To some extent, yes, but I feel freer, better about my own sexuality at this point in my life than I ever have.

Playboy: Are you saying that you felt bad about sex previously?
Jong: Oh, I think it's very clear in all my writing that for a long time I thought having pleasure was something to feel guilty about. My own adolescent sexual experience was fraught with guilt. I truly believed I was the only person in the world who ever masturbated, who ever finger fucked. I think I discovered masturbation to orgasm when I was about 13, and I was sure nobody else had ever done it.

Playboy: Do you get off as well with masturbation as with intercourse? Or do you agree with another Greer dictum, that "a clitoral orgasm with a full cunt is nicer than a clitoral orgasm with an empty one?"
Jong: I much prefer an orgasm with a cock than without one. That's the best there is. But I think the distinction between vaginal and clitoral is totally mythic. Because, as far as I can see, every orgasm starts at the clitoris and ends up in the vagina, and it doesn't matter whether the orgasm is induced by someone manipulating the clitoris with a hand or going down on you or putting his penis inside you. It was Freud who decided there were two kinds of orgasm. What did he know? He wasn't a woman. I would love to get him back here and ask him to explain it.

Playboy: Demonstrate it?
Jong: God, no. Just explain. He said that a clitoral orgasm was immature and a vaginal orgasm was mature, and I think he probably meant that a

woman who got satisfied by having a penis inside her was more "mature" than a woman who got satisfied by having her clitoris rubbed. What he was really saying was that whatever is good for men is "mature." I think the whole fuss is totally without foundation.

Playboy: Some women swear they get their best orgasms with vibrators.
Jong: Really? Warm flesh is nicer.

Playboy: Is it true, as reported in *Newsweek*, that some San Francisco sculptor sent you a marble penis?
Jong: It was a sculptor from Los Angeles and he sent me a marble penis to be used as a dildo.

Playboy: Did you?
Jong: Marble makes a very cold dildo. But you know how it is with writers—anything for research.

Playboy: How big was it?
Jong: About life-size.

Playboy: Now we get into the whole thing about prick size. Does it really matter?
Jong: Well, I remember in college they used to say it's not the size but the stroke. My personal suspicion is that it's both the size *and* the stroke, but any answer to *that* question is going to make men all over America feel terrible—because every man has a subjective view of the size of his own genitals. Most men are going to tend to feel inferior, even if they are in fact well endowed.

Playboy: As women are self conscious about their breast size?
Jong: Exactly. I always thought that I had very small breasts, but I've been told by a number of men that, while they're not enormous, they're a pretty respectable size.

Playboy: Did you ever want big jugs?
Jong: Who didn't? But the nice thing about mine is that they stand up.

Playboy: Women's libbers are sometimes described as bra burners. Do you see any connection between liberation and brassieres?
Jong: None at all. I rarely wear a bra myself. I frequently go without any underwear at all. But I can get into stuff like Frederick's of Hollywood lingerie for fun. I enjoy wearing make-up; I like sexy clothes. I don't think that's a true feminist issue at all. And no bras were ever burned by anyone,

in fact. That's a media myth—one of many used to discredit feminism, or any revolutionary movement.

Playboy: You have, whether you've intended to or not, been taken up as something of a guru by elements of the feminist movement. Do you see other feminist issues as bogus?

Jong: No, but I do get pissed when certain famous feminists say, "No more alimony" or "no more child support." They don't know what it's like to be 38 years old and have three kids, never to have graduated from high school or college, to have devoted your whole life to helping your husband up the corporate ladder, and then have him walk out with somebody else. I feel I'm in a privileged position in currently making a living writing, but a lot of women are not that privileged. They've spent their whole lives catering to men and children, and now they are supposed to start from scratch. It's impossible to expect that. Look—there are so many ways in which *successful* women are discriminated against; imagine how bad it is for the *average* woman.

Playboy: Another burning feminist issue is abortion. What's your feeling about that?

Jong: Obviously, I think women should have the right to determine whether or not they need an abortion. I mean, that should be a basic premise. I *personally* have a lot of negative feelings about abortion.

Playboy: You mean you couldn't have one yourself?

Jong: Psychologically it would very tough on me because I'm 33 years old and have never had a child. I never lie about my age, by the way, with the result that friends of mine who are five years older than I appear to be five years younger. But things happen to women who are past 30 and have never had a child; we get kind of crazy on the subject.

Abortions—I think there will always be abortions. The question is whether there will be legal, safe abortions or back-street abortions. That's why the Right to Lifers infuriate me so. Their attempts to stamp out abortions by legal measures means that only rich women will have safe abortions, and poor women—the Puerto Ricans, the blacks, the college students—will die on kitchen tables. Or get blood poisoning or perforated uteruses. And I think that's just unconscionable.

Playboy: Before we leave the subject of the dogma of women's lib, let's bounce this statement from an unnamed male observer of you: "A feminist who admits to liking men is comparable to a Nazi leader who says he loves Jews."

Jong: I *hate* it when people polarize us like that. I don't see why being a feminist should be inconsistent with loving men. I suppose the trouble is that a lot of women, in order to love a man, feel they have to submerge their own identities. So if they want to be themselves, they have to give up loving men.

Playboy: Do such women come on to you sexually? Have you gotten letters from women propositioning you?

Jong: No, I haven't gotten many propositions from women. I do remember getting a letter from three women who said, "Dear Erica, do you want to be made happy beyond your wildest dreams? We are dykes and we can make you happy. Please call us at such-and-such telephone number."

Playboy: Did you call?

Jong: No, I never did. But I don't get many overtures like that—I think probably because my work seems so heterosexual that a lesbian would assume I wasn't interested. I've been criticized for that, by the way. For example, the feminist journal *Off Our Backs* did a very, very vituperative review of my first book of poems, *Fruits & Vegetables*, and the gist of it was that the trouble with Erica Jong was that her mind's not open to bisexuality or to lesbianism. I think that's a silly criticism to make of a writer's work, to judge somebody on his or her sexual orientation.

Playboy: We take it that yours is pretty exclusively heterosexual?

Jong: Well, I must say I feel there should be utter freedom for gay people, that they're unfairly persecuted. I could say to you that some of my best friends are gay, except that it would sound stupid. But I, myself, really *am* more oriented toward men than I am toward women.

Playboy: Somehow you sound as if you're apologizing for that. Do you feel you must?

Jong: Well, in this day and age, one almost has to apologize for not being bisexual.

Playboy: Do you dig centerfolds of nude men, such as the centerfolds in *Playgirl*?

Jong: I'm not particularly turned on by these photos, but I think that's because I look at those men and think, "God, I know how absolutely dumb he's going to be." One of the things that turn me on in men is intelligence.

Playboy: What makes you think a man's dumb just because he poses nude? Are you really a female chauvinist pig?

Jong: Oh, those men always say they're posing nude to further their acting career or something. Besides, they never have erections! Real men excite me more than pictures.

Playboy: What turns you on about real men besides intelligence?

Jong: Touch. And a real, live nude man walking across the room toward me turns me on immensely.

Playboy: Some women, to the surprise of social scientists, are now admitting that they are aroused by pornographic movies. Are you?

Jong: My reaction to porn movies is as follows: After the first ten minutes, I want to go home and screw. After the first *20* minutes, I never want to screw again as long as I live. Those endless blow jobs in slow motion, to me, are just tedious. The funniest porn film I've ever seen is one of two little girls in pigtails—they're really women of about 30, but they're dressed as little girls in pigtails, with short skirts and knee stockings—making love to a man in an ape suit who has an enormous black plastic penis that gets longer as they pull on it. One night I sat down with some friends in an apartment to watch some other porn films and we got so bored with running them forward that we decided to run them backward—so we could see the ejaculations returning and the cocks getting soft and the pants getting zipped.

Playboy: Was that a turn-on?

Jong: No, but it was funny. None of those films was a turn-on, really. I found *Behind the Green Door* a turn-on for a few minutes, but then it got repetitious.

I have been very turned on at times by erotic art, if the quality of the art is good. One thing that really turns me *off* is crummy prose, like you get in porn novels, "And then he pumped his hot pole into her wet pussy." It's so mechanical. Gigantic sexual organs thrusting at each other as if they didn't have people attached to them. Like those pictures in *Screw*.

Playboy: You're not a fan of Al Goldstein's *Screw*?

Jong: I read your interview with Goldstein and I think he came across as a totally obnoxious human being from beginning to end. Both ends. *Screw* did publish a perceptive review of *Fear of Flying*, though. In the main, what I object to in *Screw* is those pictures of those huge sexual organs taken out of context from the rest of the body.

You know, a friend of mine had a book of what people call wide-open beavers, crotch shots, that he got in Copenhagen. It was just page after page of cunts. A black one, a white one, a Chinese one, with garters, without garters, with crotchless panties. And they were all pretty similar. The color of the hair or the skin might be different, but they were pretty much alike. Some people apparently find this sort of thing an object of fascination. I don't.

Playboy: Your heroine in *Fear of Flying* is certainly fascinated with looking at her *own* cunt.

Jong: I can't imagine anybody growing up who hasn't had the desire to see her own cunt. I certainly did: I remember in my adolescence, like Isadora, putting my head through my legs and looking at myself backward in the mirror. It was just an object of intense curiosity for me.

Playboy: But not beauty?

Jong: I may be killed by the feminists for saying this, but I think many women have the basic, gut feeling that their genitals are ugly. Maybe it has to do with the fact that your cunt is hidden, that you can't see it. Maybe it has to do with the fact that it has secretions and sometimes there are odors that are not pleasant. One of the reasons I think women are very gratified by oral-genital relations is that it's a man's way of saying to you, "I like your cunt. It's good to me. I can eat it."

Playboy: Is that the idea you were expressing in Isadora's fantasy of wanting her husband to go down on her while she was having her period? Is that one of your own unfulfilled fantasies?

Jong: I don't know whether I would really want to do it, but it does seem like it's a tremendous pledge of love. Do you love me enough to do anything? That's really what that's about. Do you love my menstrual blood? Would you eat my shit? Stuff like that. I don't think anybody actually *wants* to. You just want to hear the person say, "Sure I would." Reassurance.

Playboy: Isn't that some kind of power play?

Jong: No, I think it's sort of asking for acceptance. One doesn't have to go on and *do* it.

Playboy: Wouldn't you say there is rather a lot of emphasis on menstruation in your writing—your novel and your poems?

Jong: A lot? Every 28 days. Why not? I just think that for a woman it's a very, very important thing, that rhythm of menstruation. It's a kind of connection with your own mortality. Maybe it's hard to conceive of one's own death, but I don't think it's that hard to conceive of aging, or menopause. And one thing that's absolutely finite is your childbearing capacity. So every time a woman has a period, she knows that she is 28 or 27 or whatever number of days closer to the end—menopause, aging, death. It's a kind of biological time clock, a constant reminder of mortality.

Playboy: A moment ago, you referred to vaginal odors, and certainly a multi-million dollar industry devoted to feminine-hygiene sprays and such has sprung up in recent years. Yet many women put down these products and the advertising that promotes them. Do you?

Jong: I think those advertisements are terrible. My agent called me up one day and said some company wanted me to do a commercial for cunt wipers of some sort, and I said, "Don't even tell me who they are or how much money they're offering. I don't even want to know."

Playboy: Would you have been tempted by the money?

Jong: No, I was shocked that anybody would ask a writer to do something like that. *Nothing* would have made me do the commercial. Anyway, what's wrong with soap and water? Bring the bidet to the New World! There's another thing I've always wanted to write to *The Playboy Advisor* about: OK, if you decide, as I have, that the form of contraception with the fewest side effects is the diaphragm and jelly, what do you do about oral-genital sex? The jelly anesthetizes the tongue and tastes terrible! Why don't companies come out with some kind of yummy-tasting contraceptive cream—grape flavor, maybe?

Playboy: There *are* flavored douches and male genital sprays on the market.

Jong: But that doesn't solve the contraceptive problem. And I really don't want to take the pill. I don't believe one should fuck up one's body with chemicals. I might take a sleeping pill occasionally, if I'm on tour and can't relax in an unfamiliar hotel room. And I used to always carry penicillin tablets, because I have the greatest clap phobia of anyone in the world. I've always been terrified when I've slept with somebody I didn't know well. I guess I'm just an alarmist, because when I travel someplace I take V-Cillin K, Lomotil, and my diaphragms.

Playboy: Diaphragms, plural? You have several?

Jong: A whole collection. I'm planning to send them to the Smithsonian.

But—although this may go against the way people see me—I really haven't done much sleeping around. I was always preparing for it, just in case a really terrific guy came along—carrying around diaphragms in my briefcase and stuff like that—but the *number* of men I've slept with in my life is very small.

Playboy: How many have there been?

Jong: Not many. I don't notch my bedpost, so I don't know, exactly. I do, however, have a good imagination, and I can describe sexuality clearly.

Playboy: Who was your first lover?

Jong: My first husband. He was my college sweetheart, my best friend, my constant companion—a person I took courses with, long walks with, read books with, did everything with. If it had been 1968, we would have shacked up together for a year or two and that would have been it. But because it was 1963, we got married. And we were much too young and too broke.

Playboy: How old were you?

Jong: He was 24 and I was 21. We were married a year and a half, and then he had a nervous breakdown. That is the part of *Fear of Flying* that comes closest to something that actually occurred in my life.

Playboy: When did you meet your second husband, the psychiatrist?

Jong: I met him in the fall of 1965 and we were married the next year. Then I went with him to Heidelberg, where he had a three-year tour of duty with the Army.

Playboy: Like Bennett Wing, in *Fear of Flying*. Those were three years that Isadora Wing obviously hated. Have you been accused of being too rough on the Germans in that book? And why did you, or at least Isadora, lump the Viennese in with the Germans?

Jong: I know that makes the Viennese very, very angry, but I see them as being alike, Teutonic. Both Germans and Austrians were extremely anti-Semitic.

Playboy: Were you being fair to them to generalize to such an extent?

Jong: I certainly wouldn't do it if I were writing non-fiction. But because I was writing a novel in which I was talking about people's gut feelings, I think I had the right to do it. You see, I had never been particularly conscious of being Jewish. My family was cosmopolitan; nobody cared much about religion. I never had been to a synagogue. All my life, I have had friends who were not Jewish—lovers, husbands, even. But in some way, that German experience changed something inside me, in that I came to understand what it means to have an identity you would fight for, and I began to burrow into those feelings. I wrote a lot of poems in Germany, and many of them dealt with being a victim and with rage. And from that I moved into writing about female rage and all those unexpressed negative feelings I had about my family, about men, and so on.

Playboy: Didn't you have other means of venting your rage? Specifically, didn't you, like Isadora, undergo an extensive period of analysis?

Jong: I was in analysis for eight years. I didn't have as many analysts as Isadora did. I had three. I'm not really sure why I spent eight years in analysis; one reason was that I was married to an analyst and it seemed to be the thing to do. I was greatly helped in a lot of things in analysis, though. I did suffer from writer's block and I was terrified of flying. I'm not anymore. Analysis really did help me enormously. It freed me to write about things that matter deeply to me. If you can learn to be authentic and honest about your feelings on the couch, you can bring that authenticity into your writing.

Playboy: One prominent New York psychiatrist made headlines recently when he was convicted of prescribing sexual relations for his patient, with himself as a sex partner. What's your opinion of that technique?

Jong: I'm totally against it. I think it's like child labor. Exploiting the helplessness of somebody who depends on you. When a person goes to a psychiatrist and puts his or her life into that person's hands and then gets a pass out of it, I think that's utterly immoral. And the psychiatrists who rationalize it as good for the patient are the lowest of the low.

Playboy: What's it like being married to a psychiatrist?

Jong: It probably depends on the psychiatrist you're married to. They do tend to bring their work home with them, I think, and sometimes you feel you're being analyzed in the bedroom. And this sounds like a frightful generalization, but in the marriages of most psychiatrists I've known, there's an awful lot of daddy-baby stuff. The psychiatrist's wife plays a role: "Take care of me, Daddy." And the psychiatrist, in turn plays a role: "I am the good daddy. I will protect you." For "protect," read: "control."

Playboy: Is that what finally broke up *your* marriage?

Jong: It's very hard for me to talk about that marriage. But I'll say this: It was not the success of *Fear of Flying* that broke it up; my husband was immensely supportive of my writing, always. In fact, it was he who insisted that I use his name in my writing. I remember pointing out at a much earlier period in our lives, long before *Fruits & Vegetables* was published, that if I ever became a really well-known writer, it would ensure us much more privacy if I used my maiden name. But he was adamant about my using his name, Jong. He wanted this identification with me, as a bond between us— and he was relentless in his insistence. I think if he hadn't been so strong on it, I would have used my maiden name. Anyway, he was always proud of my work, proprietary, almost, and he never objected to the book. He read it all before publication and endorsed it heartily. Who can ever say why a marriage breaks up? We didn't share the same sense of humor—that's *part* of it.

Playboy: How would you describe your sense of humor?

Jong: I see the world as a tremendous circus. I am very anti-elitist, anti-authoritarian. My real view of the world is a satirist's view; and more often than not, I find the games we play to gain status very foolish. And I want to share that laughter with somebody; I mean, I can't get on with people who take all that bullshit seriously.

Playboy: And your husband did take it seriously?

Jong: *Most* people do, and I think he did more than I did.

Playboy: Is he a Freudian analyst?

Jong: Ask *him.*

Playboy: We wondered because Freudianism is an extremely authoritarian discipline. If you're such an anti-authoritarian, how could you ever get mixed up with a Freudian analyst?

Jong: Mixed up is the key phrase there. I don't believe in systems, and I don't believe in breaking the world down into two types of people or two types of orgasms or any of those things. I do not want anybody to feed me any kind of orthodoxy, whether it's Catholicism or Seventh-Day Adventism or Calvinism or Freudianism or anything else. Doctrinaire Marxists bore me. Doctrinaire Gestalt therapists, doctrinaire sexologists bore me.

Playboy: What is your opinion of Freudian theories of sexuality?

Jong: There are a number of things in Freud's writing that lead me to believe he was extremely frightened of sexuality, very hung up and guilt-ridden.

Playboy: Specifically, how about one of Freud's most controversial theories: Do you believe in penis envy?

Jong: *That* has a certain lilt, like a singing commercial for peanut butter. No, I believe that women envy the power men have in our culture, and well we might: I don't think we literally envy the *organ*. We don't have to; there's so much else we can envy. We can envy the fact that men make more money; we can envy the fact that society is structured for their benefit; we can envy the fact that they can go out to restaurants unescorted without getting pinched in the ass.

Playboy: We thought you *liked* getting pinched in the ass, or is that only Isadora's predilection?

Jong: *Isadora* likes it. Isadora—she's incorrigible. I like to be pinched on the ass, but only by some people. And I want to pick the people. Isadora has a lot of weird tastes that I don't share. Most of her fears, though, are mine. Or *were*. I've outgrown many of them.

Playboy: What besides your fear of flying?

Jong: I'm no longer afraid of being alone. That panic Isadora feels: "Oh, my God, he's going to leave me and I'll be alone"—that actually is the irrational female panic that is ground into us from our earliest days and reaffirmed during our adolescence. God forbid that you should be without a date Saturday night! God forbid you should be alone on New Year's Eve! God forbid your man should leave you! And then you discover, well, being alone is pretty nice. I like my own company. If I don't have a date on Saturday night, I'm reading a terrific book. I'm going out with a woman friend or a man who is not a lover but whose company I enjoy. It's not so terrible. Life goes on.

Playboy: You're in the process of getting a divorce. Why do you think so many marriages are breaking up these days?

Jong: Women are tired of bending, so they break up. I think that in some cases, divorce comes about through a healthy desire to fulfill one's own individuality. In other cases, it may be part of an endless quest for what is unfillable anyway. The things that used to hold the family together don't exist to the extent that they did. Childbearing is optional, and even if you do have children, it doesn't take the whole of your life because one child, or two children or even three children, is not a total lifetime's work in the way that it was when women had 14 children. I mean it doesn't go on as long.

Playboy: You have been quoted as saying that you have finally decided you'd like to have children.

Jong: I think I would. I certainly have waited and waited, as long as one can wait; but I don't believe I will get out of my childbearing years without having at least one child.

Playboy: And it doesn't matter to you whether it is born in or out of wedlock?

Jong: Not at all. I'd rather be unwed than in a state of deadlocked wedlock. I don't think marriage guarantees a woman anything she can't have outside marriage—in terms of security, child support and the like. I only wish tax and inheritance laws did not discriminate against the unmarried. Unfortunately they do. Other than that, I can't think of any reason one should be married. What can marriage offer me? It certainly doesn't guarantee that I won't stop loving somebody—nor does it ensure the continuance of a relationship. In some sense, it puts a sort of dutiful obligation on both parties that may make it harder to love, freely. I'm not absolutely sure of this, but it's possible that if you feel locked together in a certain way, your love feels more obligated than freely given. If you only live with somebody, it is taken for granted that you do so because you want to *be* with that person. Nothing in this world is more secure than that.

Playboy: Do you agree with those who claim the trouble with modern marriage lies in the nuclear family? Would you rather live in a commune?

Jong: Boy, if I could find six people with whom I could live happily, I'd be glad to have a commune. But I think it's hard enough to live with one. It's practically a miracle when you live harmoniously with anybody. You know, theoretically I always said I would like to have a variety of people in my life, a variety of men. And yet I always wind up pretty consistently with one man and am monogamous for long periods of time. Ziplessness unzips me. Monogamy helps me work and function and write. I think it's just that there are so few people in this world whom one can really love, whom you feel that tenderness toward. It doesn't happen to me everyday. More often than not, I've felt a sort of intellectual contempt for many men. I know that sounds terrible to say, but I can remember, from the time I was an adolescent, thinking, "Oh, gee, he's so attractive, but he's so *stupid*!"

Playboy: Are you saying you couldn't go to bed with a man you didn't respect?

Jong: Oh, I could and I have, but I've always felt sorry afterward. For me, it is so much better to have a warm, companionable relationship.

Playboy: What would you consider an ideal relationship?

Jong: I have a new love poem that expresses it. It's about giving. I think we've always been afraid that if we give too much it will turn the other person off. And sometimes it does. Unfortunately, there are a lot of men—some women, too—in this culture who are terribly afraid of commitment. But I would think that if you could find somebody who was not turned off by it, you could just sort of renew each other, and that would be life's greatest pleasure.

Playboy: Isn't there a contradiction between what you've just said, about commitment and monogamous relationships, and what you, through Isadora, had to say about the excitement of being unfaithful. The eroticism of sloppy seconds, so to speak?

Jong: It's not fair to blame me, three years after writing a book, for my character's views. Sure, one of the fun things about adultery—at least for a little while—is the sense that you're getting the best of two men. There you are, having a little affair and then going home to your husband; fucking two men in one day. The only trouble is it's very superficial. It really turns out you're not getting the best of either man. You're just getting a little piece-that's a pun, I guess—of both. Infidelity seems like a tremendous turn on at times, but you really don't get much out of it. It's much better to have one really rewarding relationship than to have several fragmentary ones.

Playboy: Do you think total marital fidelity is possible?

Jong: I think it's unreasonable to assume that one's mate is always going to be faithful. You *know* that people are not going to go for 20 years without ever fucking somebody else—for whatever reason; maybe just to assert independence, to prove you aren't caged. Sometimes out of a genuine compulsion. Or overwhelming attraction. It's unreasonable to assume that there won't be such occasions. But I'm the worst person to talk about that, because I'm very jealous. I'm really fascinated with jealousy and the effect it has on a marriage. There's something of that in my new novel.

Playboy: Some married couples deal with this problem by permitting a certain amount of sexual freedom. How would you feel about open infidelity? Wife swapping or consensual adultery?

Jong: *I* feel much less threatened by it than by secret infidelity, and I think maybe in this respect, I'm like a lot of other people. The thing that gets me the most crazy about infidelity in the way that it's practiced in a conventional marriage is the secrecy. It re-evokes all your childhood terrors about things going on between the adults behind locked doors. When you find out that someone has been cheating on you for years and that night he was supposedly off studying for such and such he was really . . . that's what makes *me* crazy.

Playboy: You don't subscribe to the "What you don't know won't hurt you" school of thought?

Jong: No, I don't, because I've had it both ways. I would have gone along with that idea until I actually experienced it, found out that things had been going on behind my back for years. And suddenly I understood all the over-head conversations, all the innuendoes, whose car was parked in front of whose house—all those things—and they just came down on my head with sickening force. After that, I really felt that I would rather know, painful as it is. I think lying corrodes a relationship. When you start lying to each other, you start with little things, lies by omission. And the lies grow and that ruins the relationship. I would rather have things in the open.

I *don't* mean that you ought to call home from a business trip and say to the man or woman you're living with, or your husband or wife, "Darling, I just slept with So-and-So." I mean, you don't do that on the telephone. You wait until you're back together and talking in a kind of loving way.

Playboy: What about, "Darling, I *want* to sleep with So-and-So"?

Jong: I honestly think that would be less threatening than keeping it a secret. But sometimes you take the steam out of the fantasy by speaking about it, and then you find you don't want to do it. But you see, if we all did that, there would be less fucking of other people out of rebellion and more doing it for the pure pleasure of doing it.

Playboy: Do you think that a lot of fucking is done out of rebellion?

Jong: Yes, absolutely, in conventional monogamous marriages. And when you read a lot of the novels of adultery that have been written by women, you see that pattern. Very often the woman finds a lover who's not nearly as good in bed as her husband. Certainly, in *Fear of Flying* that's the case; the woman finds an impotent lover. He can't even get it up most of the time. So what's the need that's being fulfilled by this man? It's the need for rebellion, for saying, "Look, I'll show you." And I have talked to many, many women who have had affairs—sometimes persistent, constant affairs throughout their marriages—and they tell you overwhelmingly: "My husband is really a much better lover: He satisfies me more often; I reach orgasm more often with my husband; we're more attuned to each other." And so you ask, "Well why the lover?" And they say, "Ah, I feel great. I feel alive. I feel reborn." What is going on that makes her feel that way? It's being appreciated again, not being taken for granted, being rediscovered as an individual, being validated in the eyes of a new man.

Playboy: Do you have a need for validation in the eyes of men?

Jong: I don't believe I do, but I think that's the way many women live. I think validation comes very much from my work. But I must say that my sense of joy and being one with the world comes from having love in my life. I can live without it, as I've said, but I really don't want to. I'm so much more *crotchety* when there's no man I love in my life.

Playboy: In several articles that appeared earlier in the year, you were described as being depressed. Was the lack of a man in your life the real reason for that depression?

Jong: That may have been part of it, but I think mostly it was sheer exhaustion. I was inundated with mail after *Fear of Flying* came out, so much that I couldn't cope with it. This is something nobody can understand without going through it. Imagine opening your apartment door and finding a stack of mail that comes up to about mid-shin: four galleys in search of quotes, six books from editors saying, "Will you please write something about this?" 20 letters —15 of them from strangers, two from good friends, two or three requests for speaking engagements. It's amazing how many causes come out of the walls the minute your name becomes known. The Zionists of Upper Beverly Hills, the Feminists of Lower Mamaroneck, College Women in Search of Equal Pay. And they're all worthy causes, but nobody could keep up with them all. That was particularly difficult for me to deal with, because I'm the girl who can't say no. At first I tried to answer all the mail myself. I could categorize it, put it in big cardboard boxes: interesting fan mail, dumb fan mail, invitations to "stop for tea if you're ever passing through Secaucus."

Playboy: What were some of the interesting letters?

Jong: Well, I get certain categories of letters that interest me. There's the letter of heartfelt appreciation: "Thank you very much for writing that book. You wrote about my thoughts and feelings." This type sometimes comes from a woman and sometimes from a man: almost equally between both sexes.

Playboy: Men identify with Isadora?

Jong: Absolutely. A lot of men are surprised when they find that women have the same feelings they have. I don't know *why* they're surprised. When I was a kid and read *Great Expectations*, I identified with Pip. I identified with any number of famous characters from literature—Tom Jones, Robinson Crusoe, Gulliver, for God's sake. I never thought that I couldn't identify with them because I was a girl. And yet it surprises men that they should pick up a book about a female and be able to identify with her. But men and women *do* face similar problems, like those Isadora faced: the difficulty of separating oneself from one's family, of achieving a sense of adulthood; the dilemma of wanting to be sexually free and yet wanting to be grounded in a safe, secure relationship. That's not a female thing alone. And men will say to me, "I feel just like Isadora. I feel I am Isadora." Or sometimes, "I'm glad that you wrote about the feelings of women so that I can see that *my* feelings are not so different. Perhaps the sexes are not as far apart as I thought." I find that kind of letter very touching.

Playboy: Do you get letters that aren't so touching? Hate mail, for example?

Jong: Rarely. I once got a crazy letter from a man that said, "Dear Erica, I would like to tear your poems into little pieces and lick them off your body," which struck me as destructive, though I suppose he meant well. Perhaps the *oddest* letter I've ever received was from a former nun who wanted me to meet a young man, perhaps have an affair with him. I think she was in love with him but didn't have the nerve to do anything about it herself and was sort of using me as an intermediary.

Other letters come from men who want to meet me. Sometimes they will say things like, "I have a wonderful 30-acre farm and I'm very wealthy. With a very long cock." No, they don't say that.

Playboy: They don't?

Jong: They don't use the word cock, but sometimes they talk about what good lovers they are.

Playboy: In your own writing, you call a cock a cock, but not all writers—or publishers—are so explicit. Some months ago, *The New York Times* printed an article by Henry Miller praising your work, and at the end there's an italicized footnote: "The *Times* requested and Mr. Miller consented to alterations of some of the language in this article." One of the words the

Times seems to have found it necessary to excise was bastard. How did that strike you?

Jong: As absurd. They wouldn't use the word lay, either. Or horny, which I though was even funnier. I think writers should have full linguistic—even cunnilinguistic—freedom. But there are some people who scan down a page of prose, and if there's one cunt on that page, that's all they see. It's almost as if the thing were surrounded by a neon halo. This astounds me, because swearing was never taboo for me. It always seemed like an interesting way to make language emphatic.

Playboy: With freedom, linguistic or otherwise, goes responsibility. Do you feel that writers bear special responsibilities?

Jong: My own, as I've said, is to be honest. Beyond that, I've always felt that writers should strive to be part of the common run of humanity, that they cannot be elitist. That's what bothered me so when I started having to delegate things, hire a secretary, get an answering service, retain an agent. I had always answered my own phone, my own mail. And I had to sort of reshuffle my head, tell myself, "OK, it's not terrible to have an answering service, to pull the phone plug out. You're still a nice girl." Once I made those decisions—and got out of New York—I felt much better.

Playboy: Why did you have to get out of New York? What's a nice girl from Manhattan doing in a place like Malibu?

Jong: Hmmm. That's another whole book. I often wake up in the morning and don't know why the hell I'm in Malibu or how I got here. I think I'm probably a diehard New Yorker and that New York is so in my blood that I can't survive too long away from it. But it was really getting to me. I used to think that writers who say that they couldn't function in New York were being phony, because I wrote four books in New York. I had never anticipated what happens when you have a best seller, that you are suddenly on tap for the entire world. So it became necessary for me to get out of New York. I don't know if Malibu will become a permanent place for me. I somehow doubt it but who can tell? Right now, I'm feeling more like a gypsy than ever before in my life. I have never had so few possessions as I have right now. I have three cartons of books and papers, and four suitcases. I bought a portable typewriter and a couple of reading lamps at Sears Roebuck. Everything else is either borrowed or rented.

Actually, this is the first time in my life I've lived for myself. Simply, not to worry about *things*, or about what people think of me, whether I'm pleasing people or not. Being able to choose my friends from among people I really love. To be with a man I really love, someone to whom I'm extraordinarily close, with whom I can spend hours talking, giggling, laughing and kidding around, flinging jokes back and forth.

Playboy: We assume you're talking about Jonathan Fast, the writer with whom you are sharing a home in Malibu.

Jong: Right. I think when I first met Jon, I had the sense that I was living with my other half, a sense I'd never had with another man, ever—that this was the other side of my personality. We are not exactly alike, but there is this tremendous kind of sharing of a way of looking at the world.

I had always assumed that men and women were sort of adversaries in a relationship, probably because of the experience I'd had before. The idea of living with someone without that sort of plea bargaining and competitive strife—I was astounded to find that that kind of a relationship could exist. I had convinced myself that it was impossible and unfindable. But it's not. And that's a delight. I must say. We support each other in our work, too. Jon pushes me to work; he's much more disciplined in his writing habits than I am.

Playboy: Which are you happier writing, poetry or prose?

Jong: I like doing both, but I think I enjoy writing poetry more. The sense of exhilaration is more acute. With a novel, you have to keep your eye on the thing for months and months, sometimes years. You have to keep track of the characters. You give a character red hair on one page, you don't want her to have brown hair two chapters later. So you have to keep rereading what you've written. I reread *Fear of Flying* so many times that now I can't even *read* it anymore. I don't think I could make it through one chapter.

Playboy: Before long, you'll be seeing it onscreen. Did you ever think of playing the role of Isadora in the film version yourself?

Jong: Me? I'm not *thin* enough! I'm sure the book's fans will feel whoever plays the role is miscast, but then, given the way Hollywood functions right now, it's a wonder they didn't get Robert Redford and change the heroine's name to Isadore.

Playboy: What's your new novel about? Is it a sequel to *Fear of Flying*, with Isadora once more the heroine?

Jong: No. But the way I put together a novel is so anarchic and it goes through so many major versions that I never can say till the very end of the process what exactly it will become. I can tell you that it deals with a woman who has all the conventional female hang-ups and finally learns, as we all finally learn, that she has to be her own savior.

Playboy: Do you feel you're *capable* of writing outside of your own experience? Must you write at least partly autobiographically?

Jong: I'm fascinated with the idea of writing a fairy tale, or science fiction, or a panoramic historical novel. But right now I have a compulsion to write what I call "mock memoir." I feel that for the first time in my life, by doing so, I'm doing something that's not only pleasurable for me but socially useful.

Playboy: You mean you feel you have a message to transmit?

Jong: Yes, oddly enough. It sounds almost corny to say that, but I do. And that message, in the broadest terms, is: Be honest about your own life, your feelings, your fantasies, your sexuality. I really believe that women writers are in a unique position, in which we can uncover stuff that has been buried for centuries. And I'm not ready to stop doing that.

Playboy: Do you see an increasing vogue for so-called confessional writing by women?

Jong: It's often called confessional writing by male reviewers, but I think the word confessional in this instance is a put-down. It implies that what these women are doing is just sort of spilling out whatever they have in their guts and that there's no craft involved in the writing.

Playboy: How would you describe it, then?

Jong: I think it's a kind of confrontation with self that women are exploring for the first time. Women are confronting their own sexuality, dealing with things inside themselves they've been afraid of dealing with before: their own aggression, their negative feelings toward their families, possibly toward their men; part of it is an exploration of healthy anger, and there's something important about being in touch with your own anger and moving from there to love. I think this is what is new in writing by women, and that's sort of the contribution I feel I can make.

Playboy: Are you working on anything else right now, besides your novel?

Jong: A book of love poems, which is going to be called *The Long Tunnel of Wanting You.* They are erotic poems. One of them is about giving one's lover a blow job before being interviewed on television.

Playboy: And what effect does that have?

Jong: It loosens the tongue. Makes one feel very sassy. It's a wonderful poem, if I do say so myself. I'd rather have you print my poems than interview me. But I guess Playboy doesn't print poems, does it?

Playboy: Well, we might print a poem about that.

Jong: It begins,

> My mouth seeded with your sperm,
> I talked back to the interviewer.
> It may also be this way with God.
> Approach with a mouthful of stones,
>   you will be mute;
> But speak semen and seed and the
>   words will flow.
> Is heaven a television show?
> Everything points to it. . . .

and it goes on like that.

Playboy: Your love poems are graphically candid, not to say earthy, and yet the public's image of a poet is of someone ethereal, fragile. Wouldn't you agree?

Jong: I'm not responsible for the public's false image of poets. The poets *I* know tend to be very full of their own sexuality. A lecherous lot. Male poets, especially. They go on tours, traveling from college to college, and they tend to use their poetry as a way of seducing college girls, teachers, and other poets. They're desperate to get laid; they always come without their wives. In both senses of that word. A really terrific poet, of course, is supposed to be able to come just writing a poem. The muse screws.

Playboy: The muse screws? Are you able to come just writing a poem?

Jong: My head comes—in a manner of speaking.

Playboy: At least your poetry has brought you other rewards. *Loveroot*, your latest volume of poems, made publishing history of a sort by making a Book-of-the-Month Club alternate selection this month.

Jong: I hope all the people who buy my poems simply because they think I'm an outrageous celebrity will really discover they *like* poetry.

Playboy: Do you see yourself as an outrageous celebrity?

Jong: Well, you see me, you see the way I live. I'm not an outrageous person at all; I live rather quietly. But certainly that's not my image. I'm shocked by some of the things I read about myself in print. I begin to sympathize more and more about people like Eisenhower, who never made a statement to the press that you could understand. Therefore, nothing he said could be held against him. But certainly I can't restructure my whole personality because now I'm the subject of interviews. It would go against everything I stand for. I *am* outspoken. I *am* candid. And if an interviewer is out to get me, I will come out sounding awful. I didn't understand at first that such people were directing their hostility at Erica, the commodity, not at Erica, the person—who is five years old inside, insecure and scared in the middle of the night like everybody else.

Playboy: Why should Erica Jong, the famous author, feel insecure?

Jong: Fame can *make* you insecure. I mean, if your status can change so radically that people who previously would not even return your phone calls are now sucking up to you, asking you out to lunch, dinner, breakfast, bed, you have to develop a tremendous sense of insecurity about the world. At a time like that, you need your friends more than ever and you find out who your friends really are.

Playboy: So who are they?

Jong: Special people, people whose values are real. That's one of the things I like about Henry Miller, that his values are real. He will treat as equals a famous writer and some kid who has never published anything. He will be interested in both of them.

Playboy: How did your friendship with Miller begin?

Jong: It all started when he wrote me a letter after having read *Fear of Flying*. He wrote, "You have written a female version of *Tropic of Cancer*. You have done for women in your book what I have done for men in *Tropic of Cancer*." He raved on about the book and then he said, "Use any portion of this letter you wish with your publishers. Xerox it as many times as you want; send it anywhere you want." And as if *that* weren't enough, he wrote another letter to the publisher, saying the same thing. I was absolutely knocked out by his tremendous generosity. But Henry is like that. I first met him in person when I flew out here last fall to work on the screenplay of *Fear of Flying*, and since then, his house has been like a home to me. There are certain people who are never spoiled by fame, who never become aloof and who always remain folks. Henry Miller is like that. Anne Sexton was one of those. Actually, Anne and I saw each other only a few times, but we corresponded a lot and there was instant rapport. There are certain people in this world whom you meet and know you love, know that you could call them in the middle of the night and talk about anything. Anne was that kind of person: a very vulnerable lady without any of the protective coloration of fame. I miss her.

Playboy: Have you ever felt low enough to do yourself in, as Anne Sexton did?

Jong: Yes—but I don't think I'm a potential suicide. I *identify* with suicides, I could write about one. I know what they're feeling and I know why they want to shut off the world. They just feel so much pain that taking each breath is painful. I think that's what happened to Anne. But I don't think that I would ever actually do it.

Playboy: Why not?

Jong: Well, perhaps because I tell myself, "Well, the depression will lift. They always do. Ride it out." Perhaps because I think that it's just a terrible waste and because at just those times in my own life when it seemed that everything was falling apart, suddenly things got better. All last summer and fall, I was as low as I have ever been. I thought there was nothing to look forward to. I *thought* about suicide. I was in constant turmoil, partly because my marriage was dying and I didn't have the guts to admit it to myself. So I just sat there immobilized, in pain. And then it all came together for me.

Playboy: What pulled you out of it?

Jong: A couple of things. Making the decision to dissolve the marriage. Learning to live with the demands put upon me by this whole fame thing; realizing that I really was very lucky to be able to do my own work and make a living at it, to be able to choose my friends from the people I really loved and not to have to kiss ass to anybody.

The assumption is, I think, that when you become "famous"—and I always want to use that word in quotes, because it really doesn't mean anything—is that people expect you to be different. A lot of friends drop away for that reason. J.F.K. is supposed to have made a statement about that that was marvelously quotable. One of his friends said, "Well, now that you're President, Jack, you're not going to have time for your old friends." And he said, "Oh, yes, I am. The White House is a terrible place to make new friends." I think that's true of fame also. Fame is a terrible place to make new friends, 'cause you never know who's asking you for what. I mean, you never know whether the man who's making himself so charming wants to publish your new book or wants to take you to bed or just likes you as a human being. And that's kind of sad, because fame is not one of the things that really matter.

Playboy: What is?

Jong: Well, in the cosmic scheme of things, how hot you are today, or whether your picture is on the cover of a magazine, or how much money you get for the movie rights to your novel, matters *not at all*. It's nicer to have fame, success, than not to have it, just as it's nicer to be comfortably fixed than poor, but the things that truly matter, and always matter, are: Can you write a poem that will last, like one of Emily Dickinson's poems? Not will they put your picture on the cover of a magazine, but can you write something that people will be reading to each other 100 years from now? Can you really love people, care about people and give yourself to them? Those are the things that matter. And all the rest is total delusion.

Erica Jong

Barbara A. Bannon / 1977

From *Publishers Weekly* (14 February 1977), 8–9, 12. Reprinted with permission of *Publishers Weekly.*

Just as Isadora Wing divorces her psychiatrist husband of many years in *How to Save Your Own Life,* the sequel to *Fear of Flying,* moves out of New York's Upper West Side "forever" and finds love and happiness with a younger man, Josh, at the novel's ending, so too has the lifestyle of the author of the novel taken on a whole new look.

Divorced from her own psychiatrist husband, Erica Jong is living now in an East Side high rise apartment with Jonathan Fast, also a writer, the son of Howard Fast, and a man who bears a striking physical resemblance to the description of Josh in the novel. "We are immensely happy," she says of the relationship. Jong, Fast and a toy white poodle named Poochkin are about to move into a country home in Weston, Connecticut, because a schedule for writing "is too difficult to maintain in the city. We're too gregarious."

Together Jong and Fast have written a screen play, *Love Al Dente,* a romantic comedy set in Italy, which she describes as "Irene Dunne and Cary Grant brought up to date." Fast has two science fiction works under contract to NAL.

The fact that both *Fear of Flying,* Erica Jong's best selling first novel, and the new *How to Save Your Own Life,* due from Holt in a few weeks, have appeared to mirror events in the author's own life has led a certain number of readers to confuse Isadora-Erica completely and assume they are totally interchangeable. Not so, says Erica Jong firmly.

"Isadora is an alter ego. She is always much more critical than I am. She is 100,000 times more audacious, more outrageous. She has the snappy comeback. I only think of one hours later. Only the more unsophisticated readers take each book as all gospel truth about me and write me letters asking, 'How can I get in touch with the psychiatrist on page 89? He sounds as if he could help with my daughter's problems.' The sophisticated reader who has read Colette, Proust, Henry Miller knows that what I am writing is a mock memoir, allowing for a complete range of interpretations in between fact and fancy. This kind of writing is hardly my invention, after all. The mock memoir is not so shocking and new."

Basically Erica Jong thinks of herself as "spiritually" a poet, although fascinated with the process of writing novels. She was published as a poet some years before *Fear of Flying* and won the endorsement of Louis Unter-meyer and Muriel Rukeyser, among others. "There is more sheer euphoria in writing poetry," she says. "The psychological process of writing novels changes your own personality as some memory from early childhood sud-denly possesses you."

Grace Griffin, to whom *Fear of Flying* is dedicated, sent some of Jong's poetry to editor Robin Kyriakis, then at Holt, "They were acquiring new writers there then, and felt like taking a gamble on a new poet." Jong recalls. "Aaron Asher, also then at Holt, encouraged me to write both poetry and fiction. I was frightened to write about a female and was trying a novel with a leading male character. Aaron said: 'You are evading women's feelings. What you have to do is bring into your fiction the same honesty you have in your poetry.'"

Fear of Flying was not originally planned to have a sequel. *How to Save Your Own Life* started as a book about someone other than Isadora Wing and then she took it over. "At the end of *Fear of Flying* you were left truncated, up in the air about what was going to happen to Isadora next," Jong says. "I wanted to establish that such a woman could move on into a *good* relationship with men, that it was not impossible for her.

"How do I feel about the reception *How to Save Your Own Life* may get? I'm petrified. I feel as if a guillotine is hanging over my head. Now I'm trying to be philosophical about people waiting to attack me. A lot of this kind of thing is merely envy of people who earn money.

"I think I have taken a lot of the fire for writing so openly about women's sexual drives and needs because I came first. After all, Lisa Alther had plenty of it in *Kinflicks* too. Some men are very upset about this in my writing and the anti-hypocrisy stand I have taken. Many men are very pig-headed. I've tried very, very hard for honesty in my own life. I think people betray each other more in sex by thinking 'women are different from men' in their needs. Monogamy has always been harder on female sexuality. Men had to believe they owned our bodies to assure themselves of a legitimate line of succession.

"As for the lesbianism in *How to Save Your Own Life,* there was a time in the Women's Movement when you had to be either a lesbian *or* a heterosex-ual. I wanted to show that men and women can be friends as well as lovers."

Part of the sales success of *Fear of Flying* in both Holt hardcover and NAL paperback editions was due to the tremendous amount of time Erica Jong gave to doing personal publicity for the book. Now she says, "I'm only going to do a few major network television shows and I will go to England for a week or so for Secker and Warburg. You want the truth? I would like not to do any of this kind of thing."

Jong's editor at Holt is now Jennifer Josephy but she also singles out for special praise her paperback editor at NAL, Elaine Geiger. "Elaine, who has been my dearest friend and fan, did a lot of the line-by-line editing on *How to Save Your Own Life*. What I want from an editor is never any heavy censorship, but somebody who will help counteract the paranoia endemic in publishing, basic hand-holding."

To bring the cycle of Erica Jong's personal life up to date for her readers, *Fear of Flying* will be brought to the screen, probably by Columbia Pictures. There is talk of Ingmar Bergman being interested in it. Erica, who, like Isadora, became embroiled in lawsuits over the filming of her book, says, "I wasted a great deal of money on lawyers. I now think it is more important to do new work than to fight."

Her real-life ex-husband, Allan, "is happily remarried. His life has gone well. He got married a month after the divorce became final although he greatly opposed the divorce. He has always been very supportive of my book, and wanted me to use his name, Jong, so that it would become my official writing name. He identifies himself as the person who helped me become a writer."

As to where Jong wants to go next in her writing—such writers as Kathleen E. Woodiwiss and Rosemary Rogers had better look to their laurels. She is researching right now an 18th century historical novel, "an epic story of a woman looking back at her life, from the time she was born in Queen Anne's day, to the romantic poets, all of whom she has known. It will be a literary spoof, a romp. I'm very eager to prove I can write in another genre." One thing Jong promises: authentic historical accuracy, which she believes most of the current writers in the field lack.

Will there ever be another Isadora book? "I would love to keep this character alive," she says, "but I am becoming interested in religious meditation and yoga these days. Maybe I'll try *Isadora Finds Enlightenment*. I am bored with writing about women's sexual fantasies.

Erica Jong

Rozsika Parker and Eleanor Stephens / 1977

From *Spare Rib* (July 1977), 15–17. Reprinted with permission of Rozsika Parker.

Q: In *Fear of Flying* you write about all the "itches" that marriage creates, you say "How could you sit on a train fucking total strangers with your eyes? How could you do that to your husband? Did anyone ever tell you that maybe it had nothing to do with your husband?" You make it clear that you blame marriage itself for the problems couples have, yet in *How to Save Your Own Life* you seem to be saying find the right man and live happily ever after. Isadora leaves Bennet for Josh—Mr. Right. Have your ideas on marriage changed?

A: I would never stand for a relationship with someone where fidelity was legally enforced, where it wasn't understood that there might be times when we would not be faithful to one another. It's a very different thing to go lovingly into a monogamous relationship because you are fond of someone and want to be faithful, than to enter into something that at heart is an economic contract in which the woman is selling her body, womb and services for a livelihood and social status.

Q: But you've said that free choice hardly comes into making the decision to live as a couple—"It's heresy in America to embrace any way of life except as half of a couple". And you go on to describe the suffering that comes from living isolated with one other person, yet you are still saying it's the answer?

A: You know it's so dangerous when we read novels as polemics. Just because *How to Save Your Own Life* has a happy ending, I'm not saying unequivocally that women can all find true love and happiness, and that if they are unhappy it's because they haven't found the right man. I'm more subtle than that. I'm not that dumb. Also there's the dark side to Josh and Isadora's relationship. There's love, there's a romantic readiness, there's an opening but there's also a kind of rivalry developing. Even in this relationship which is so close there's the snake in the garden, discontent.

Q: What makes it romantic is the notion of the lover being your other half, a sort of long lost brother. If we search the world and find this person then we've got a good chance . . .

A: In some way I believe that. I believe it is possible to find a man who is a friend as well as a lover. I think men and women are brought up to hate each other, and they fulfill their programming all to grimly well; they become enemies and their lives divide down the middle. But if one finds a kind of liberation—and God knows it's hard enough because we are all very culture bound. If you reach a point where you don't need a man for social status or money, only for affection, good comradeship, and, hopefully, good sex, you may choose a much better sort of man than you would have had you needed someone desperately. Mostly in their twenties women are looking for a daddy, for a protector. In their thirties they look for a companion and that's already an improvement. But speaking personally, and I will speak personally without saying that I've done everything in the book which I haven't, or that I'm indistinguishable from Isadora which I'm not, but in my own life my relationships with men have never been better. It's partly because I now think that if I have to live alone, I'll live alone. I'm not so afraid of it. And as soon as I stopped being afraid the good things started to happen in terms of relationships.

Q: That connects to what you wrote in *Fear of Flying* about the dangers of a woman looking for a man to complete her: "If we haven't the power to complete ourselves, the search for love becomes the search for self annihilation." Isadora says that her greatest illusion was to imagine that Adrian Goodlove was her double, and here she is in *How to Save Your Own Life* welcoming Josh as her long lost brother.

A: Well, in the beginning of an infatuation you tend to feel that the person is your long lost other half. As the relationship develops you discover you are very different. If it survives, you grow to like and honour the differences. If it doesn't survive the infatuation period, then it just smashes to bits. In *How to Save Your Own Life* I've written about the initial period. The subject of the book is really *how hard it is to leave,* how frightening it is to change your life. As a love story it's barely recorded, it's hinted, suggested, recorded in poems.

Q: Let's go back to how you lost your fears. Isadora's fear of flying was one aspect of her feeling that if she stopped worrying for a moment everything was going to fall apart. How was it that another woman poet's death,

Jeannie Morton's, cut through her fear of flying so that she no longer felt she had to worry to keep the plane up?

A: It's sort of ineffable isn't it. In the book it's not explained and maybe at the time I wrote it I didn't really understand it. I think there comes a point in life—usually tied up with the death of people we love—when you lose the fantasy that you can control everything. I mean we go through our adolescence and twenties thinking we can control absolutely everything and going mad when we can't, and then there comes a point—I think it has to do with the ageing process, losing dear friends, the death of a parent or some irrevocable illness, when you say to yourself, "I will try to make my life as good as I can for myself, but to some extent it's in the lap of the gods." You become much more of an existentialist. It has to do with recognising your own death someday through the death of a friend. The strange thing is it's very liberating. It's like always being afraid of your thirtieth birthday and when you get past it you think, "Oh it's marvellous, why didn't somebody tell me that the worst things is anticipating it." That's the way I feel about death. Also Jeannie acts out a part of a suicidal wish that Isadora has. She is an aspect of Isadora.

Q: You were quoted as saying that you wanted to show that women needn't be "spinsters or suicides," that they could have both love and work.

A: I wanted to create a role model that was positive because I think we've had tons of negative ones and retribution fantasies. In the 19th century novels I admire—*Anna Karenina, Mme Bovary*—the heroine makes one little stab at independence, rebelling against her husband in the form of an affair. Rebellion against patriarchal society always took the form of a sexual affair because women's sphere of action was so narrow—there's no other place where she can rebel. So Anna goes off with Vronsky and ends up a suicide. In the 20th century you see so many women writers carrying on the same old thing. The woman will always be punished. She doesn't do very much but the punishment is hideous; death, a baby run over, sterilisation, the only way Kate in Edna O'Brien's *Country Girls* trilogy manages to deal with her womanhood is by having her organs ripped out. It's not a positive role model, OK? (laughter)

Q: But how positive is Isadora's solution, going from one man to another?

A: But you see, I think that the crux of the book, the message if you want to find one, is not in the erotic epilogue, nor in the poems, but when she goes back to the hotel and writes those notes to herself. Renounce useless guilt.

Don't make a cult of suffering. Live in the Now. Always do the things you fear the most. Trust all joy. I won't put down love either because I really think it is very soul expanding to love another person, whether you call it romantic love or whatever. And I don't think human beings were meant to live without other people, although there may be times in one's life when one should quite happily live alone. There are different stages but the point is to lose the fear and to sort of have a risk taking attitude towards life.

Q: Yes, I agree with that, but I think romanticism has been very destructive for women. You have to draw the good things out of it—being close to somebody, intimacy, sexual ecstasy. But we haven't really found a way of expressing those outside the romantic framework.

A: Yes, but it's such a shame that everything is so fraught for women nowadays. I've seen people come to blows over my books. I've seen myself bitterly denounced as being reactionary.

Q: Isadora says she writes to be loved. You books seem to arouse real love or real antagonism. Does this upset you?

A: For much of my life I've written for approval, but I'm sort of moving out of that now. I have certain tasks this year and one is to stop caring so much what people think of me. Am I number one on the best seller list or number five? Were the reviews good or bad? I think all this was given to me as a lesson by God, or the Muse, or whoever you believe in, to teach me a kind of indifference. I mean that indifference in the Zen sense.

Q: Several of the things you have said do suggest a mystical or Zen Buddhist attitude to life. Would you say you have moved towards that . . . moved through psychoanalysis?

A: I'm much more drawn towards religion than I ever thought I would be, and I'm much more drawn towards mysticism than I ever was. Not that I think answers are to be found in meditation, but I would like to cultivate a kind of engaged detachment that the Zen Buddhists talk about. So that one can stand above the stream of life and see the circus of the world without becoming too enraged by the injustices and the excesses, and yet struggling to combat them. That would be a solution for me—not a final solution, but much better than where I've been before. I've had some hard knocks because of the backlash against the success of the first book. And many men are outraged by *How to Save Your Own Life* because it is an instance of a woman actually changing her life, and doing this awful thing of finding a younger man—a man with no money and a beard. This is practically worse than being a lesbian; men can sort of dig lesbianism, it's a turn on, they think it's very cute and really want to get in bed with the two of you. But they can't deal with the idea that you might want another, younger man—that's really upsetting. But despite all of this I've found myself in a much greater state of calm. I will go to a hotel room in a foreign city and be really depressed because I've had an interview with some hostile son of a bitch, and I'll do breathing and meditation, take a long bath and enjoy the peace. This is new to me—this ability to enjoy the loneliness that isn't lonely.

Q: Whereas Isadora would have masturbated several times and made long distance phone calls.

A: Yes, however much you draw on your own feelings and experiences in a book, by the time you've written it you've already moved somewhere else.

Q: Did you find it hard to write another book after the success of your first?

A: Yes, it was ghastly. I knew that no matter what I did next I would get a lot of shit. I knew that if I did a book that was totally different, say a historical novel, everyone would have said, "Oh, why did she give up Isadora, she should have developed her, after all she left her in the bath tub and it wasn't clear which side of the fence she was on." If I wrote a sequel they would all say, "Oh the lazy woman's way out." And if I didn't write a book for eleven years, they would say, "See one shot author, we told you it was one shot." So I gritted my teeth and said, "You're a professional writer, professional writers write a book every couple of years, whether they want to or not. That's your life, how you make your living, so by God you've got to get through number two."

Q: Do you also see writing poetry as a profession?

A: Poems are divinely inspired! (laughter). Maybe I feel I'm a poet first who happens to write novels. Sometimes I feel that my novels support my poetry habit like somebody being a rock star to support their cocaine. No, I do feel very serious and passionate about writing novels. When you write poetry, you preach to the converted; people who read it are poetry freaks. But when you write a novel you reach the big world, you cause a stir and you really make people reconsider their lives.

Q: You really think that novels can change people's lives?

A: Oh yes, I do. Well, not directly, but I frequently get letters from women who say, "As a result of reading your book I began to think about my marriage and I've now left my husband." I think that's why a lot of male critics don't like my work.

Q: But your work has been described as a breakthrough for women in that you've written very explicitly about sexuality. Why do you think it has been so hard for women to write about their own sexuality?

A: If you sat in on some of the interviews I've been through you'd know— the flack is incredible. I come home sometimes and say, "I'm never going to write another word about sex as long as I live." Anaïs Nin said that the reason she had eliminated all the stuff about her love life from her published journals was because she had seen what had happened to Violette Leduc, and that a woman who writes about sex is not tolerated. And Boy! It hasn't changed much. Now they are claiming that we are all climbing on the bandwagon to earn royalties because a lot of these books have been successful. There was a piece by Francine du Plessix Grey in the *New York Times* where she said, in the famous old tradition of the woman writer turning on her sisters, that women writers are stuck in the body trap; now they've discovered writing about sexuality, all they can write about is sexuality and it's become boring and . . . I think Francine is a brilliant writer but what she's doing here is internalising male criticism of women and spewing it out against other women.

Q: Didn't you find it very difficult to write about sexuality? All our images of what is erotic have been male defined.

A: It was terrible. I wrote *Fear of Flying* in a constant state of tremour. I was so scared my hands and feet kept getting cold. I kept thinking, "What are you doing, what are you putting on the page, you nut, you can't publish this." And then I would say, "So you won't publish, but you'll just get it down and then you'll put it in your desk drawer. Unless you see it through to the end you'll never believe in yourself again." I had started so many novels that I hadn't finished—this was one book I was going to finish *for myself.*

Q: So you were very aware that what you were writing about was taboo?

A: Definitely. When I was writing the second one, partly as a result of *Fear of Flying,* it had become more acceptable, almost chic. Then I felt a very different kind of pressure—the pressure of knowing that anything I wrote next was going to be hated and nothing was going to be seen for its true value. So at that point I said, "OK I will write this book for 1990, by then people won't be over-reacting."

Q: Many women will react against the way you treat lesbianism in your second book—you present a very negative picture.

A: Well, the sad fact is that I'm not presenting a picture of lesbianism. The awful thing about writing a novel is that people think you advocate and/or disapprove of everything in the book. I was really doing a send up of that whole period in the Women's Movement in the United States when everyone said, "If you don't try it once whether you like it or not, you're not a good feminist." I think that's absurd and an insult to people who are inclined to be gay, or seriously gay.

Q: But very little has been written about sexuality between women. Your book might be the only account of a lesbian sexual experience that a woman could ever read. Sure you're entitled to say what Isadora felt about it, but why make her lesbian lover the baddy—the one who hides Isadora's love letters from Josh?

A: She was not being spoofed as a lesbian but as a user, a sort of rich girl who uses writers for her own agrandisement. You try on different modes in different books and people always try to nail you—saying that's your position.

Q: I would nail you as reaffirming heterosexuality. Given that you're saying we have to change so many things about ourselves, about society, one of the things we have to fight against is the absolute imperative to be heterosexual.

A: It's unfortunate my book is seen as an attack on lesbianism. I didn't see it that way. It was a very satirical and broad thing, I mean no-one has ever used a bottle of Dom Perignon to my knowledge. I thought that would tip everyone off that it was just wild parody. I recognise that lesbianism has been a way of independence for many women, of having shelter in the world without seeking it from patriarchy.

Q: Would you say politically that you see men as directly oppressing women? Do you think that male power is what we struggle against?

A: No, it's patriarchy and it's carried on by women as well as men. Our mothers are often the greatest teachers of patriarchy, and you see women in power who are just as patriarchal as men. It's much more subtle than that. In the early days of the movement we assumed that if you put women in positions that men have held, you would eliminate sexism. But in a misogynous society even women are misogynists.

Q: The few times that women's liberation is mentioned in your books, it's in a kind of satirical way at the end of some sexual exploit. It's very much an individual's attempt to pull herself up by her boot straps. I don't get much awareness that there are lots of other women who are thinking about thee things.

A: Well, I never got a lot of nourishment from the movement. I've always been a person who loved other women and had women as friends, but the first time I ever came intellectually to blows with another woman was after the movement began. There was such incredible pressure. And there was this awful feeling that if you wanted to do your own work, if you said, "I'm sorry, I can't come to the benefit/poetry reading on Monday, Tuesday, Wednesday, Thursday, Friday nights, because I'm writing a novel," you were selfish, not contributing enough, too interested in your own career. You had to be out there stuffing envelopes, you had to be doing this and doing that, and what you were best at—writing—was the thing that got lost, there was no time for that. I made a very conscious decision that I had more to give by writing novels.

Erica Jong: Writing about Sex Is Harder for a Woman

Robert Louit / 1978

From *Magazine Littéraire* (February 1978), 44–45. Reprinted with permission of *Magazine Littéraire*. Translated by Charlotte Templin with assistance from Christine Guyonneau and Peter Witteveld.

After a number of fruitless attempts with the tape recorder . . .

Robert Louit: Are you adept with machines?

Erica Jong: Not all of them. I love my old B.O. [typewriter], but I always write out my books by hand and then give the manuscript to a typist. I always write on a yellow pad. I can compose a book review at the typewriter when I want to be brief and to control the length of the review. That's journalism. But for my books I use a typewriter only at the last stage. Writing by hand is more natural for me, more "organic." After the manuscript is typed, and I look at it again, I see what needs to be changed. I can make corrections. Each time it's a new text.

RL: So you do several revisions.

EJ: That depends. For my two novels I continued to revise certain chapters while others remained unchanged. I cut a lot, pruned. *Fear of Flying* was much longer. I cut about one hundred pages of the part that takes place in Paris. I was afraid of boring the reader. It was very dark . . . the dark night of the soul. I kept very little of that.

RL: Why did you think it was necessary to expunge that element? It's true that the tone of your novels is rather optimistic, or at least not at all despairing.

EJ: Not everyone is of that opinion. But I didn't cut because it was dark. I felt an obligation to my reader not to bore him. I can't stand boring writers.

RL: Who can?

EJ: That poses a big problem for me. Certain people don't take my books seriously because they are entertaining.

RL: You think people still judge books that way—on one side are serious books and, on the other, entertaining books?

EJ: Definitely. The *New York Times* or the Nobel Prize Committee only approve of books that are unreadable and boring. It's a school of criticism. It extols Thomas Pynchon, Saul Bellow—who is not a bad writer. What they like about him is that he cites Hegel every two lines. And if you cite Hegel frequently, that makes you a philosopher. What bores me the most is high brow, academic literature. The novel of Bellow's that I like best is *Henderson the Rain King*.

RL: I agree—along with *The Adventures of Augie March*. It is true that with age Bellow has become the great man of American letters, a little pompous and highbrow.

EJ: That's what I mean. I don't want to criticize him because he has had a real influence. It's the academy that annoys me too often. They confuse the literary and the boring. Thomas Pynchon, for example, whom no one reads, not anyone I know anyway. This rule remains: if you entertain, you are not serious. Do you know who bores me? Thomas Mann at his most somber. Not Melville. It's not that an author tries to be comprehensive, to portray every aspect of society, that bothers me. Consequently, I love Doris Lessing. I forgive her for her lack of humor because she describes society so marvelously. In her own way, she writes the *Bildungsroman.* I wouldn't write that kind of book, but I respect an author who does. I have nothing against the scrupulous desire to depict every aspect of society. It's deliberate obscurity that annoys me.

RL: What do you think of the nineteenth-century novel?

EJ: We have very little patience with long novels because so many things interrupt our lives. Television, the telephone. The rhythm of life is different. Nowadays it is difficult to read a novel like *Clarissa*. It wasn't so difficult in the eighteenth century. Technology has also changed our way of reading and writing. I would never be capable of writing a novel like the nineteenth-century novel. I live in my own time, but I love those novels a lot. If an author believes that the world can be contained in a book, he tries to do it. But few believe that today, and that's why one finds thin books of 200 pages, abridged versions. One can no longer believe that a book can contain the world. I'd love to revive the nineteenth-century sensibility—when it was possible to believe that a book could contain everything. I'd love to be able to do that in my books—but so many things intervene.

RL: That's why some writers have tried to transform the nature of the book itself, like William Burroughs with his fragments. Do you find such books readable?

EJ: That didn't start with Burroughs. One finds it in Lawrence Sterne, with his typographical games. It's interesting. I'm not as opposed to it as I used to be when I hated typographical games. But it does not excite me. I don't care for concrete poetry. I don't think those games amount to very much. I happened to write some poems that I played with on the page. That was supposed to be like Chinese music, meant for a Chinese lover and played on strange instruments. I toyed with it, but it didn't do a lot for me. I'm happy one can experiment with poetry nowadays. Previously poetry was too rigid, too rule-bound. Whitman is a specific example. Whitman has had success everywhere in the world, but particularly in South America, where he inspired a school with disciples like Neruda. But he was an object of disdain in his own country. He liberated South American surrealistic poetry. He has had an enormous influence. In America there has always been a gulf between what Philip Rahv called the Redskins and the Palefaces—the writers of the salon and those of the Wild West. I think the latter have found favor in Europe or in South America, but in our country, academic writing has gotten the upper hand. In the United States, Bellow has more admirers than Henry Miller, although Miller has probably had a greater influence on the rest of the world. Miller is still criticized by the establishment. As recently as last autumn, William Gass criticized Miller harshly in an article in the *New York Review of Books*, in connection with the publication of *Genius and Lust*, the anthology of his work edited by Norman Mailer.

RL: Writing about sex does not always make for success.

EJ: When a writer writes about sex, that is all that is remembered of his work. People don't see the rest. Once when I was told that Miller was a pornographer, I took a copy of *Big Sur* and read a passage, without saying he was the author. People guessed it must certainly be Emerson or Thoreau. No one thought of Miller. The important theme of American literature is anti-authoritarianism, it seems.

RL: Miller loves Emerson and Thoreau, as he wrote. He's their heir. Do people criticize you for sexual writing?

EJ: That's why I mentioned it. I'm fed up with talking about it. But that's very likely because I'm a woman, young, and don't as yet consider myself a *grande dame*. Perhaps one day, when I am seventy years old, with white hair

and a body like Margaret Meade's, it will be better for me. But as long as
I'm young and pretty, things will not be easy. People confuse me with my
writings. Writing about sex is harder for a woman. Even more now, because
we have supposedly completed our sexual revolution. I have not experienced
that kind of criticism in France, Holland, or Sweden. But in Great Britain, in
the United States, and in Germany, the reviews of *Fear of Flying* were very
puritanical. In France and Holland, my books were received as literature. In
Sweden, I may have been chided for not dealing with the war in Vietnam,
something that concerns the Swedes. In the United States it's rather, "The
sexy blonde has written another book."

RL: What harm is there in being a sexy blonde?

EJ: None, except people don't believe she can think.

RL: In *How to Save Your Own Life* there are reflections about the sixties
that strike a pessimistic note—the sexual revolution has taken place, but traditional sentiments like jealousy are still with us.

EJ: Does that surprise you? Jealousy interests me because it is very imme-
diate, primary. One of my intentions was to describe jealousy from a female
point of view. That has almost never been done to my knowledge. Everyone
should be able to experiment with his or her sexuality at about age twenty
because it's the age of madness, of sexual madness. We control ourselves too
much. We don't give ourselves time to experiment. Most people discover that
they don't want to live that way during their entire lives because it's not
satisfying. They prefer stable relations with one person. But first of all, one
does have to experiment. The good thing about the sixties was that people
were not forbidden to experiment: All the students could make love or do
drugs. Most of those people are now settled, married. Personally, I was
caught between two generations during the sixties. I didn't belong to the
generation that did drugs and took part in protests, but I was young enough
to have friends from that generation. I envied the freedom of people five
years younger than I. I envied the Woodstock generation. It had an almost
mystical experience. But they finally understood that sex was not a response
for everything. They acquired a sort of receptivity—to God, to mysticism
through drugs. I envy them.

RL: That's what one finds in *How to Save Your Own Life*. Your characters
suffer from a mild generational time-lag. One of them takes cocaine but in a
ritualistic way. The orgy doesn't come about naturally.

EJ: That's true, but I'm not a true fan of orgies.

Erica Jong

Diana Cooper-Clark / 1981

From *Interviews with Contemporary Novelists* (London: Macmillan, 1986), 115–143. © Diana Cooper Clark 1986. Reprinted with permission of Diana Cooper-Clark and Macmillan Ltd.

DCC: What do you like best and what do you like least about your work?

EJ: That's a very tough question. I think what I like best about my work is that it has authentic energy and passion, and I try to preserve the energy and passion even at the risk of technique. As a college student and as a graduate student, I was very literary, and the work I loved best was highly structured verse, Nabokov's novels, things that were puzzles and literary games. As I got older and as I began to write myself I began to hate that graduate-student quality in contemporary literature. I came to distrust that writing of fashionably obscure books to be unravelled by literature students. And I discovered that what was most important to me in literature was the quality that makes the work of Whitman so great and makes the work of Mark Twain so great—energy, life, perhaps even vulgarity. To me, *that* is the important strain in American literature. I find the crabbed, cerebral strain in American literature to be the antithesis of what our spirit has brought to the world. I mean if we are going to write that way, we might as well be English.

DCC: Or French.

EJ: Well, French literature is another problem, although certainly many French writers are terribly cerebral at the expense of the heart. What I like best in my own work is its naturalness, its closeness to life. At times I've become upset when I've reread *Fear of Flying* and thought, "what a damn shame to have become famous for a book that is so full of wisecracks, and so full of itself." And yet I know that that kind of book was important for a woman to have written at that period in history. Also, it has undeniable exuberance—not a usual thing, especially for women. Women writers are always so terribly constrained by "What will people think of me? What will Daddy think? What will Mommy think?" Historically, they often silenced themselves. The curse of the woman writer is the need for social approval. It was absolutely necessary that somebody come along and break down those barriers. And I was the one whose fate it was to do that. I was speaking not only for myself but for something that was brewing in the atmosphere at that time.

86

And by God, there are still so many women writers who are afraid to question authority. Ultimately, I think that, as with all writers, my strengths and my weaknesses are so intertwined that I myself cannot separate them. If I load myself with self-consciousness and I say, "Don't be vulgar, don't be this, don't be that," I won't write at all. So I have to write to my strengths, although I certainly see the weaknesses in my work as well as anyone; perhaps better.

DCC: Do you ever fear the silences of Hardy, Melville, Hopkins, that Tillie Olson talks about in *Silences?*

EJ: I fear being silenced by critics. I fear my own depression when I'm attacked. I fear the retribution that falls on a woman who writes about sex. I fear the retribution which falls from the literary establishment. I fear the Bible-thumping puritans who all want to silence women who write about passion. I don't think I write so prolifically. My output has not been so large. On the contrary, most writers spend most of their life in various kinds of neurotic rituals. They spend a lot of time drinking, they spend a lot of time in bad relationships. I write about two-and-a-half pages a day when I'm working on a novel. I work about six or eight hours a day, four to five hours of which is really creatively productive. I don't think that's a lot. I don't think two-and-half pages a day is much for someone who's a full-time writer. I do think that the output of most writers is so pathetically small because they make fetishes out of their weaknesses and they don't work most of the time. That's the truth, and it's very sad. People work to a fraction of their creative ability. I think that even I don't work to a fraction of my creative ability. I hope that someday I will.

DCC: You've said: "Learning is good for a poet as long as she doesn't become a professional scholar." What do you mean by that?

EJ: Read everything you possibly can. If you are going to be a writer, the chief way you learn your craft is by reading and writing. And read everything. Read Smollett and Defoe and Dickens and all the poetry you can. Read archeology and the history of religions and the Bible and everything that will give you a sense of language and everything that will give you a richness of knowledge and self-knowledge. One of the writers I admire is Robert Graves—and it's partly for these qualities of expansiveness. He's somebody who's written novels to make a living, and poetry because the Muse inspired him; but he's written about the history of poetry, archeology, religion, myth, and the White Goddess. I think he's an inveterate sexist but I can still learn

from him. He doesn't write the kind of poetry I write, his concerns are not
the same as mine, but I love his kind of Renaissance spirit. That's the kind
of writer I really want to be. The trouble with being a professional scholar
(as I found when I was doing my never-completed Ph.D. in eighteenth-
century English lit. at Columbia) is that scholars are asked to write books
about books *about* books, rather than books. I don't want to spend my time
arguing with some scholar who says that *Tom Jones* is really a Marxist para-
ble. I don't think that what's interesting about Swift, let's say, is whether we
decide he's an ameliorist or a pessimist; what's interesting about Swift is not
what scholars decide about his themes but that he's an incredibly energetic
and vigorous writer who has the gift of life in his writing. That's why his
books are read today. The Marxist or the Freudian or the structuralist debate
doesn't interest me much anymore. I think such debates are artifacts and, as
such, they're bullshit.

DCC: Do you think the "Death of the Novel" debate is artifact?
EJ: Yes.

DCC: Do you think that people like Anaïs Nin who write books about the
future of the novel are doing something useful? Do you see any need to
prophesize about the future of any art form, the future of the novel, the future
of poetry, giving death chants for either form?
EJ: I think it's wishful thinking on the part of blocked, self-hating writers.
The critics and the academics in this country have managed successfully to
kill poetry as a popular art by demanding that poetry be crabbed and difficult
and impossible to understand. They have so put over the notion that poetry
be impossible to understand, that they have, in fact, killed the chances for
poetry to ever be a popular art form again. They would like to do the same
to the novel by exalting Thomas Pynchon over anybody who write intelligible
prose, and I think that if given their own way, they would be a greater danger
to literature than the people who pay Judith Krantz three million dollars!
Because I don't see the pop-novel as a danger to literature. There'll always
be publishers eager to make a buck out of what they think will be the new
profitable trash. And that frightens me far less than the desire to force upon
the public work that is unreadable. So I'm not bothered by the huckster aspect
of the paperback scene. It's unfortunate that those book deals get so much
publicity because it gives the impression to young writers that there's just
money, money, money; whereas most writers in this country make an average
of two thousand dollars a year from their work. Most of the members of the

Authors Guild of America average 2.5 thousand a year from their writing and work at teaching or advertising or something to make a living. There are perhaps a hundred writers in America who make a living from writing fiction. I am one. Vonnegut, John Updike, and Philip Roth are a few of the others. You can count them, really, on just a few people's hands. This, by the way, also accounts for the viciousness of the criticism that commercially success-ful writers receive. It accounts for it almost better than anything because the only word to explain it is "envy," really.

DCC: There seems to be a rage for order in criticism. But new art forms are always evolving. Would you agree with Archibald MacLeish or Dylan Thomas that it is almost impossible to define art or to create categories for art?

EJ: If you study the history of literature, you see that certain art forms decline and others arise. In the seventeenth century, the novel was considered a trashy, low, literary form, suitable for serving-maids who wanted to pervert their minds. In the early eighteenth century, before Richardson and Fielding, the novel was also considered trashy. Who would have dreamed then, that in the twentieth century the novel would have become *the* great art form and the modern successor to the epic? Eighteenth-century writers were always apologizing for writing novels at all. Fielding apologized for writing anything so low as a novel, and he called *Tom Jones* an epic to elevate it. That's why I think we should be wary of making these predictions about high and low art, because we really don't know. The novel is alive and well as long as people buy it and read it. The fact that Judith Krantz can make three million dollars is proof that the novel is alive and well. Maybe her novel isn't one of the enduring ones, but the novel is a lively form, and let's say it's read by lots of people. What the successor to the novel may be, I'm not sure. For a time in the sixties, wishful journalists asserted that the novel was dead and journalism was the coming form. Indeed a lot of novels were influenced by this, including my own first two, *Fear of Flying* and *How to Save Your Own Life* (which I wrote as sort of mock-memoirs). I tried to make those first two novels seem not like novels but like autobiographical projections. I succeeded so well in fact that nobody believes they *are* novels [*laughs*].

DCC: Do the literary and academic efforts to create structural responses to art really in fact create a Tower of Babel? An excluding language of semi-otics, phenomenology, structural fabulation, and on and on . . .

EJ: Those things have nothing to do with the creative process except to impede it. If a novelist is stupid enough to listen, they create self-consciousness which is the enemy of art, the enemy of creation. I cannot see that that does anything to help the writing of books. Maybe it's good at some point in your life to help organize your view of literature. When you're a student of literature in college and you're confronted with this mass of material for the first time in your life, and you can't understand it, it may then be useful to have certain constructs to help you absorb it. It is important to understand whey the novel rose to dominance in England in the eighteenth century (based upon the rise of the new reading class and so on). I think it's helpful to look at the nineteenth century and try to understand why a novel of interior psychological exploration should have arisen in that particular century. That's interesting. But the other more arcane kinds of constructs that literary critics think up, are useless self-indulgences. I think they help academics get promoted and that's about all. They have a certain limited utility as teaching tools but I don't think they have any use artistically at all.

DCC: "Open form" aesthetics, which became increasingly popular in this century with the influence of the East in particular, created a new sense that art is anti-Aristotelian, anti-teleological, anti-beginning, middle and end. Literature in this century, perhaps starting with D. H. Lawrence or Joyce, and continuing with Susan Sontag in her book *Against Interpretation,* is calling for a literature that is more transparent, and a critical structure that is what Sontag calls, "Descriptive rather than prescriptive," and here and now, the organic. What do you make of all those ideas?

EJ: It's shocking that there's been so little experimentalism in contemporary literature. I think it's shocking that here we are, fifty years or sixty years after *The Waste Land,* after *The Waves,* after *Ulysses,* and almost nobody is publishing novels using the kind of freedom from narrative structure that those early modernists tried to teach us. I find it rather amazing that so many of us are still writing novels in a nineteenth-century literary tradition. I'm all for experimentation. I am not anti-Dada or anti-open form or anti-non-linear narration (if you can make it *interesting* and *readable*). I hate the idea that everybody's going to go back to writing sestinas for a new generation of new critics. I see a whole reactionary trend in the arts right now, and I think we should stay open to experimentation. But we should not use experimentation faddishly. We should use it to develop our own styles. I don't believe that there must be a beginning, a middle, and an end in a novel absolutely, and I'm sympathetic to open form, but a novel has a reader, and you can't make things so hard for the reader that the reader won't finish the book. I mean if you want the reader to read your fucking book, make it readable! I want to be read. I don't want to turn off my reader on page one. And the purpose of a story, a plot, a beginning, middle and end, is not to fulfil some crazy formalistic Aristotelian rule, but to get the fucking reader to read the fucking book. The reason for having suspense, for having sympathetic characters, for having a readable story, for doing some work for the reader so that the reader can enjoy the book, is to get people to read your work so that you can communicate with them! Therefore you *must* create some principles of organization to lure the reader from page to page. Why talk about it from an abstract intellectual point of view? Let's talk about it pragmatically. When you read *Great Expectations,* you want to know what's going to happen. When you read *David Copperfield,* you wade through a lot of stuff that's boring because you want to find how it turns out. When you read *Anna Karenina* you go through all that information about farming in Russia because you want to know: will Anna and Vronsky get together? Those are very simple practical reasons for having a plot and a story, a beginning, a middle, and an end.

DCC: That makes sense [*both laugh*]. Is the best criticism empathetic? Doris Lessing speaks of a critic who is the alter ego of the writer. She says, "Writers are looking for the other self, more intelligent than oneself, who has seen what one is reaching for." Have you ever encountered any critics like this?

EJ: I have never encountered such a critic. The problem with most critics is that they have never actually written a novel, nor published one, nor do they know the problems a novelist faces; they are in a different world. They seem not to know that the novelist is dealing with certain things, such as, "How can I get the reader to turn the page?," and they seem to think that this is irrelevant, whereas to me that is the most relevant of all.

DCC: So are the best critics other writers?

EJ: Well they would be, ideally, except that the economic and literary rewards of writing are so capriciously distributed, that other writers are likely to be jealous. Other writers who have had less success than oneself, tend to be eaten up with envy. If they are teachers whom one has superseded, they may also have their own jealousies. If they are other women and they feel there is only room for one token woman in our male-dominated literary scene, they may be jealous. So, ideally other writers are the best critics, but

in practical reality they often attack one simply because they feel so threatened themselves.

DCC: I have often seen two types of book reviewing and criticism. One
practises a kind of "kill—tear—maim—rip" of which I think Lance Morrow
in his review of *How to Save Your Own Life* is one type of piranha—
EJ: I didn't read it—

DCC: Just as well. The other kind of critic is a sort of "protect—baby—
suckle—pamper." Canadian critics writing about Canadian literature are
often a type of "help the cripple" criticism [*both laugh*].
EJ: We don't have that type in the States. In America we go out of the
way to attack success and we have a whole form of journalism based on
gossip and attack. Apparently it sells magazines. Apparently it lets people
get their frustrations out against the people they envy; famous people,
whether actors or writers, or musicians. That's a very destructive journalistic
trend. It literally destroys some of the people against whom it's directed—
Jean Seberg, Marilyn Monroe, Truman Capote, Tennessee Williams . . . the
list is long. I do think it is an incredibly dangerous thing. Writers are best left
alone. I don't think writers have much to learn from critics, truly. I mean I've
never met an ideal critic. Sometimes I have had wonderful essays written
about my work, usually by sensitive young writers or older writers, beyond
jealousy, or sometimes academics who are particularly sensitive and who
take my work very seriously (yet also playfully). I've been very grateful for
that kind of intelligent consideration. But I never really learned anything
from your garden-variety critic.

DCC: What are your prime considerations when you are writing a book
review of somebody else's work?
EJ: [*sighs*] Oh dear! I always keep in mind how hard it is to write a book,
even a bad book. Even the typing is a chore [*laughs*]. I realize that the stamina
to sit down at a desk every morning at nine o'clock and to work in solitude
isn't given to many people. It's not something to be laughed at, slashed at,
made fun of. I'd rather not review a book than gratuitously attack it. I'm not
much into attack. Because it seems to me that one so transparently reveals
one's *own* smallness when one attacks. It may not seem that way to others,
but when I read a vicious attack on someone's work I always see envy, envy,
envy written all over it, and I can't help thinking, "How can that person want
to reveal to the world how envious and narrow and small he is?" I'm too

proud to want to reveal those feelings. I have them just like anybody else at times, but I don't want to reveal them to the world. That doesn't seem like anything I want to be known for.

DCC: But aren't there ways of evaluating literature without being petty, vicious or mean? Aren't there ways of saying that this book is better than that book and this is why, without being small?

EJ: I guess there are, but you see so few examples of that sort of criticism. One has to write about the characters, one has to write about the language of the book, one has to write about whether the book has a heart or whether it's an empty shell. *Those* are the things that are important in a book. I can tell you in a minute when I read something whether it lives and breathes or whether it's dead. I can tell you, for example, that *Catch-22* lives and breathes and that *Something Happened* is a shell, although they were written by the same man, at different times in his life. *Good as Gold* is alive. That's what matters to me about books.

DCC: Many feminists today seem to respond best to a literature that reveals ideal role models: energetic, life-affirming women who are capable of taking their lives into their hands, as opposed to the perhaps more realistic portrait of women who are confused, and emotionally and philosophically ambiguous, or, in fact, complacent women who don't even care about these choices. Do you think feminist critics give bad reviews to writers who don't create these ideal role models; I'm thinking here of Roberta Tovey asserting in her review of *How to Save Your Own Life* that the ending endorses what she calls "the power of the male"? I'm also thinking that *Fear of Flying* was what you called a saga of unfulfilment, so you were *not* trying to portray ideal role models; you were talking about one woman's life and the way she tries to sort it out.

EJ: I don't know the review you're talking about because I deliberately didn't read the reviews on *How to Save Your Own Life;* I didn't think I'd survive them if I did. All I can say is that there's a difference between literature and utopian inspirational prescriptions; and feminist activists (like the Marxists of the thirties) don't care about *literature.* They are looking for inspirational writing that will help women rise up from their despair. This is all very well and good but it has nothing to do with literature. I understand the *desire* for inspirational writing, "I am woman, hear me crow, blah blah blah . . . I am strong, I am invincible, I will overcome, we shall overcome, blah blah blah." That's useful at certain points in the struggle. There's a need for that. But it has nothing to do with literature. Literature has to do with accuracy and truth. It has to do with representing, with as much accuracy as you can tolerate, the situation of women as you see it. It cannot help but partake of the conflicts you perceive in your own heart. Do you have a fantasy about a man under the bed? Well then, you write a poem about it. You don't say to yourself, "Is the fantasy about the man under the bed perhaps an expression of my oppression as a woman and perhaps a woman who is not oppressed will not have such a fantasy?" That may well be, but it is your job as a writer to write about the truth of the heart, not the societal changes you *hope* will come in the future. Find me a woman who is strong and invincible (who isn't a cartoon character like Wonder Woman), who you'd like to read a novel about. Let those feminist critics come out of their collectivist cowering in the closet and write a goddamn book about an invincible strong woman who is not dominated by men, and let that book be something that ten million women around the world want to read! Will they read it? I mean, will it relate to their lives? It sure doesn't relate to my life. My life has been a constant struggle of self-stunting stereotypes, of falling in love with men who were very sadistic, and then having to escape various cages of my own making, of educating myself to freedom because I was *not* born free. And I think I'm quite a characteristic woman of my time. I've had a great struggle towards freedom and a lot of women identify with *Isadora* because she is struggling. She is in conflict, as most of us are. Besides, with Utopian literature, there is another problem. If you start out with a heroine who is strong, invincible and not in conflict, what the fuck are you going to write about? Where's your story? From the simple point of view of the storyteller, there is no story without conflict; there is no story without struggle. There is no story without change and growth. I mean, what they're asking for is something you would only ask for if you had never tried to write a book. It's meaningless. It's silly. It's almost a giggle. I've been told by certain feminists: "Isadora should not have gone back to Bennett at the end of *Fear of Flying*." Well maybe she shouldn't have, but that has nothing to do with writing a novel. That "should" and that "shouldn't," has nothing to do with literature.

DCC: Are there any female writers now who don't seem to elicit the critical antagonism you do? Why?

EJ: Well, my father calls me up and asks, "Darling, why don't you get reviews like Joan Didion?," and I explain patiently why, and I *do* understand why. Joan Didion is an excellent writer, but she doesn't really question the female role. Her women are invalids and cripples. She is a brilliant prose stylist; her essays are beautifully formed. I read them with great pleasure, I must say. Her novels interest me very little, because I'm weary of novels about women who are invalids, who are mental cases, who are self-destructive. But I think she appeals to a certain kind of male-oriented critic because she doesn't question the proper sphere of woman—the proper sphere of woman is to lie in bed and be an invalid. She says it about herself when she talks about her migraine headaches. She says, in effect, "I am not robust." In the patriarchal culture we live in, there are certain acceptable roles for women, and one of those acceptable roles is to be perpetually ill. And you will find that women writers who accept the invalid role, the sick, suicidal, self-destructive role, encounter far less controversy than women who assert that females are strong, that females are sexual, that females are whole. Mary Gordon's *Final Payments* is an example of a really fine piece of work that also does not question the traditional female role. And I think the book was praised not so much because it was excellent (which it was), but because it showed a woman submerging her whole life and identity in her father. Perhaps unconsciously, all those critics who were so shocked by sexuality in my work, *loved* the idea of a young educated woman submerging her identity in her father. Often when books are madly praised, you must look through and see what is going on psychologically. This takes nothing away from Mary Gordon who is a wonderful writer, an extraordinary writer. But she is not a revolutionary one. The revolutionary writers tend to get axed.

DCC: How do you feel about Diane Wakowski refusing to be included in all-woman anthologies?

EJ: It's understandable, after centuries of oppression, centuries of denigration of women poets, that some women poets should feel that they don't want to be classed with the women poets! I understand her feeling, but I think it's a misguided attempt to remedy sexism.

DCC: Many women feel that art exhibitions like "Retrospectives of Women through the ages" are a negative thing, simply because they categorize women as "female artists." You don't see "Retrospectives of Male Artists through the Ages." When Sarah Caldwell was invited to Russia as a "female conductor" to be exchanged with another female conductor, she wrote back and said, "Look, I'm just a conductor."

EJ: It's entirely understandable that these women don't want to be ghettoized; I don't fault them. I don't fault Wakowski, I know what motivates her.

But essentially we're quibbling. We live in a society that is very oppressive to women, and women creators, and I think that any way we can make ourselves visible, we ought avail ourselves of. We should be pragmatic. We shouldn't get ourselves all screwed up in all kinds of ideological disputes at this point. We don't have the luxury to do that right now. Of course, to be known as a "woman" artist is a denigration, but it's not as bad a denigration as being totally invisible, which is what has happened to most women artists in the past. I think we have to have a sense of humour about this. We can't *afford* to be purists yet.

DCC: I agree. You've talked about writing myths. You've said that you're writing "a mythology of continuation." What are the "myths" that "expand human consciousness" in your work?

EJ: When I was working on *Fear of Flying,* I was very struck by the fact that there seemed to be a "proper" ending for women's novels, and that proper ending was always suicide or madness. If you look at the novels by and about women (and I'm not just talking about novels by women, but also novels about women by great novelists like Tolstoy and Flaubert) you find that womanhood inevitably ends in madness or death. I felt it was very important to write a novel about a woman, that didn't end in madness or death. And I feel that that was a very revolutionary thing to have done at the time. And I honestly believe that a lot of the flack that I've received has to do with the fact that my heroines do not die and do not self-destruct. I refuse to accept the idea that women must be cripples or invalids. You can argue about whether women ought to wind up in the arms of a man or in the arms of a woman but that's less important than whether they wind up *alive!* I don't know if you've ever read Wendy Martin's brilliant essay "Seduced and Abandoned in the New World: The Image of Women in the New World" [see *Women in Sexist Society,* ed. by Vivian Gornick and Barbara K. Moran, 1971]. Martin argues that women in literature usually die for their one attempt at independence. The weight of tradition is extraordinary when you start looking at it. I mean you see it even in the "liberated" women writers of the last couple of generations. Look at Mary McCarthy's *A Charmed Life.* Look at the independent, strong woman who has to have an abortion and dies in the last paragraph of McCarthy's novel because she can't decide whether the baby belongs to her ex-husband or her present husband. Look at that as a "myth" of an intelligent woman destroyed by patriarchal values. Look at that and weep, and then you will understand why *Fear of Flying* created such a

furore, such a ruckus, because on a mythological level what I had said was
that women can live, *women can have sex and live, by God!* It's sort of
pathetic that you and I can sit here and have to say that that's a radical idea.
I mean it's pathetic and sad, but there it is.

DCC: You use the "mythology of continuation" also in *At the Edge of the
Body,* which is quite different I think from what you were doing before. In
your excellent article "Creativity Versus Generativity," you speak of a literary history of childless women. In what way would literature change, if
women who are mothers by choice and desire were writing to a much larger
extent?

EJ: Well, because patriarchy split women into the whore and the madonna,
it became necessary (both for practical reasons and for reasons of sheer survival, both physical and mental) for those women who wanted to be creators
to swear off family life or procreation, and for those women who were mothers to completely submerge themselves in motherhood. It need not be so. If
we had a sane and rational society, we would be able to have babies and write
books. There is no reason why we can't. Maternity is not a form of invalid-
ism. I wrote like a demon while I was pregnant. I enjoyed my pregnancy. But
I also had a husband who cooked and who did all kinds of things around the
house and who completely assumed that the house was as much his responsibility as mine. I had enough money to hire a nurse for my baby when she
was born. Because I was established in my career, I did not have to choose.
So it was not easy for me to do both, but it was *possible* for me to do both.
And it would be possible for most women to do both, but we've been really
robbed by patriarchal culture. The waste of life-power, of woman-power is
tragic. As a result, most of the women who have been creators have been so
at the expense of their generative function. And consequently, they've been
fearful of maternity, fearful of men because men might trap them into maternity, fearful of families because family life might smother their creativity,
and all of this is quite understandable. I probably would have been the same
had I lived in that age and had no contraception and no money and no legal
rights and so on. But that doesn't mean that it's *natural.* I think that when
you have a generation of women who have been creators and mothers both,
there are going to be experiences in literature that we will not have seen
before. In my novel, *Fanny,* which is an historical novel, I have a section
dealing with birth and pregnancy and the kidnapping of a small baby that I
think could only have been written by a woman who is a mother. In a way,

it's the most moving section of the book. I could never have written about this as well, if I hadn't experienced motherhood. I could have written it, but I could never have written it quite the way I wrote it, from research alone, or from reading diaries of pregnant women. And I think literature has been pushed in the direction of male concerns for centuries, for twenty-five hundred years to be exact, and I think it is time for that to stop.

DCC: I've heard so often Karen Horney's point of view that men created because they couldn't have babies, which, as you've pointed out, are quite different experiences. Art is conscious. Giving birth is not.

EJ: Many women believe that and it becomes a self-fulfilling prophecy. My oldest and best friend from college (who's a highly intelligent woman) says, "When I'm pregnant I can't do anything creative." Now, she's a brilliant woman, but what it is that leads her to believe that (I think she's just been brainwashed by male culture) has created a situation in which she does stop work when she's pregnant. When I became pregnant, I feared a cessation of my creative drive, but in fact I was extremely productive, and I think I wrote better than I am writing now. I wrote with tremendous fire and tremendous passion because I felt almost as I had the Muse inside me. Maternity is an amazing experience. And I secretly think that men and male culture have denigrated it because they can't have it. "If we can't have it, it must be bad and it must impair your creativity," they said. I think, on the contrary, maternity enhances creativity, and we've been lied to. Moreover that lie has been enforced by sheer brute force; the throwing of women out of academies, the firing of pregnant women, and such atrocities. If women are so naturally weak during pregnancy, why all the obstacles? It's rubbish!

DCC: I like that. To change the subject, Karl Shapiro wrote that many American poets wrote prose, not poetry. It's another one of those statements.

EJ: I think it's kind of silly. Most poets in any age are not inspired by the Muse. I prefer Robert Graves' distinction to Karl Shapiro's. I think the test of a true poem (as Graves says in *The White Goddess*) is whether or not it is true invocation to the white goddess (the mother goddess who is the goddess of creation, of destruction, of provenance. The triple-aspected-goddess). One knows a true poem by whether or not the hair stands up on the back of one's neck. And, alas, 'tis true that, most poets in every country, in any age, do not write muse-poetry (in Graves' sense). They write clever anagrams, rhymes, verses. They write topical trivia, or prose, or fashionable cant. But it's not truly muse-poetry, for that is always a very rare commodity. And even a poet who has written muse poetry at some time or other, may not always write it, because the Muse comes and goes as She wishes.

DCC: What are the elements that constitute your decision to write a poem or a novel?

EJ: A novel starts out with a situation and a question. A novel is usually an exploration of a situation and a character, while a poem usually starts with an image and a poem is an epiphany. They are totally different kinds of writing. With a novel I'll begin by saying, for example, "What if a young woman in conflict, trying to break away from her family, has an unsatisfactory love affair with an impotent man, travels across Europe, loses her husband, but finds herself as a result?" A novel starts with a, "What if?" And then I say to myself, "Who is this woman? This woman is very intelligent, very well-educated, but emotionally confused, tied to a conservative husband on the one hand, tied to a family who is trying to thwart her on the other hand, and at the same time she's an artist, she has longings for adventure, and so on." She's tugged between two forces. She's in Europe, in Vienna, it's a psychoanalytic convention . . . and then I work out the details. But a poem starts with a line and the hair standing on the back of my neck. I'll get an image from the blue and I know I'm on the track of some buried memory or something in the communal unconscious that needs to be teased out. The poem is a burst of insight rather than a working out of a psychological situation. They're so different that the two kinds of writing don't conflict at all. They satisfy different needs.

DCC: You've said that you're interested in mixed forms; the mixing of prose and poetry which you have done in your novels and your poems. What are the possibilities for that?

EJ: The possibilities are much greater than have been explored to this day. I've always particularly admired a novel of Nabokov's called *Pale Fire,* which is written in the form of an epic poem with footnotes. The whole novel takes place in the footnotes! I love that sort of thing. I'd love someday to write a book in which I use both poems and prose. I tried to use poetry to some degree in *How to Save Your Own Life,* because I think it is better to tell a love story in poetry than in narrative. Perhaps one can tell a love story more truly in verse.

DCC: In a review of Anne Sexton's poetry you said that two of her worst traits are "repetition" and "excess." Do you think that there is any aesthetic value in both? Most great writers are uneven. In some cases their worlds are felt and lived in by the reader precisely because they are repetitious and excessive. The observation also seems contradictory because you've said that you use repetition in your poetry and that what you want particularly in the novel is "excess."

EJ: Maybe I criticize it in her because I see it in myself.

DCC: But it's something you like, "excess" in the novel and "repetition" in poetry. You see that as something positive in literature, yet still you pointed it out as a weakness in Sexton.

EJ: Perhaps I was being unfair. As Anne Sexton's work went on, she edited herself less and less. Which maybe isn't always a bad thing. I think perhaps her later work was too loose. But she was a great poet; I'm not saying she wasn't. In fact, when I told her she had "excess" in her work, she wrote me and she said, "Of course, I have excess, I am an excessive person." Maybe I was really criticizing myself because, at times, I share that trait with her. Often, in our book reviews we are more subjective than we admit.

DCC: I don't think that if you criticize her for what you think inhibits the poetry, that this necessarily means that you are saying she's not a good poet. What is the balance between viciously attacking a writer for no purpose at all, and standing back and saying, "Well, this isn't doing what you want it to do."

EJ: Alas, there is very little good criticism around. There are a lot of reasons for this, too. One reason is the gossip-mongering mentality of most magazines and the low level of contemporary journalism. But this infects literary journalism as well, although the literary journalists claim to be above it. But they do exactly the same sort of thing in their own way. Witness those articles in the *New York Times Magazine* about John Gardner and Truman Capote and Norman Mailer. They make writers seem like buffoons! Even the article on Updike was regrettably gossipy. And the one on Mailer was so vicious that it made me want to hug him and say "there, there." But I do think there's another reason as well. Most writers have very weak egos, and they tend to like unreservedly those people who praise them. Writers and critics tend to group themselves into cliques. And much book reviewing is merely touting one's friend's books and smearing one's enemy's books. There are very few real literary standards being deployed. I have felt the pressure. Sometimes I'll be sent a book to review and it's a bad book by somebody I'm personally fond of. What to do? I turn the review down, be-

cause I can't honestly rave about the book. But at the same time I don't want
to hurt the author's feelings if he's been kind to me in the past. That's why I
often think we are much better critics of foreign writers whom we don't know
personally. I notice, for example, that I always get a far more dispassionate
appraisal in France, Italy, England, Sweden, Holland, and Japan than I do in
this country.

DCC: I know that Isadora isn't necessarily your mouthpiece but she does
make an interesting statement. She says: "Mediocre poetry did not exist at
all." Now is that to suggest that mediocre prose is *not* a contradiction in
terms? Was Matthew Arnold right in saying that poetry is the most perfect
speech of man, for through poetry man comes nearest to being able to utter
the truth? And of course, there is the Western bias that poetry is the greatest
of the three literary genres and the novel is a sort of poor cousin.

EJ: I think they do different things. A poem can't tell you much about the
relationships of people in families. A poem can't tell you much about the
way society infringes on the individual. Not in the way the novel can. They're
very difficult to compare because they have different spheres. I think that
poetry is more precise than fiction. Poetry chronicles the *dream* life of an
age; a novel chronicles its *social* life. What I meant really, when I made that
distinction in *How to Save Your Own Life,* was that you can have a novelist,
like say, Dreiser or Doris Lessing who is not a beautiful stylist but who's a
great novelist none the less. Whereas in poetry, a person who is a clumsy
stylist wouldn't be good at all. I'm always amazed how graceless Lessing's
prose is.

DCC: She's doing it intentionally.

EJ: I don't know whether she's doing it intentionally or not. I find her a
rather graceless writer, but also a great writer. I can't think of anyone in our
age who can so involve you in the world of her novels.

DCC: But that's her point. Because life is confusing, because it is graceless, because it is fragmented, we need a style that is commensurate to whatever is being discussed. So she deliberately sets out to be clumsy, fragmented,
graceless. She feels it is pointless for critics to remark, as they did, that her
style is clumsy. Of course, that raises the aesthetic question of whether the
theory is better than the practice.

EJ: The last person I would feel myself worthy to criticize is Doris Lessing, whose achievement is immense. I look up to her as one of the great

women of our age. But I would say that I have often wished that her novels were easier to read. It took me ten years to read *The Golden Notebook* because I was so turned off by the introductory dialogue in that novel that I kept putting the book down. As a novelist I try to lure my reader into my story more seductively. I don't want to be easy, but I do want to be seductive enough to the reader to be read. I don't see that as prostitution of art. I see it as enhancement of art. But every writer is entitled to write the way she wants to.

DCC: Do writers of even loosely based biographical portraits in any way feel exempt from such depictions? Would you resent anybody if they depicted you in a novel in the same way that you loosely based portraits on Anne Sexton and Henry Miller?

EJ: Both Ann Sexton and Henry Miller should be flattered at the way they've been depicted. I don't think anybody could ever maintain that either of those portraits is anything less than totally flattering. I remember Anne Sexton's closest friend, Maxine Kumin, saying that Jeannie Morton was a very touching portrait of someone like Anne. And Henry Miller's children thought that the portrait of Kurt was very much the best of Henry. If I lived for my critics, those people who did not find the portraits flattering, I wouldn't live long! I went through a very rough time after *How to Save Your Own Life*. I never believed there was that much malignity in the whole world. I am not a vengeful person. I've always had lots of friends who were loving and affectionate. I could scarcely believe the hatred that was spewed out against me. I went through a terrible time. I felt very misanthropic. I felt as if I never wanted to publish again. I also went through a period of total sexual isolation because I had been so typecast as a sexy writer that I didn't even want to have sex again as long as I lived! But that depression has receded and I've been left with greater detachment from praise and blame. I hope that now I'm healthy enough to say: "Fuck you world!" The fact that I've stirred up controversy and denunciation is proof that I'm doing something worth while. I look back at the women writers who have been most attacked (Aphra Behn, Sappho, the Brontës, Kate Chopin) and they were all revolutionaries. If you look at the history of women writers you'll see how *horribly* they've all been treated. Look at the examples of our female geniuses and say: "I'm lucky to be alive, I'm lucky they don't burn me as a witch. I'm lucky I'm not stoned on the heath!" In another age, I would have been totally silenced, like Kate Chopin. And, of course, they *have* tried to silence me. There has been censorship of my work in many places, including my own country. We're none of us beyond that and we're going back into a period of tremendous repression. It's a dangerous time.

DCC: You consider yourself a satirist. What do you mean by the term?

EJ: I think a satirist is someone who scourges the world in order to bring it to its senses. That would, of course, be Swift's definition. Swift said also that satire is "a glass wherein people do generally behold every face except their own." That's a fair definition of satire too. But privately, I think of a satirist as someone who's disappointed in mankind (because he once was an idealist) and who makes fun in order to bring it to its senses. A satirist hopes to ameliorate the world, although the satirist will always tell you that he doesn't believe any amelioration is possible (because human beings are completely, morally destitute). Yet the satirist keeps on trying to bring them to their senses! Swift, for example, is the ideal example of a satirist. I love Swift. I even like what I know about him as a person, crazy as he was. The world tries to wear artists down. The world tries to batter them. All those creepy little conventional journalists, all the Lance Morrows of the world, try to make artists tow the mark and be good girls and boys. What they're doing is not really any different from what your mommy did when she said "girls don't do this" or "girls don't do that." What are they but spokesmen for convention and bourgeois morality? They claim to be spokesmen for literature, but they're not spokesmen for literature. It's doubly hard if you're a woman because you're trained to try to win approval, to smile, to be nice to authority figures. You have to *learn* the sheer strength not to let the bastards get you down. It's very hard. By God, it took me two-and-a-half years to get over my sense of hurt and outrage about the way *How to Save Your Own Life* was treated. But really now, when I think about it, it was a very cleansing kind of experience because it reminded me that I am a maverick, and that I shouldn't be seeking approval. The minute I get approval I should be worried that maybe I'm not telling the truth in my writing anymore. As a writer, my value is partly as an irritant. If I'm not an irritant, maybe I'm not telling the truth anymore. If I ever write a book to which Elizabeth Hardwick responds and says, "Ah, that's what women really think," I'll be very surprised if it's any good. I think Elizabeth Hardwick is a brilliant woman, and her writing in *Sleepless Nights* and in her literary essays is beautiful. But I think she's another woman writer who doesn't question the female role. And I don't think she tells the whole truth. I think she's been properly socialized to the female role.

DCC: Did you read *Seduction and Betrayal?*

EJ: Yes, I did. There are some things in it that are very good, and some things that are totally wrong headed about women. When, for example, she says about Sylvia Plath that the problems for a male poet are the same as the problems for a female poet, she's dead wrong. But the giveaway to me is *Sleepless Nights.* A beautiful book with a totally empty centre. How can she write about a character named Elizabeth who lives on West Sixty-seventh Street and talk about everything about her life except the central fact of her marriage? The whole relationship with the man who shaped her life, to whom her life as, in one sense, sacrificed, is left out. It's as though her life as a writer were sacrificed to being a muse to Robert Lowell. But this sacrifice is *not* in the book, which is precisely why the male critics all stand up and say, "Bravo Elizabeth, you never gave him away! You did the thing that women are supposed to do, you stood by your man." What distinguishes her from Tammy Wynette? I mean, *really?* Except that she's a beautiful, beautiful writer. And some of the stories in that book just break your heart. The things about the old people and the bag lady and the crazy old hotels on the west side. You read them and you weep. And then you weep again to think that a woman of such great talent should have been sacrificed to the ideal of the "angel in the house." Who says that perhaps her gifts were not equal to Lowell's? He did *not* spare her in his poems. But, Freedom, as Camus said, is the right not to lie, and women writers do not yet have that freedom. We're not supposed to say things about our husbands in public; we are not supposed to say things about our sex lives in public; we may only write about those subjects that we are allowed to write about (i.e., old bag ladies and hotels on the west side). And those we write about beautifully; we pull out all the stops. But we can't permit this self-censorship to continue! You cannot be a writer and censor yourself at the same time. And to be a good woman in this patriarchal society is to be self-censoring and self-stunting; *ergo,* the woman writer, is perforce a bad woman.

DCC: Are there are any other writers, past or present, whose comic sense you like, other than Swift?

EJ: I love Mark Twain, Chaucer, Rabelais, Colette, Keats and Blake. I discovered a lot when I did my eighteenth-century novel *Fanny.* I discovered who I still liked and who I didn't like at all any more. And I found I didn't like Pope at all any more, though I had once loved him.

DCC: You did your Master's thesis on Pope.

EJ: But I can barely stand him now. Swift, however, I like better than before. And I now find Fielding very trying—very distanced from the reader. I used to love Fielding. Now I find I can't bear the way he puts a kind of screen between himself and the reader. I once adored everything about *Joseph Andrews* and *Tom Jones*. Now, when he says, "Dear Reader, this is the meaning of this scene," I hate the Fielding narrator. I also find I like Smollett very very much. I like his vulgarity and I like all the things in Smollett that Dickens imitated (Dickens was always saying that he learned from Smollett). I like him far better than Fielding at this point in my life. Isn't that funny?

DCC: How about people in the twentieth century?

EJ: I like Salinger very much too. Henry Miller—I think he's funny and I think he's bursting with life, despite his sexism, his anti-Semitism, and all the other antisocial things that he does.

DCC: Do you like Mordecai Richler's humour?

EJ: I loved *St. Urbain's Horseman*. I thought that was a terrific novel Rollicking and funny and full of life. And full of a nice kind of vulgarity. You see I think Lessing is right in the sense that a novel has to be as crammed as life. That's what the novel was born to do.

DCC: You said that *Fear of Flying* was a female picaresque in the tradition of *Henderson the Rain King* and *Tom Jones* and *Augie March* and the *Tropics*. In what way were you thinking that it is a female picaresque?

EJ: It's a story about a young person going on the road in order to find herself. That's a very old literary form, perhaps the most ancient. It's a way of organizing a hero's or a heroine's quest. *Fear of Flying* is clearly a novel about the quest for self.

DCC: I also found that there were many structural and thematic similarities to Joyce's *A Portrait of the Artist as a Young Man*. *Fear of Flying* was the portrait of the artist as a young woman. I was impressed by the structure, the use of flashbacks, and as you said "recollections in tranquillity," the use of consciousness.

EJ: That was my original title for the book. All I can say is that *A Portrait of the Artist as a Young Man* was one of my favourite books. I think I first read it when I was fourteen. I loved that and I loved *Dubliners*. Of course, *Ulysses* is a wonderful book although it takes five years to read it. When you read *Ulysses,* you read two pages a night and annotate and try to figure out what's going on. I would like to read it again, but it is not something I would readily plunge into. That's why when I started to talk about structure before,

I said narrative structure is a ploy. In a way, it is a part of the writer's bag of tricks, and it's merely a way of keeping the reader turning pages.

DCC: I find so many of your ideas about narrative structure interesting and one of the things that struck me in *Fear of Flying* is that you called the last chapter "A Nineteenth-Century Ending." I assume that this title was ironic.

EJ: Obviously. Nineteenth-century novels end in marriage while twentieth-century novels end in divorce. Twentieth-century novels usually begin with relationships breaking apart. I was playing on those ideas.

DCC: You've been asked before about your audience. You've said that a possible epitaph could be: "She addressed her readers as if they were her friends and the become her friends." Yet you have also talked about the perverts you attract. When I first read *Fear of Flying,* my reaction was that you were talking to me partly because the novel makes highly literary allusions to writers and artists; on the other hand, you have said that there are women in Texas with minimal education who feel the same way.

EJ: I've never really understood that, but it's true. Perhaps we literary types underestimate our readers. They are smarter than we give them credit for being. Some people who read *Fear of Flying* and *How to Save Your Own Life* had never read a novel before.

DCC: I like what you said in *How to Save Your Own Life;* ". . . the aim of my writing is to utterly remove the distance between author and reader so that the book becomes a sort of semi-permeable membrane through which feelings, ideas, nutrients pass." Do you think that that happens with the reader from Texas with minimal education?

EJ: Yes I do. I don't really know why, but I do think that I found an awful lot of readers who had never really read before. I must say that I have a lot of readers who are not readers of novels *per se,* and who are not particularly literate. It comes as a great shock to me because I was really the most bookish sort of Ph.D. candidate and never thought of myself as the kind of person who would become a popular writer. Even when *Fear of Flying* was first published, the publisher thought it was a literary first novel (by a poet no less) which is why they didn't promote it or advertise it enough. Nobody thought of it as a blockbuster. Nobody thought of it as a sex-novel, by God, and it was only a year later that people were asking me in interviews, "Did you put in the sex to calculate the success?" As if I had calculated it! I wish

I could! So it comes as a great shock to me to have an audience that broad. But I like it. In a way I'd rather have an audience of people who have never read a single book before than have an audience of fabulators. Better fornicators than fabulators! [*laughs*].

DCC: What is it about the eighteenth century that you particularly admire? I loved *Fanny.*

EJ: It's before the nineteenth century and the horrible sexual hypocrisy of the nineteenth century. As you know, if you've read Boswell, life in the eighteenth century was far less hypocritical about sex than life today. Sexuality was much more in the open than it is today. The English in the eighteenth century were extremely coarse about hygenic functions, personal functions, shitting and pissing and fucking. When you go back to the eighteenth century, therefore, you go back to a period of great robustness and great vulgarity. But it is also the period in which our modern consciousness was formed. We, in the United States, have a constitution that is an eighteenth-century document. Our country has eighteenth-century ideals—"The pursuit of Happiness," for example. So I take this wonderful time in which there was so much ferment about the slave trade and the rights of women (and yet the women were legally second-class citizens they could not own property, they could not vote), and I say, "What if a woman like myself had lived in that time?" And I was able to put all the problems of women in society in relief because I was dealing with a time removed from ours, and yet through it I could satirize our own time. It was a book I had always promised myself to write. For years I had wanted to do an eighteenth-century novel in which the heroine got involved with all the great men of her time: Pope, Hogarth, Swift, all of them. And it was great fun to write—and, I'm told, great fun to read. My desire to write *Fanny* came out of my perception that there are far too few great women heroines in literature. I wanted Fanny to be a female picaro, an innocent who is educated but not corrupted by the evils of an evil world. I use Cleland's Fanny as a kind of counterpoint to show that women can be far more than the whores of erotic fantasy. I have always had great affection for *Fanny Hill,* mostly because of the sunnyness of the writing, but there is no denying that Cleland's imagery of women is extremely reductive. I wanted to show that a woman might be reduced to working as a whore, but she would not necessarily forfeit her brain and subtlety thereby.

DCC: In your "Afterword" to *Fanny,* you wrote: "In many ways her [Fanny's] consciousness is modern. But I do believe that in every age there are people whose consciousness transcends their own time and that these people, whether fictional or historical, are those with whom we most closely identify and those about whom we most enjoy reading."

EJ: It is one of the tragedies of the movement for feminine liberation (which spans the last three centuries) that each generation has to discover it anew as if the issues had never been around before. Our generation is no exception. In fact, Lady Montagu, Mary Wollstonecraft and others understood female bondage quite as well as we do. Their works are still tremendously timely. Society has not changed all that much, alas. But even with all their self-awareness, these women accepted their societal constraints as the price of their survival. Fanny does not. She has an unshakeable conviction of the importance of her own selfhood which is really rather modern.

DCC: Witchcraft is an important part of *Fanny* and you've since written a book called *Witches.*

EJ: One of the most attractive theories of witchcraft suggests that witchcraft is, in fact, the remains of an ancient matriarchal pagan cult surviving secretly in a Christian world. Although some scholars have quibbled with this theory, it seemed to me an important and richly evocative philosophical underpinning for a novel. I wanted to write a novel about female strength, female bonding, and using the witches exemplified these things underlying *Fanny* as a matriarchal myth. Women come to help other women in childbirth, in rape, in economic need. The men are incidental to the story. The male lovers are companions, but the primary importance is the mother–daughter bond.

DCC: Fanny often changes into male costume. This aspect of androgyny can be seen in opera, drama and literature. Shakespeare often has women playing men: Rosalind in *As You Like It, Viola in Twelfth Night,* and Portia in *Merchant of Venice.*

EJ: I made Fanny change into male costume throughout the book to emphasize the capriciousness of sexual roles and their immense variability. The sexual roles as we know them in our society are really metaphors for power and powerlessness. They are not immutable and biologically destined. By showing Fanny putting on and taking off roles with her clothes, I wanted to show that sexual roles are every bit as superficial as clothes—and as important.

DCC: You have said that with *Fanny* you wanted to "try an epical novel, an historio-comic epic (as Fielding would say, in which I could show through the counterpoint between past and present, just how much had changed for women and how little."

EJ: In the early seventies, it was very important for women writers to make sense of their own presence, to understand their own oppression and anger. As the feminist movement matured, it became important to see our own struggles in an historical context, to realize that the more things change, the more they stay the same, and to discover our own histories. The historical novel, like the science-fiction novel, has often been a satirical device for viewing our own world. In *Fanny*, I wanted to show both how immensely the world had changed for women, and how little. In general, I think writers tend to turn to the past for their material when the present seems overwhelming. The perspective of the past enables us to understand our own times more acutely.

DCC: What is your response to people who ask, "When are you going to create a male hero?"

EJ: People always ask me when I'm going to write about men—as if writing about women were just a warm-up for the main business which is writing about men. The question has a sexist assumption about it, albeit an unconscious one. Male novelists have often used female protagonists to represent the human condition (Anna Karenina, Mme Bovary), but when a woman uses a female protagonist to represent the human condition, critics ask "When are you going to write about a *male* hero?" It seems to me that we have had four thousand years of male heroes, and only about a decade or so of female heros. That means we still have three thousand, nine hundred and ninety years to go before we catch up!

Erica Jong

Ralph Gardner / 1981

From *Writers Talk to Ralph Gardner* (New York: Metuchen, 1989), 190–201. Reprinted with permission of Ralph Gardner.

"Unfortunately, so many modern poets, and so many modern critics, have praised obscurity in poetry, and have condemned clarity. My poetry tends to be clear. And poets who have a kind of lucidity have a potential of a large audience."

Although Erica Jong has written more books of poetry than fiction, it still comes as a surprise to some fans when they "discover" her as a poet. A bestselling poet, by whatever yardstick, measures big sales of a volume of verse.

"When I was writing *Fear of Flying*," she is quoted in *Poets & Writers Magazine,* "I felt, 'Yes, I'd like people to read me.' I had published two volumes of poetry to critical acclaim and received recognition and awards, but it was clear to me that poetry was not the language of the land."

Her most recent book of poetry, *Ordinary Miracles,* sold more than 30,000 copies—a staggering amount for a book of poems—while *Fear of Flying* (which first appeared in 1973), as of several months ago had passed the 8,050,000 mark in the United States. It is equally popular abroad, where it is translated into fifteen languages.

In a letter to the *New York Times Book Review,* commenting upon "the curious publishing history of my first novel, *Fear of Flying*," she recalled that "It is a history so atypical that it should be a beacon of hope to first novelists and publishers alike." Her book was greeted by mixed newspaper reviews, but was lauded three months after publication by John Updike in the *New Yorker,* and after nine months by Henry Miller, who cheered it in the *New York Times* as "a female *Tropic of Cancer.*" Even so, Jong believes it was her readers who "made" this book about a woman's growing-up; reaching out for independence and self-knowledge.

However, it was *Fanny: Being the True History of the Adventures of Fanny Hackabout-Jones*—the book discussed in our interview—that, I suspect, was a story she had long wanted (and was trained and eminently qualified) to write. This narrative is set in 18th Century England, an era that interested her as a student at Barnard College and later, at Columbia University where, in 1963, she received her M.A. in 18th Century English Literature. Alexander Pope was the subject of her master's thesis.

Like Isadora Wing in *Fear of Flying,* Fanny pursued an education, but Jon described her as "a naif, a picaro and at the same time a very modern wench in 18th Century dress." This red-headed young heroine also was an aspiring poet who encountered highwaymen, bawds, pirates and witches as well as some of the greatest minds of her time (Pope, Hogarth, Jonathan Swift and John Cleland make cameo appearances). Jong's answer to "What if Fielding's *Tom Jones* had been born a woman?", Fanny seems to have a rather modern feminist view and analysis of much of what happens. At a total 505 pages in hardcover, it is also her longest novel to date.

To satisfy readers who, possibly glimpsing themselves in Isadora Wing's quest for emotional and sexual fulfillment, Jong continued Isadora's search in *How to Save Your Own Life,* completing this trilogy with *Parachutes and Kisses.* Calling it "Jong's best book," the Associated Press reviewer "found Isadora weary but willing, after three broken marriages and more than her share of fame and infamy, and . . . in love again in Venice, wary but not cynical."

Along with 18th Century England, Venice has thoroughly fascinated Erica Jong. It is not surprising, therefore, that her newest novel, *Serenissima,* to be published this month—April, 1987—by Houghton Mifflin, is set in Venice. It is a saucy, erotic tale in which the author bends time out of shape as she spins her heroine, Jessica Pruitt, from the paparazzi-crazed atmosphere of the Venice film festival to the Venetian ghetto of the 16th Century, where she becomes the model for Jessica in Shakespeare's *Merchant of Venice.*

Gardner: Here first novel was *Fear of Flying,* published in 1973. To date, more than 6,000,000 copies of that book have been sold. Her latest novel will probably surpass that figure. I'm Ralph Gardner, visiting with Erica Jong. Her latest bestseller is *Fanny; Being the True History of the Adventures of Fanny Hackabout Jones.* It is published by New American Library. Erica, welcome to Ralph Gardner's Bookshelf.

Jong: Thank you.

Gardner: A lot of your readers who enjoyed *Fear of Flying* and *How to Save Your Own Life* will discover an entirely new and different Erica Jong heroine in *Fanny*. How is Fanny different from your earlier novels and heroines?

Jong: *Fanny* is a conscious attempt to create a real female hero. Isadora Wing is a woman who is tugged between being an anti-heroine and being a heroine. And I think Fanny is a true female hero. She is very strong, courageous, tough, and yet sweet and tender. I really always felt we ought to have a literature about female heroes. Fanny is my attempt to make one.

Gardner: You might say Fanny is an Eighteenth Century Horatio Alger heroine.

Jong: In a way she is. She is very like that. I mean, she rises from modest estate to great fame and fortune. She is saved by her pluck and her bravery from many terrible situations that other people couldn't get out of. And, in a sense, I identify with her, but I also feel she is an idealized self. She's much braver than I am.

Gardner: I believe Fanny's story is almost twice as long as your other novels, isn't it?

Jong: It's a very long book. A very ambitious book. It was an attempt to create a vanished world. To create a world of Eighteenth Century, or re-create it.

Gardner: Erica, you mentioned a "vanished world." That is what I enjoyed so much. I found myself so deeply involved in this vanished world. Your readers will get deeply involved in it.

Jong: I wanted you to know everything about what people ate, what the feasts were. How they went to the bathroom. What kind of contraception they used. How they laced themselves into bodices. What the sailing ships were like. Because it's always fascinated me. I'm an inveterate museum-goer and I've always been fascinated with the details of daily life in past ages. I can get lost in the Victoria and Albert Museum in London, looking at petticoats and the way they were made. And I wanted to put that kind of fascination into a book. I think that one of the things a historical novel can do is to transport you back into a vanished time and show you what daily life was really like.

Gardner: Tell us a little about who Fanny was at the beginning of her story, and who and what she became as you moved her through one adventure after another.

Jong: She's an orphan. A little baby girl abandoned on the doorstep of a great house in Wiltshire. She is taken up by an aristocratic family and given a fine literary education. She grows to beauty. She has wonderful russet hair and enormous boobs. She's the heroine of romance. As a result, we find her, at the age of seventeen, the beauty of the family and everybody is trying to seduce her. I mean, in a way, the beginning of the book is a send-up of what publishing people call a bodice-ripper. It's my spoof of that kind of novel. And, you know, in that kind of novel the heroine is constantly ravished, ravished, ravished, ravished by everyone in the beginning of the book. So this is what happened to Fanny. But, unlike the heroines of the traditional bodice-ripping romances, Fanny sets out on the road of her adventures to London. She falls in with a group of witches. She falls in with highwaymen. She works in a brothel in London. She eventually becomes a great female pirate of the Caribbean, towards the end of the book. But the difference between her and the conventional novel—the conventional heroine of the bodice-ripper—is that Fanny is a realist. She is a very tough woman inside. She's sweet. She likes men. Men are her companions. But never does she lean on them. And what she learns in the course of the book is to e self-dependent and to be strong. I think that is what I like about her—I like her better than any of my heroines—is that I like her moxie. And I like the fact that she's not a whiner or a leaner.

Gardner: Who are some of your other main characters?

Jong: Fanny's great loves is a homosexual highwayman named Lancelot Robinson. I think one of the great fantasies women always have is converting a homosexual man to a straight man. And Fanny experiences this. Lancelot, the leader of a troop called the Merrymen, is completely uninterested in her and she has to transform him. She's also aided and abetted by a black servant from Barbados, named Horatio, who speaks Latin and is very learned. He is forever throwing Latin phrases when ever the moment suits, or even when it doesn't suit. Her stepfather, Lord Bellars, is an important character because it's he who first seduces her.

Gardner: Fanny covers a lot of territory. Where do her travels take her?

Jong: She travels to the coast of Africa on a slaving voyage. Something that really fascinated me about the 18th Century is the fact that slavery was so deeply a part of the economy of England and America at that time. The fact is that people were already beginning a kind of abolition movement. There were many pamphlets written about the abuse of black people. And yet, the relations between blacks and whites, as today, were an integral part of the culture. And economically, the slave trade was the under-pinning of the success of many of the great shipping capitals—Bristol, Glasgow. Boston was built on the backs of slaves to an extent. Although we always blame the Southerners for the slave trade, it was the New England shipping cities that benefitted from it, too. So Fanny goes on a slaving voyage to Africa. Unwittingly, she's kidnapped by a slaving captain, not knowing that's where she's going. She goes to the Caribbean, where she meets the great female pirate of the time, Annie Bonny, and learns much from her. Eventually she comes back to England, but in changed circumstances. She is a different woman. She is grown-up and she is the mother of a daughter, and so on.

Gardner: To what degree do you consider *Fanny* to be a female *Tom Jones?*

Jong: That was my inspiration, really. My idea was to write about the sort of woman who really did exist in the 18th Century. But about whom, strangely enough, no novels were written. Because, although there were many heroic women in 18th Century life, the heroic ideals for women didn't exist in the novels of that period.

Gardner: What makes you decide upon the early 1700s as Fanny's time?

Jong: I was in love with that period. I had gotten my M.A. at Columbia in 18th Century English lit, and had done a thesis on Alexander Pope. Then I started a Ph.D. on that period but dropped out. I was always fascinated with the time, and with all the texture of the time. And the language of the time. I wanted to go back and do a book set in that period. It was a dream that I had had for about fifteen years. That I would eventually write a novel set in that time. I always knew I wanted to do it.

Gardner: Is your novel what you wanted it to be and what you expected it to be, or did it—at some point—take control of you and tell you what it was going to be?

Jong: It turned out kind of different from what I expected. All books do. All books that are worth anything do. I thought I would have Fanny span the century, and be writing her memoirs at the age of ninety. That proved unfeasible. You can't have this book with such a time frame. That's very hard. The book turned out to e a book about passion of motherhood, in a way. It turned out to be a book about mothers and daughters, and the wisdom they give each other. That I didn't expect.

It also turned out to be a deeply Oedipal novel about a girl who's really in love with her father. Again—you know—one of the absolutely imperishable female fantasies. I was very surprised when I discovered how incestuous the novel was. It was like a kind of self-analysis. I think one of the interesting things about writing a novel is that it is a sort of self-analysis. And you discover all the strange psychological fantasies—the quirks that you have—when you're writing a book.

Gardner: Erica, not only is *Fanny* set in 18th Century England, but you've written it in the speech pattern of that time. Tell me something about the research that must have gone into this book to enable you to do it—technically—as you did.

Jong: I had to get a feel for the language of the period, and I had to get the kind of sentences that they wrote, in which were Latinate sentences with balance and antithesis. That is the quintessence of the 18th Century sentence. All the 18th Century writers were trained on the classics. Mostly Latin. More Latin than Greek. But if I had really written a book that was in the style of Fielding, let's say, it would bore the modern reader. Swift doesn't bore the modern reader, but Fielding does. So what I had to do was to give you the feeling that you were reading an 18th Century book, and yet, make it bright and updated and fun so that you wouldn't be bogged down, because there are a lot of people who would rather kill themselves than get through *Clarissa,* or even *Tom Jones* or *Amelia.* One reads *Joseph Andrews,* by Fielding, but few people ever finish *Tom Jones.* They see the movie.

Gardner: Did your research take you to England?

Jong: Many times. I'm lucky in that I have a lot of friends in England who took me on research trips. And I was able to do research there at museums and libraries. Also, I live in Connecticut, not far from Yale. So I was able to use the Beinecke Library, which has a great 18th Century collection.

Gardner: I've read 18th Century books and found the language slow-paced and—as you said—boring. You successfully created the pattern, but at the same time produced a fast-paced, vastly entertaining novel. How were you able to do that?

Jong: I was aware of that problem when I started. I thought if I just wrote a pastiche, I would lose my readers. I didn't want to write only for 18th Century scholars. I felt that I have an audience. I'm lucky—I'm blessed—in having an audience, and I wanted to make the book fun to read. So I sort of tackled that problem head-on. We tend to write our novels like movies today.

We cut from scene to scene, cinematically. We are all influenced; I mean by *we,* novelists are influenced by the advent of the film. We don't write in the way the 18th Century novelists wrote, with digressions and epistolary fragments interwoven. That would bore us. So what I had to do in *Fanny* was to bring that liveliness—that cinematic writing—into an 18th Century novel. I was very conscious of the problem as I was working.

Gardner: Here's a quote in which you say you created Fanny as "a 20th Century woman placed in 18th Century England." To what extent have you made Fanny a 20th Century feminist in old-time England?

Jong: I don't think feminism began with my generation. In fact, there was an important feminist movement at the beginning of this century. There was an important feminist movement in the 19th Century. In the 18th Century and in the 17th Century. It's one of the sad truths about woman's status that we have to keep fighting the battle over and over and over again. And there were many women in 18th Century England who were quite feminist. But I wanted the modern reader to be able to identify with Fanny, and feel her fighting the battle for women's emancipation. I don't think she's out of her time in doing that. But I also made a conscious attempt to make it possible for a modern woman to identify with her. I think modern women do.

Gardner: You've also said about Fanny—here I quote you again, Erica— "I wanted to try an epical novel in which I could show through the counterpoint between past and present just how much had changed for women, and how little." How much and how little have you found has changed, in light of your novel?

Jong: We still live in a prostatocracy, as I call it. I mean we still have men debating in Congress what women should do with their bodies, and whether they should have safe abortions or not, and when life begins. So, in that sense, our world has not changed so much. I mean, as long as men are making the rules for what women do with their uteruses, our world is not a world of equality. But I think that, in many ways, there is more freedom. I felt we had come to a point when we had a decade of cant about women's liberation. A decade of cant that made everybody believe that real change had happened.

But really—underneath—the underpinnings of society were not so different. And I thought it would be fun to show that satirically in a novel about a vanished age. Because, really, Fanny is as unfree as the modern woman. And as free as the modern woman. In other words, her freedom depends upon her own pluck. Nobody gives her her advantages. I think that's still true of women today.

Gardner: Have you found that readers are searching for some kinship between Fanny and Isadora Wing, your *Fear of Flying* heroine?

Jong: I think it's obvious that the same person wrote the book. The three books. I seem to be preoccupied with certain things in all my books. I'm preoccupied with life as a quest for knowledge. I'm preoccupied with the problem of integrating mind and body for women. For being intelligent and yet sexual. Two things that have always been tough for women. We've always been asked to be either totally sexual objects or totally brain. I maintain—and my heroines maintain—that one wants both! And why not? That's what life is about. So I think that Fanny and Isadora are sisters.

Gardner: Much of your writing reflects relationships between mothers and daughters. How does that work into this narrative?

Jong: *Fanny* is a book that is written for a daughter by a mother. The mother is writing her memoir for her daughter, saying, "Darling, when you grow up you'll read this and learn about life." The whole book is addressed to the daughter. Of course, I think of her getting this huge manuscript of a thousand pages, or whatever it was in handwriting. In fact, it was two thousand pages, because I write longhand, and looking at it and saying, "Oh, God. My Mother. What a bore!" and never reading it. I imagine the daughter, Belinda, never reading it. But the desire of a mother to protect her daughter from all the things that may befall a woman on the road of life is very strong. And that's the passion behind this memoir.

Gardner: How long did the actual writing of *Fanny* take you?

Jong: It took me four years to do the book and I would say the actual writing was about two-and-a-half to three. The rest was research time, warm-up time, casting about for what I wanted to do next, and so on.

Gardner: You are unique as both a bestselling novelist and a bestselling poet. I get the feeling that each of your poems that I read had its own very specific inspiration. What or who have been the inspirations of some of these poems?

Jong: Poems come out in funny places. They come aslant at us in life. Sometimes you read something in a newspaper and it sets your mind going. Sometimes you see a painting. Sometimes it's just a strange feeling you wake up with in the middle of the night. The tangible evocation, the tangible inspiration for a poem is not always what really comes out in the poem. What the poem does is to create an epiphany to try to unify your life in some way. To try to make sense of it. It's quite a different kind of writing from novel writing. Very different.

Gardner: Do you switch easily from one to the other? Do you ever do both simultaneously?

Jong: I often stop when I'm writing a novel and write poems for a week or so. Often. Although with *Fanny,* that was such an all-absorbing kind of book that I didn't. But usually I switch back and forth between the two forms because they don't serve the same purpose in my life. What I do think is interesting about novel-writing, though, is that once you've settled on what the book is going to be, you can set yourself a task of so and so many pages a day. You can't do that with poetry. You really have to wait for the inspiration to come. You can write novels as a trade, once you've settled on your theme, but you can't write poetry that way.

Gardner: How much Erica Jong biography might we find in your poetry?

Jong: You'll find a funny, slanted biography. You'll find bits and pieces of my life. But it wouldn't be reliable for the biographer because they're transformed.

Gardner: I'm told that when you visit university campuses to give poetry readings, you attract larger audiences than rock stars and big-name comics. How do you account for this interest in poetry?

Jong: Some of my audience came out of curiosity to see "that lady who wrote that book," I must say. I mean *Fear of Flying. Fear of Flying* was read by millions of people, which is very rare for a novel. And I think maybe some of the people who came to the poetry readings just wanted to see who this monster of depravity was. Then they stayed to listen. And many of them were won over. But there is a deep audience for poetry out there. Unfortunately, so many modern poets, and so many modern critics, have praised obscurity in poetry, and have condemned clarity. My poetry tends to be clear. And poets who have a kind of lucidity have a potential of a large audience. But our literary culture despises lucid poetry at this particular juncture in history, and only likes poetry that needs to be extricated by a professor. So the way they turned off what could be the natural audience for poetry is unfortunate.

Gardner: Well, how much of this good contemporary poetry do you feel is reaching audiences today?

Jong: Modern poets have become kind of troubadors. They go around campuses and they reach people in the flesh, so to speak. They read their poems aloud. I think that's very good, because poetry is an aural medium. I think that when you hear a poem read you understand it better than when you read it on a page.

Gardner: A number of poets have told me they feel fortunate if their books sold five thousand copies. Yet yours sell in many thousands. What do you suppose creates the phenomenal popularity of one poet's work, while many others go virtually unnoticed?

Jong: I think that my poetry hasn't sold hundreds of thousands in hardcover, but in paperback. My poetry has ridden, to some extent, on the coattails of the novels, ad the name that was created by that. But also, the poetry is very intense. Very lucid. It speaks to concerns that people can deal with. It's not obscure poetry. Some good poets are obscure. Some good poets are blessed with lucidity and I'm lucky in that I have the potential of being a popular poet, because my work is easily understandable.

Gardner: What do you feel is the market for poetry in America today?

Jong: Not big enough. Unfortunately. We're in a period now when the determinations about the lives of books are made way in advance. If a big book chain doesn't order a book—and most of them don't order poetry—then the print order is small. The advertising budget is small and everything down the line is small. Therefore, you've probably had the experience—we've all had it—where a friend published a new volume of poems and we go out to one of the big bookstores, and they don't stock it. We'll find it at Books & Company or we'll find it at the Gotham Book Mart. But we won't find it at the big chain bookstores. This is unfortunate.

Gardner: When writing poetry, do you do much revising?

Jong: I do a lot of revising. Constantly. And I often write the poem in several stages. There'll be an initial outburst of inspiration, then I go back and re-work and re-work. Sometimes it takes years to get it right.

Gardner: How long would you estimate it takes you to write a poem that covers a page in a book? In a minute I'm going to tell you why I ask that question.

Jong: I am sometimes amazed at how quickly you can write a first draft. I've written first drafts in fifteen minutes. They come like *that!* Like a dream.

Or a waking fantasy. And I get it all down. Then it may be years in revision. Why do you ask?

Gardner: Because I asked Rod McKuen the same question when he was on my show, and he said, "Well, let's see. How old am I now?" He figured his age and said, "That's how long it took me to do this poem, because everything I've been and everything I've done becomes a part of every poem I write."

Jong: Of course. That's true.

Gardner: Do you do much rewriting on a novel?

Jong: I rewrite constantly. Constantly. With *Fanny,* because I was working in this vanished language, I revised every chapter as I went along. Some chapters came out close to what they would later be. Some were written ten, fifteen, twenty times. Just tremendous numbers of times.

Gardner: What have readers told you they enjoy most, or find most significant about your literature?

Jong: I would say the one thing, the note that's struck always by people who write me letters, is "thank you for your honesty," and the most frequent comment I get is "your work is not licentious; your work is not pornographic. It is honest. I have never read a book that was as honest, before." That's the note that is struck again and again. And apparently, the reason for my readership, basically—my detractors will say I've exploited sex—but I don't think my readers read me for the same reason Harold Robbins readers read him. I think they read me because they want to see a kind of honest view of life, told from a woman's point of view. And they find it very rare and very refreshing. That's the sense I get.

Erica: Being the True History of the Adventures of Isadora Wing, Fanny Hackabout-Jones, and Erica Jong

John Kern / 1981

Reprinted from *Writer's Digest* June 1981: 20–25.

Erica Jong burst upon the literary scene during the early '70s, a period of political and social fragmentation. Her first novel, *Fear of Flying,* was immediately embraced as the bible of the burgeoning women's movement. A satirical, sexually explicit work, it polarized the critics and electrified the book-buying public. After the smoke had cleared, it had sold more than six million copies in 20 countries, and it had garnered some impressive praise. John Updike, writing in *The New Yorker,* spoke of the novel's "sexual frankness that belongs to, and hilariously extends, the tradition of *The Catcher in the Rye* and *Portnoy's Complaint.* It has class and sass, brightness and bite." Nora Sayre added: "A magnificent novel. Eric Jong has written about women in a completely new way."

The overwhelming success of *Fear of Flying,* however, turned out to be a mixed blessing. Although it gave Jong financial security, it also produced a backlash against her next novel, *How to Save Your Own Life.* The confessional style of her first two works gave reviewers an inviting target. "I have been bedeviled by deliberately hostile critics," she stated bitterly after the publication of her second book. "My situation as a writer has never been one of sheer acceptance."

In spite of her contentious beginnings, the last few years have seen Jong's life come full circle. After weathering a second divorce and a protracted lawsuit with Columbia Pictures over the film rights to *Fear of Flying,* she remarried, settled in the Connecticut suburbs and gave birth to her first child. "My work now shows a much more reflective mood," she says. "It is the product of a person who has come to terms with existence and who has reached a certain maturity."

Jong's contentment is certainly reflected in the pages of her latest novel, *Fanny: Being the True History of the Adventures of Fanny Hackabout-Jones.* Unlike her first two books, *Fanny* is a joyously entertaining romp through the Fieldingesque world of the 18th-century England. Written in the form of a book of advice from a mother to her daughter, the novel chronicles Fanny's rollicking adventures as a ravished orphan, witch, highway robber, whore, loving mother, kept woman and famous pirate. "When I was younger I couldn't even conceive of sitting still long enough to write a novel," Jong says with a chuckle. "If someone had told me when I was 22 that I would someday write a 500-page book set in 18th-century England, I would have thought that they were crazy. I really think *Fanny* is the best book that I have ever written."

Yet, Jong didn't start her career as a novelist. Throughout the late '60s and early '70s, Jong had an uncommonly successful career as a poet, and then established the themes that would later dominate her fiction. Long before the publication of her first novel, her poetry expanded the boundaries of feminist literature and, in the words of Anthony Burgess, explored the "pains and occasional elations of the Modern American Female."

She is still novelist and poet, but she has also taken another role: that of film producer. She will co-produce the film version of *Fanny,* which should prevent problems such as those that prevented the filming of *Fear of Flying.*

The first thing WD interviewer John Kern noticed as he approached Erica Jong's home in Weston, Connecticut, was a brown Mercedes coupe in the driveway with a license plate that read, WING-IT. "Apart from this reference to Isadora Wing, the heroine of Jong's first two novels," says Kern, "nothing about the staid environs indicates that it is the residence of a famous writer. Though perched on the side of an isolated cliff overlooking the Saugatuck river valley, the inside of Jong's home is the epitome of domestic tranquility. Her daughter's toys and yellow canvas playhouse dominate one corner of the high-ceilinged living room. At any given moment, her husband, writer Jonathan Fast, would stop by from his office above the garage to discuss babysitting schedules and other household arrangements.

"Fast is the son of author Howard Fast, and his own books include *The Inner Circle* and *Mortal Gods.* Both Fast and Jong were born and raised in New York City, but came to Connecticut because of their fondness for country living, which they developed living in California for a time. Their mutual profession gave them the ability to live wherever they wanted, so they looked for houses across the country—from Lake Tahoe to Key West—until a friend introduced them to their western-style home.

"Amidst this well-ordered backdrop, Jong curled up on her couch with a glass of white wine and talked in calm, almost blissful tones. Considering her reputation as a novelist, both the familial setting and her serene manner come as something of a surprise. So it is appropriate that our first topic of discussion was surprises."

WD: Were you surprised that *Fear of Flying* turned into such a cause celebre?

Jong: Totally. Before the book was published, everyone kept telling me that first novels never sell. They further discouraged me by saying that a literary novel about a Barnard girl would never make it. I had to fight to convince my publishers that it was commercial. Sometime later, after it had sold six million copies, everyone then accused me of adding the sex to make it sell. It was a very sobering experience to go through and it made me very philosophical about the nature of success.

WD: What *is* your philosophy about success? Do you consider yourself successful?

Jong: Well, I know that the outside world considers me a successful person. I would say that a successful person is someone who is completely happy with both work and personal life. But I don't think anyone fits that definition. I mean nobody except an idiot is completely happy with all their personal relationships and work.

I have no regrets about what I've done with my life. I don't regard writing as just a trade, but really as a calling. I feel that I was to be a writer and I consider myself a success in having found the thing that I was put on this earth to do. But I would be a fool if I thought that I had succeeded in every area of my life.

WD: How have you changed in the past ten years? Has success changed you?

Jong: I'm much less neurotic and my life is much more together. In fact, at the risk of sounding terribly arrogant, I will say that I am one of the few people I know who hasn't been ruined by success. I will admit that I was caught up in the confusion created by my own celebrity for about a year or so after *Fear of Flying*. But the question is, How do you handle it when that intensive period of celebrity is finished? I think that you have to rededicate yourself to your writing and work more fervently than ever before.

WD: The fact that the book sold six million copies must have eliminated any fears that you may have had about being able to reach an audience. After a success of that magnitude, what fears remain?

Jong: A success like *Fear of Flying* creates a marvelous sense of freedom and there is always a great joy in making money for your work. But it is also very frustrating because a lot of people who tell me that they love the book have never heard of my poetry. The reputation of a notorious novel tends to dwarf everything else. Most people think of me only as the author of *Fear of Flying,* but I hope that will change with my latest novel. It's awful to feel that a book you wrote when you were 28 is the one with which you'll be buried.

WD: The late Henry Miller once said that *Fear of Flying* was the female counterpart to his *Tropic of Cancer.* Do you think that is true?

Jong: The *New York Times* obituary described Henry as an "artesian" writer, which I thought was a very felicitous phrase. In that respect I think that the statement is true. I consider myself to be a natural writer in the sense that everything surfaces from the unconscious. Henry was right in comparing *Fear of Flying* to *Tropic of Cancer* in that both books throw away literary inhibitions. I was writing from the gut about female fantasies in the same way that he was writing about male fantasies.

You must remember that I grew up in a time when most important American novels were written by men. Most distinguished women writers tended to write in male-dominated prose. They did not write books that only a woman could have written. My generation of young female writers discovered its own character and found that we could dictate the form and content of our own fiction. It was given to my generation to come along and show that we had sexual feelings. It was given to my generation to assert that territory of honesty which had long ago been established by men.

WD: When you were working on the book, were you ever worried that it might be dismissed as pornographic?

Jong: No. When I was writing *Fear of Flying,* I was aware that I was working in a literary tradition. I have a good education and nearly did a Ph.D. in English literature. I knew that what I was writing was not any more sexual than what D. H. Lawrence did in *Lady Chatterly's Lover* or Philip Roth did in *Portnoy's Complaint.* I did not think of sex in my book as dirty. I sensed that people might be shocked because it was written by a woman. But I had no idea what an enormous double standard they had—that what was pornographic for a woman writer was literature for a man. I was quite astonished when I saw what Middle America thought of *Fear of Flying.* I really didn't think the world was that reactionary.

WD: You must have received some interesting mail after *Fear of Flying* was published.

Jong: Oh God, I could publish a book of the mail alone. I received all kinds of grateful letters from women who said that I had freed their sexuality and made them feel less lonely. Many men even wrote that I had helped them to better understand women. However, I also got the other type of mail. I would get requests for soiled underwear and liaisons at the local motel. A number of the letters I received were full of kinky sex and anti-Semitism. But I think that women who write about sex get a different type of response than men. There is a tendency on the part of a certain type of naive reader to assume that an author who has written this type of book is available for one-night stands.

WD: Your second novel, *How to Save Your Own Life,* was subject to some pretty savage notices. It almost appeared as if the critics were reviewing you instead of your book. Was it a great disappointment?

Jong: When you have a first novel that sells six million copies, anything you do after it has to be a disappointment. You set a standard that you cannot compete with and the pressure it puts on you is almost unreal. So, if your next book "only" sells two million copies, everyone thinks of it as a failure.

I went through a difficult period. I was coming off a notorious bestseller which wasn't just a blockbuster like *The Thorn Birds.* It was a book that signaled a switch in the female consciousness and encouraged women to change their lives. It was a book that a lot of men and reactionary women could blame for something that was happening in America that they didn't like. There was a great deal of pent-up anger about the new narcissism and women's rights and it was all taken out on *How to Save Your Own Life.*

Despite my brassy exterior, I am a pretty vulnerable person and it was a very painful experience. I could scarcely believe all of the hate and personal character assassination that were in the reviews. But I lived through it and it turned out to be very strengthening.

I think that I receive a lot of hostile notices because I have been held responsible for the emergence of women and female sexuality. Of course, it's not true. I only wish I were responsible; it would be a great honor. In any case, my work has been identified with women demanding rights in the bedroom and I think that many men and women had a lot of mixed feelings about that and it led them to attack my work.

Our society is still very uncomfortable with the idea of successful women.

Underneath all of the lip service that this country gives to the women's movement, I believe that it is still very sexist. So, if a woman is conspicuous and
writes about sex and makes a lot of money, both men and women tend to be
very hostile toward her.

WD: Do you have any plans to turn Isadora's adventures into a trilogy?

Jong: I'm not sure. I have in the back of my mind an idea for a book about
Isadora at 40 or Isadora in Connecticut, but it seems kind of schticky. Besides, when a book becomes that famous you tend to get very self-conscious.
I think that my creativity would be inhibited. Isadora is no longer just a
character in a novel but has become a symbol of a million things. I would
feel that I would have to live up not only to what I think Isadora is, but to
what she has become in the public mind. In any case, I wrote *Fear of Flying*
ten years ago and my notions of a novel were very different from what they
are now.

When I first began writing it was much more instinctive. Now, my work is
much more thought out. I recognize the importance of a strong story line in
a way that I didn't before. The story is the armature of the novel. You can't
have a good novel without a good story. You must have that frame to build
the novel around.

WD: You spent four years writing your latest novel—*Fanny.* After invest-
ing so much time and emotion in a book, how would you have coped with it
if it had failed instead of becoming a bestseller?

Jong: I always expect my work to fail. It's almost a protective magic that
I use: expecting the worst in order to ensure success. I know how fickle the
writing profession can be. I suppose that if my book failed I would be very
disappointed, but I don't think it would change the direction of my life. The
nature of being an artist is to have hits and flops. I could have avoided all of
these risks by becoming a college professor. But I certainly would have
avoided all of the wonderful things that have happened, too.

WD: What inspired you to write a story set in 18th-century England?

Jong: I have always loved 18th-century English literature and had studied
it in college. I promised myself 15 years ago that I would write a Fieldingesque novel set in that period. I knew that it would take a lot of time and
research and that it would have to be done at a period in my life when I was
calm and financially secure enough not to have to worry about turning out a
novel every year. The idea for the book really started with the simple ques-

tion, What if Tom Jones had been a woman? Given all of the problems that women faced in that era, I thought it was a delicious idea that presented limitless opportunities.

Also, I thought *Fanny* would be a wonderful thing to try after being known for contemporary fiction. It enables you to do a historical recreation of a period and make a whole different set of satirical points. But beyond that, if you set a novel in 1740, it gives you a great opportunity to show how much has changed for women and, in turn, how little. After all, the real purpose of the historical novel is to satirize current society through the lens of the past. I have long felt that the historical novelist had missed a great opportunity to write the ultimate feminist novel.

Despite all of the carriages and petticoats, *Fanny* is the most radical book I have written. Unlike Isadora, who is always in pain and conflict, Fanny is a true heroine. She gave me an opportunity to show what women can be at their boldest and that is something that I really enjoyed.

WD: Did you find the research difficult?

Jong: I love doing research. It was the best part of working on the book. A novel like *Fanny* could never have been written without the patience of a number of librarians. The ones in Connecticut were especially helpful to me. I went over to the Beinecke Rare Book and Manuscript Library at Yale and used every other library from the Pequot to Columbia University. I even went down to the South Street Seaport Museum in New York City and studied all of the wonderful models of the sailing ships of that period.

WD: The book is written in the style of an 18th-century novel. Do you find it difficult to write in that style?

Jong: When I first started, I didn't think that I could write a whole novel in that style. But once I had completed 50 pages, I found that I could not write in any other way. I felt like I was in a trance. I started writing letters to my friends and business associates in 18th-century English. I even had to refuse all magazine assignments because I couldn't write in my normal style. It lasted for almost four years. I invented a voice that had the flavor of 18th-century England but was really contemporary. *Fanny* is a modern novel in that it moves very fast. It is not paced like Fielding's books, which were meant for a time when people had hours and hours to loll around their country homes.

WD: Were you apprehensive about fictionalizing historical characters like Alexander Pope and Jonathan Swift?

Jong: I was very apprehensive. But I think people understand that *Fanny* is a novel and that Pope and Swift are introduced as comical characters. You know, even biographers don't agree on what they were really like. I think that a novelist, as well as a biographer, has a right to take a position. Anyway, I think it is clear that I was being ironic with the characters. My heroine is, of course, partially a creature of wish fulfillment. She is very heroic and much braver than I am. But I think that she is a true depiction of what it was like to be a woman 250 years ago.

WD: Still, you must admit that a character as headstrong and independent as Fanny is not your typical 18th-century woman.

Jong: She is a very modern wench in 18th-century dress. But if you read the lives of some of the women of that period, you will discover that there were many who were like her. In the afterword of my book I write that the people we most enjoy reading about in history are the ones who transcend their own time. If you read some of the diaries of the women of that era, you will see that they did transcend their own time. Women like Mary Wortley Montagu and the pirate queen Anne Bonny were pretty amazing.

WD: *Fanny* is much more lighthearted and humorous than either of your two previous books. Would you say that this is more a reflection of the material or of where you are in your life?

Jong: Well, you find me at a pretty good time in my life. I am happier than when I wrote either *Fear of Flying* or *How to Save Your Own Life,* which is a very dreary book about a marriage coming apart. So, maybe that's why *Fanny* is so humorous.

I have long felt that there is too little humor in contemporary fiction. The number of women who have written funny books about the conditions of women can be counted on the fingers of one hand. I feel that almost anyone can write a droopy, depressing novel, but I am one of the few women who can write a truly funny book about my own sex. I think that the humorous vision of life gives you a philosophy that the wimpy, whiney outlook doesn't permit.

WD: You have also published four books of poetry. How do you think your poetry has changed over the years?

Jong: I think that it has become much more contemplative and philosophical. I think that I have always had that bent, but I feel that it is becoming much more apparent. I am older and I think that in a funny way as you age you become much more yourself—you become the person you were meant to be. But I think that I have always had a strong philosophical bent.

WD: The mood of your latest collection, *At the Edge of the Body,* seems to be very reflective.

Jong: Yes. I was thinking specifically of that book of poetry. But I am also thinking of the new book that I'm finishing, which is about witches. It is partly written in poetry and partly in prose. It is a beautifully illustrated art book with a short text and will be out sometime next fall.

WD: How long does it generally take you to write a poem?

Jong: I usually compose it at one sitting, but then I may revise it. Sometimes they are written extremely fast—often as quickly as a half-hour. But then you may go on working and polishing it for months and months until you get it right.

WD: Where do you get your inspiration for your poetry?

Jong: The inspiration can come from the observation of something in nature or reading something in a newspaper. It's usually an inner thing that is triggered by an outer event. Sometimes you don't even know what outer event has triggered it. Sometimes it's just a feeling. Sometimes the line sort of drops down into your pen as if automatically or like a dream.

WD: What do you think of the current state of American poetry?

Jong: I think there are some fabulous poets around. I don't think that they are the ones who are recognized as the great poets of our age. I was a great fan of Robert Lowell, Anne Sexton and Sylvia Plath. But a woman like Muriel Rukeyser, who I think is one of the great poets of our time, is very little understood or recognized. I don't think that poets' reputations are always commensurate with the work that they have done.

WD: What advice would you give to someone who wanted to become a poet?

Jong: I would tell them to read it constantly, go to poetry readings and buy new books of poetry and try to understand which ones are good and which ones are bad. I would also advise them to write all of the time and to keep a notebook with ideas and lines for poems. They should even keep a "dream" notebook for dreams that could turn into poems.

WD: What are the differences in discipline between writing poetry and prose?

Jong: They are very different and they don't conflict with each other. There is a sense that poetry comes from the intuitive part of the brain. It is much more pleasurable and euphoric than writing a novel. You feel that you are tapping into the source of unconscious creativity. Nearly every poet that you talk to will tell you that it is, in a sense, an automatic process.

Writing a novel is a much more conscious thing. It's a daily job. You go to your desk at nine in the morning and work until three or four. I would say that one day out of ten you feel euphoric and the words just fly off of your fingers. The other nine days you wonder how the hell you are going to move your heroine from one place to another and what adventures will take place along the way. You find that a good part of your day is taken up inventing and devising and that most of the time you don't think it is any good.

WD: I gather that you find the writing process laborious.

Jong: For the most part. But the thrill of writing is what emerges from the process. For instance, you suddenly realize how someone like Fanny is related to the other characters in your fable and it often shocks and surprises you. I think that the joy of writing a novel is the self-exploration that emerges and also that wonderful feeling of playing God with the characters. When I sit down at my writing desk, time seems to vanish. I think that it's a wonderful way to spend one's life.

WD: Is it important for a writer to have a rigid work schedule?

Jong: I think the most important thing for a writer is to be locked in a study. And I am a rather serious writer. I usually write in my office on the third floor of the house. I write every day from about nine in the morning to one in the afternoon. I set myself to the task of writing ten pages a day in longhand, which comes out to about five typewritten pages. The rest of the day I spend talking on the phone with my publishers, promoting my books and answering my mail.

WD: You recently became a mother for the first time. Have you been able to reconcile that part of your life with your writing?

Jong: Becoming a mother has really changed my life and made me much more mellow. I worked on *Fanny* straight through my pregnancy. I went back to work five days after having a Caesarean and finished it between nursing. Balancing the two was exhausting, but having a baby hardly interferes with the creative process.

WD: You and your husband lived together four years before you were married. Has marriage changed your relationship?

Jong: To a certain extent I think that legal marriage tends to make you take each other for granted. But maybe it's just being together for years and years that changes a relationship. Jon and I have a marriage that's so good it's almost scary to talk about. We really are good friends and we share everything and support each other. We have the kind of marriage that the women's movement would hope that every woman would have someday.

WD: Yet, a few years ago you wrote that you didn't envision any place for the institution. Has the success of your marriage changed your mind?

Jong: I still don't much like what marriage stands for in our patriarchal society. The marriage laws in our culture still derive from the notion of women as property. I really believe that the whole nature of the institution as we understand it is evolving in a line with some of the things that my generation of women writers have been writing about.

I see hope for marriage as it is being restructured, but not as it was ten years ago. If marriage is seen as a woman taking a man's name, trading her sexual services in exchange for a man's keep and selling her reproductive rights for a house, then I think it's horrible. But if you see it as an equal partnership with shared responsibilities, then perhaps the institution can be saved.

WD: What are the advantages and disadvantages of being married to another writer?

Jong: It's great and it's terrible. What's great is that you both have a great deal of flexibility. In our case, both parents can be involved in the child-rearing and the home. It's a lot easier for each of us to get our work done, especially when we have deadlines. What's terrible is that you tend to get very stir-crazy and house-bound since you have your home and office in the same place.

WD: What have you and your husband been able to learn from each other as writers?

Jong: My relationship with Jon has gone through many phases. The first few months were absolutely euphoric. But I think we both have discovered that we are rather different people. Jon has a marvelous sense of humor that puts everything into perspective. When I'm going off the deep end, he will crack a joke that makes it absolutely clear to me that all the things I'm worried about don't really matter all that much.

We read each other's works in 50- or 100-page blocks and then offer criticisms. We both believe in a "kind but honest" approach. When Jonathan finishes something of mine that he doesn't like, he usually says, "It's not your best work." When he tells me that I know it's just terrible.

WD: There was quite a bit of divisiveness surrounding the recent American Book Awards. Many writers boycotted them because of the way that they were structured. What are your feelings about that?

Jong: Well, I will say that I think all awards are silly. You can't say that I. B. Singer is better than Henry Miller or Vladimir Nabokov. They are quite different and have very different views of the world. The purpose of the awards is to get people to read books. What the American Book Awards are trying to do is to make the publicity better than it was in the past with the old National Book Awards.

WD: Don't you think that part of the problem with the industry is that the publishing houses are being swallowed up by conglomerates?

Jong: I don't think that conglomerates are destroying the book business. I feel that the book industry would have gone under without the infusion of money from the conglomerates. Although it is not chic to say so, my own career has been helped by conglomerates. My editor at New American Library saved *Fear of Flying* from oblivion. In fact, she also encouraged me to write a book in 18th-century English. She is an employee of a conglomerate and she sure as hell is not trying to get me to write like Judith Krantz.

The problem is that the fate of a book is often determined before it has even been published. There is a tendency to base the advertising budget for a book on what was paid to the author in advance.

WD: What are you working on now?

Jong: I am working on the book about witches I mentioned, and I am working on a new novel that I don't want to talk about lest I jinx it. I always start several books between books.

WD: How does that work?

Jong: I usually take a year of making false starts between books. I start one book and shelve it and then start another. I am never really sure which one is the false start and which one will turn out to be the one that I will want to write. Usually the false starts end up getting absorbed into the manuscript of the real book.

WD: Is there a common theme that runs through all of your work?

Jong: The common theme that runs through all of my work is the quest for self-knowledge. A poet friend of mine named Michael Benedikt, who used to teach my poems at Sarah Lawrence, said that what amazed him was how often I used the verbs "to learn" and "to teach." My work seems to be about using life as a learning process. In my poem "The Buddha in the Womb," I wrote, "Flesh is merely a lesson / We learn it and pass on." In a way that is my answer to those people who say that I write too much about the flesh. I think that could be my epitaph.

Erica Jong's Fear of Forfeiting Feminism's Gains

Elaine Woo / 1981

From *The Los Angeles Herald Examiner* (October 25, 1981). Reprinted with permission of the Hearst Corporation.

Erica Jong earned the title of "the female Henry Miller" in 1973 for her frank treatment of female sexuality in the best-selling feminist novel *Fear of Flying*. Last year, she again won critical acclaim for *Fanny,* which is set in the 18th century. Her latest book, *Witches,* explores the ancient rituals of witchcraft through poetry, prose and sumptuous illustrations. Jong, 39, was interviewed by *Herald Examiner* staff writer Elaine Woo.

Question: What is it like being Erica Jong—successful novelist, noted feminist, wife and mother? Does it sometimes feel like there are too many expectations to live up to?

Jong: It's very difficult. I feel that I live under tremendous pressure on all sides—you know, the pressure to be writing, pressure to be mothering, pressure to be running a house.

I think it's nearly impossible to be a successful woman and mother and all those things—although I adore being a mother, and I love my career. But there has to be 48 hours in a day to do it all. And there are very few men who are willing to make the compromises that it takes to be married to such a woman—very few men feel they *ought* to be making those compromises.

Q: That's still true, even after 10 years of the women's movement?

A: Yes, I do think that. It's very hard, and I think that the likelihood of winding up alone is great. The world has gone backward as far as feminism if concerned, not forward, in the last few years.

Q: Can you give me an example?

A: We see an attack on abortion and contraception, which was unthinkable eight or 10 years ago. Seven years ago when the right to free abortion was won, we thought we would never see an attack on abortion.

I think that men are less conscious of being feminist now than they were

10 years ago. There's a kind of backsliding into the habitual male chauvinism, as if feminism was merely a fad. Women's expectations have changed
and men's haven't, and so there will probably be a giant collision at some
point.

Q: Isadora Wing, the protagonist in *Fear of Flying,* said she wasn't going
to have children. Did you ever feel that way?

A: I sort of took for granted that I was going to (raise a family). When I
was a kid, I always thought I would have a child. Then I went through a
period in my 20s when all I was concerned with was my career. And at that
point, I thought I was never going to have children.

Q: What changed your mind?

A: I don't know. I reached the age of 35, and I found myself adopting all
the stray dogs in Connecticut. And I decided that I'd better have a child or I
would wind up with 15 stray dogs. I suddenly wanted to be a mother.

Q: Does your daughter, Molly, have the benefit of parenting from father
as well as mother?

A: Molly has a father who is very involved in raising her. Right now her
father and I are separated, albeit perhaps temporarily. But we both take care
of her—she's had a lot of fathering from Jonathan (Fast) and a lot of mothering from me. She's always been raised in a household where both husband
and wife shared the parenting.

Q: So equal parenting hasn't been a problem in your household?

A: Well, I'll tell you, it's been extremely hard. We've had such tremendous
pressures on both of us. We've both been writing books and we've both been
raising a child. The pressures have been immense.

Q: Do you think we're moving away from the Superwoman model—the
idea of a woman who can have a demanding career and be a successful wife
and mother at the same time? Recent books like the controversial *Cinderella
Syndrome* and *Unfinished Business* are discouraging in that regard; they're
telling us women are really afraid of succeeding and being independent and
that women are more likely to suffer from depression than men.

A: I don't think we're going to go back to the model of the little happy
housewife in her cottage who doesn't fulfill her own aspirations. But it's the
same old story: We are integrated in a society of men and women, and yet
the social structure is advantageous to men having love and work, while
women only have love and the fruits thereof—i.e., children.

This will be true until we have institutions for child rearing. Until the institutions that make feminism practical become a reality—a day-to-day reality—we're just talking theory.

And we have been talking theory now for the last 10 years without much substantive change. A lot of young women have gotten promoted. You see more women's faces on television, you see more female executives in some fields. But we have not really seen the kind of major change in the institution that would really make it possible for men and women to have equality.

Q: Betty Friedan said recently that she thinks that there has been too much of an emphasis on issues that stress the victim mentality—pornography, for instance. She thinks it is the wrong thing to be concentrating on right now.

A: I agree. I don't want to stress the battle against pornography—pornography is a side issue. I think the main issue is the way men and women relate in the home and who takes care of the children.

You can't just say, "Be a lesbian separatist and don't have children," because most women *do* have children. And you can't go around demanding that women not have children as an article of faith—that's ridiculous. What would happen to the human race? You have to confront the problem of raising those children and still having women out there doing the work of the world.

Q: What direction is women's writing taking these days? Have there been any breakthroughs in the last five years, like a *Fear of Flying?*

A: I can't find a trend in women's novels now. A lot of the feminist writers of the last 10 years have fallen by the wayside—the ones who were polemicized to a certain point of view. You see among women writers today a much greater freedom, and it's because of women's position as the outsider. That's one of the reasons women's writing has become so exciting.

And it has really changed the direction of men's writing in the last 20 years. I mean, you could not imagine a man writing the way John Irving does if there had not been a feminist revolution. You could not imagine a man making movies like Paul Mazursky's movies. Feminist writers changed the way men creators work.

Q: What got you interested in witchcraft?

A: I got interested in it when I researched *Fanny.* I wanted Fanny to fall in with a coven of feminist witches, because I wanted my heroine to have every possible experience available to a woman at that time. So I began researching witchcraft, and I learned that witches belonged to an ancient, pagan, matriarchal cult of feminists that evolved underground in the Christian world.

Q: You have suggested a parallel between the medieval witchhunts and some of the problems women face today.

A: If a small, fanatical group manages to pass a "right to life" amendment, we are going to have a situation that will be an absolute mess. Doctors will not know how to interpret the law—whether they will possibly be indicted for murder by installing an IUD. It's going to be a legal and medical nightmare.

The people who are going to be hurt by it are women—and probably young women. And probably women who are in their prime childbearing years or in the universities. Or teenagers who get pregnant and have no recourse.

I can't compare that to starving and burning women, naturally. But there is an analogy in that women are punished for their sexuality and men are not.

Q: One feminist scholar has suggested that women should mourn on Halloween because the witchhunts of the 16th and 17th centuries were equivalent to a holocaust for women. Do you agree?

A: Well, in a way they were like the holocaust for women. I'm not suggesting we're having another holocaust for women coming up, although I see all sorts of dangers in our society right now. There are renewed outbreaks of anti-Semitism all over the world, and attacks on women are increasing again.

There is a kind of end-of-the-world feeling about the stage we're in right now culturally, and talk of atomic wars and surviving atomic wars. One has the feeling we're entering a period analogous to the period that preceded the First World War or the Second World War—that we're on the brink of another conflagration, maybe the last. All of which is pretty damn scary.

If only we could have feminized our culture—if we could have had a nurturing, feeding, childbearing culture instead of the male culture, which is aggressive and dominant. We may have saved civilization. It may well be too late. We may be trying to introduce the feminine into our phallic civilization too late.

Q: You sound extremely pessimistic.

A: I think this is a very pessimistic period right now, the early '80s. I hope things will turn out.

One positive thought: Women are never going back to a slave-master relationship. But until we change the institutions of society, we are never going to be equal.

Erica Jong

Wendy Martin / 1983

From *Women Writers Talking,* edited by Janet Todd (New York: Holmes & Meier, 1983), 23–32. Copyright @ 1983 by Holmes & Meier Publishers, Inc. Reprinted with the permission of the publisher.

Wendy Martin: What authors have influenced you the most?

Erica Jong: It's so hard to answer that question. We tend to digest our influences, absorb them and bury them. When you are a young writer, at the beginning of your career, it's easier to determine the influences of other writers. For example, when I was in graduate school, I thought Nabokov was the cleverest writer in the world; now I find him rather arch and overclever and I tend to admire more the writers who have more heart and passion. One eats up influences in the course of one's career. Nabokov was a sad muse for me because he reinforced a tendency to be artificial, and it was precisely artifice that I didn't need. In fact, it's precisely artifice that most writers don't need, especially those who come out of graduate school. I have had to rebel against my earlier influences. In poetry today, there is no woman writer who has not been liberated, whose work has not been opened up, by the so-called confessional poets like Lowell and Plath and Sexton—particularly the latter two who showed women that we could write honestly about being women, that we could write honestly about the madness of families. *Now* I think that Muriel Rukeyser was a better poet than either Plath or Sexton, and a grander poet in the tradition of Whitman. The people who influenced me as a young writer are not those I necessarily admire most now.

Wendy Martin: Would you say that you are more committed to poetry than fiction, or to both genres equally? Which do you prefer?

Erica Jong: Until the time I wrote *Fanny* (which is the first book in which I really combined the novelist with the poet—that is, the person who tells a story with the person who is besotted with language), until *Fanny,* I would have said that I was a poet who fell accidentally into writing novels and who accidentally became successful at it and was able to make a living at it. Until *Fanny,* I would have said I felt myself more truly a poet than a novelist, I felt that my true being was in poetry. Now I feel much more equally divided; I feel that I *am* a novelist, that I write novels not just to support my poetry

138

habit, but because there is something about the *process* of writing a novel that is incredibly revealing about one's own motivations. It's a kind of meditation, a tremendous revelation of self. I don't think I could live without writing novels any more; it's become an inner need.

W.M.: The novel, then, gives you the luxury of a large space in which to work?

E.J.: The poem tends to be an epiphany, a kind of revelation; the novel deals with societies, families, the interweaving of lives, the way fate tricks people and reveals their lives quite differently than they had anticipated. The poem can't do that. The epic poem could do that, but we don't write epics any more.

W.M.: There are many writers who started out in another art form. Henry James wanted to be a painter, I believe. Several writers have found to their surprise that they achieve a higher level of craftsmanship in drama rather than poetry, for example. So, as you write, you discover what your true skills are, or your preferences change.

E.J.: But I really enjoy writing poetry and think I can do things in poetry that I can't do in fiction. I don't think it's necessary to choose a major; life is not a graduate school.

W.M.: You used the word enjoy; you "enjoy writing poetry." Would you say that is true in writing novels as well, that there is a sense of pleasure as you are actually writing and thinking through the plot and the character development?

E.J.: It's infinitely pleasurable. There is nothing like being right in the middle of a book which has taken over your life. I don't think I ever enjoyed writing anything as much as I enjoyed writing *Fanny*. I was completely absorbed into a vanished world, or into creating a world that never existed. It was even more enjoyable than writing about the contemporary world. It was almost as if time were suspended for me. I can't say that everyday novel writing is pleasurable. Most mornings you get up and you go to your desk and struggle to get the pen to the paper. It's often difficult getting started in the morning; nine days out of ten, you feel that what you are doing is dull, but one day out of ten, you seem to be straddling the spheres and hurtling through space and everything seems easy and magical and wonderful. Nonetheless, even on the days when it is hard, it is such an absorbing way to spend one's life that I guess it is a happy thing to be doing.

W.M.: Even with the anxieties that go along with the creation of the characters and the fear that your audience won't like it? How do you manage to balance those kinds of concerns?

E.J.: I center myself into the writing of the novel; I try to suspend all thoughts of audience or critics. I try to pretend that I'm writing just for myself, for my own ears, and my own eyes. This was much easier to do when I wrote my first novel than it is now. When I wrote *Fear of Flying,* I could always say, it will never be published. I will go back and get my Ph.D. I just have to do this for myself because I don't want to be one of those people who never finishes a novel—like that awful character in one of Camus' books who is always *starting* a novel but can't get past the first sentence; I had to do it for myself.

W.M.: Now that you know that you have an audience and you know that your work will be reviewed, are you able to circumvent whatever anxieties that causes by focusing on what interests you? What you would like to read about if you were the ideal reader? How do you keep yourself centered?

E.J.: That is the hardest problem I face; it's the hardest problem that *any* well-known writer faces—especially in mid-career. That is precisely what's wrong with being very well known. I try to purify myself of all expectation when I write. I try to remember that one doesn't know one's audience; one discovers an audience. Maybe there are certain romance writers like Rosemary Rodgers or Barbara Cartland who can determine the demographics of their readers, but with other kinds of books, you never know the audience; it may be immense. *Fear of Flying* was thought to be a very uncommercial book when it was first published in hardcover. It was all I could do to get the publisher to do anything for it, to advertise it, to publicize it. They were very wrong. The paperback publisher believed that it could reach an enormous audience and promoted it as if it were very commercial—as indeed it proved to be. But all of that is hindsight; nobody knew that at the time of initial publication. I was always arguing with my hardcover publisher to take another ad.

W.M.: So writing and publishing a novel is a process of discovery. You are never quite sure how it is all going to turn out, if any given novel is going to be well received, or even who is going to read it.

E.J.: You don't really know. The only guarantee you have, and it's not an absolute one, is that as you develop a name, people want to read your next

book. And even that doesn't always work. Well-known writers have sometimes published books that haven't sold.

W.M.: Would you describe your study to me? Is your desk filled with a
jungle of books and papers or is everything in neat, alphabetically arranged
piles?

E.J.: I work with piles of books, stacks of papers, but I can find everything.
My desk is the size of a kitchen counter; it's L-shaped and on it there are
books; galleys; poems in progress; a novel in progress, sometimes two; letters, often unanswered. It's not chaotic, however.

W.M.: So there's a sense of lots of ongoing projects, and the desk accom-
modates all of them. Describe your average writing day. Do you have any
rituals that you begin your writing day with? Any superstitious habits that
you have? Do you keep a predictable schedule? Do your writing hours vary?

E.J.: In the last few years I have tried to work normal hours; that is, from
nine A.M. to two or three o'clock—perhaps with a short break for lunch to
see my daughter Molly. I unplug the phone; but that hasn't always been the
case with me. I have only tried to normalize my life since Molly was born
and because Jon works those hours; it's nice to be able to goof off with Molly
in the afternoons. Often, I still do my best writing at night. When I'm beginning a new work, or writing poems, I'll often get up at night to write from
midnight to three. When a book is coming out and there are constant phone
calls and demands, and when I have numerous public appearances to make,
so that my writing schedule is really interrupted, I have to be ferocious and
unplug the telephone. When things get really hectic, I work at night when
everybody is asleep. *Fanny* was written from about nine to three every day.
Toward the end of the novel I worked *all* the time; the book became absorbing. But generally I try to keep the old school hours.

W.M.: Does it help to live away from Manhattan? Has your move to the
country been beneficial in terms of giving you a little more time, or making
you feel more relaxed? Do you think a more pastoral or natural setting is
helpful? Or do you care?

E.J.: I couldn't have written the last novel in New York. There is no way
I could have written *Fanny* there.

W.M.: Why not?

E.J.: Time is too fragmented in New York. In order to write about the eighteenth century, I had to create a world in which people lolled about in great country houses and read two-thousand-page novels.

W.M.: Then you needed open space to project your own imaginative interpretation of the period. The insistent modern rhythms of Manhattan would make it more difficult to sustain a vision of a different time. But trees, after all, are constant through time and enable you to make those imaginative leaps a little more easily.

E.J.: I found that to be true even though Connecticut isn't really like England.

W.M.: Do you think that living in the country will continue to be helpful? Is living in Connecticut an aesthetic choice or is it a practical choice?

E.J.: I think my life is easier here. I can divide my days between writing days and days when I go to the city and do other things. I can't live in New York and have lunch with people and also write. I'm too gregarious; I like people; I like parties. When I live in the city, I never get any work done.

W.M.: How has Molly affected your writing habits? Do you have to discipline yourself more carefully?

E.J.: It has been such a transformation—the needs of the child change so much from infancy to toddlerhood to little girl-dom. It was a constant change for the first three years of her life. I think that I was very afraid that having a child would make it difficult for me to work. I was hell-bent on showing everyone that having a child wasn't going to impede my progress; in fact, showing the internalized mother in me that it wasn't going to impede my progress. But what I didn't count on was my own attachment to Molly. When you wait until your mid-thirties to have a child, your desire to be with the child becomes stronger. The other things that you might do with your time seem less important. I've allowed myself to slack off in my schedule recently because I want to be with her more. I went racing through *Fanny* while I was pregnant and then nursing the baby. I conceived Molly while I was in the middle of writing a book which was written in the form of a letter of a mother to her daughter. The pregnancy was the prophecy of the book confirmed.

W.M.: Do you ever feel a conflict between your nurturing and achieving selves? Do you find that you are with Molly and thinking of the next chapter or that you are in your study thinking about the plot but wishing that you were with her?

E.J.: There is a pull. I try to arrange it so that Molly goes off to the beach with her nanny when the weather is good or off to a playgroup or to nursery school or someplace where she has an activity during the hours I'm working; it's much better for her and much better for me. when she's off doing something appropriate for her age and I'm at home, I don't feel tugged.

W.M.: You are able to claim the space for your work.

E.J.: Because of Molly, we've now built another study that is completely separate from the house. Nevertheless, when I hear the car pull into the driveway when the nanny brings her home for lunch, I run downstairs to be with her. I *want* to be there; if it's a break in my concentration, so be it.

W.M.: Would you want Molly to be a writer?

E.J.: I don't know. I'd want her to be what she wants to be. I must say that the household I've created here is not very different from the household I grew up in. My mother and grandfather were both painters; they worked at home, and I grew up watching them paint. In many respects, that's what Jon and I have here. We both work at home and our child is being raised in that atmosphere. Maybe that is one of the things that makes a person able to function as a free-lance, creative worker. Jon grew up with a father who was a free-lance writer and a mother who was a painter; both of them worked at home.

W.M.: So having parents as models for independent work who don't make the distinction between work at the office and at home was important to you. Many children never see their parents working and therefore work is a mystifying activity. Children who actually see the parent working have a great advantage; for them, work is not a magical event but is something that is done day in and day out.

E.J.: I have made it a point to let Molly into my study and to take her on book tours when I can. I took her on the book tour for *Fanny* and she sat with me in B. Dalton all over the country while I signed books. She has been with me to a lot of my professional activities. I think it has been good for her.

W.M.: When Molly grows up, she will undoubtedly realize that you were very widely read, and that some of your novels were quite controversial and that the erotic aspects were considered startling, even shocking to some. How do you feel about this? What do you think her response will be?

E.J.: It's hard to say. Many writers' children avoid reading their parents work and don't want to think of their parents as novelists but as parents. One's family is really the worst audience for one's work always because they are too close to it and can't read it dispassionately. That goes for parents, siblings, and children as far as I can tell. And who knows what the world will be like then; maybe Molly will go through a prudish phase and resent me because she thinks I'm very notorious, maybe she'll go through a phase where she won't want to read my work at all. When she becomes an adult, I hope she'll be inspired by my own particular odyssey in the way that I've come to be inspired by my grandfather's odyssey, my mother's odyssey, my father's odyssey. However, I didn't appreciate them until my thirties; when I was younger I rebelled against them. Perhaps she'll repeat my pattern, and it may even be a healthy pattern.

W.M.: What do you think about the reviews of your work that are critical of the explicit sexuality in your writing? Do you feel vulnerable? Do you feel that your erotic passages expose you to criticism and attacks?

E.J.: It's not only the eroticism that exposes me to attacks; women writers have *always* been treated quite differently than men writers. If they write about sex, they are treated like sluts or tramps. It goes back to Aphra Behn and any women who were presumptuous enough to use that masculine object the pen—which was seen as representative of the penis—God only knows why. Women writers were always considered insufferable and presumptuous, and that hasn't really changed. The amazing thing is that ten years of feminism hasn't changed it either. We live in a very puritanical and very sexist country. Sometimes responses to my novels have been so abysmally stupid, so gossipy, so prurient, so ignorant, that I wouldn't dignify most of them with the word criticism. Abroad, I tend to get a much more intelligent press.

W.M.: Even so, it must take extraordinary courage to write so openly and frankly about sexual subjects. Very few women have ever done it. Didn't you have some inner doubts that you had to overcome before you felt free to write about sex?

E.J.: With every book that I write I have to go through that process again. Every time I start something new, I realize my fears and insecurities. I feel very vulnerable; that's why I've used the ploy of pretending that I'm not writing for publication but for myself. It's been very hard. Most women writers haven't written freely because of their need for approval. Most women artists want more approval than men, yet they get far less. That is the situation of the woman artist, it seems to me; as women, we are socialized to need approval, but we are often treated with great savagery. I feel frightened when it's time to publish a book. But during the time I'm writing, I try not to live in the future. I try to write as honestly as I can without concern about running the gauntlet of reviews.

W.M.: When your work is described as popular, as appealing to a wide audience, what is your reaction?

E.J.: It used to be defensive. When *Fear of Flying* was published, I was defensive about its popularity. I had won awards as a poet, had wanted to get a Ph.D. in English, and felt contempt for best-sellers as people do in that academic environment. But as the years went on, and I met my readers, I began to consider it a great *privilege* to be read. For example, when I met college students who had copies of my book that were dog-eared and underlined and stained with coffee, I was thrilled. It then seemed to me that the people who criticized me because I was popular were envious; they would have given their eyeteeth to be read. On one of my first book tours, I met blackjack dealers in Reno who never read a novel until *Fear of Flying*. The distinction between literary and popular is made by academics and it's a tragedy for literature in this country. The notion that novels that are popular cannot be good is quite idiotic, and it's killing the novel. If you go back to the major British novelists, they were all popular.

W.M.: What do you think that the relationship of art and politics is? Is art political or is it beyond politics?

E.J.: Art should not be political in the narrow sense; it would be a great mistake for a writer to serve a particular party line, to write for the Communist Party (as certain writers did in the thirties), or to write about that latest phase of feminism. For example, many women of the sixties and seventies turned out propagandistic novels—they were too worried about toeing the correct party line from a feminist point of view. In an integral way, one is political, but politics is expressed through individual experience, not through polemic. The novel *does* reflect political concerns—racism, sexism—but as the individual feels them, not in a doctrinaire way. A critic should never say, "I didn't like your novel because Isadora Wing doesn't leave her husband and go to a feminist commune"—that kind of criticism is absurd.

W.M.: Do you think that art changes life? Does art create social change? Can it? Should it?

E.J.: It can in a deep way, in a way that is not easily seen. I think that poets *are* the unacknowledged legislators; they *do* change society—not in a decade but over the centuries. You see this process clearly in the eighteenth century;

there were tracts about the abolition of slavery, gradually the movement gained force, but it took a lot of time before there was any degree of consciousness of civil rights. Novels do augment this process and change what people think.

W.M.: What do you think the concerns of women novelists will be in the 1980s? If we can say that the exploration of self, autonomy, the meaning and reassessment of relationships were central to the sixties and seventies, are there parallel concerns for the eighties?

E.J.: A lot of the women novelists seem to be running scared right now. In America we treat social movements as if they were a branch of show business; right now, feminism is not considered good box office. Black liberation and Indian rights are no longer good box office. Instead of thinking of these movements as expressions of the need for social justice, we tend to ask, "Will it play?" I think a lot of women are running away from the confessional or autobiographical novel because it has been attacked as "narcissistic." There is a great casting about for the style of the eighties, but it hasn't been found yet. Off the top of my head, I think there will be a lot of books about motherhood written from the perspective of women who combine both work and childrearing. And a lot of novels about families—and what family really means.

W.M.: For many years, raising children was thought to be an inferior activity. Now women are looking at their experience and saying, "Yes, but this is what we do, and it's important."

E.J.: Many of the baby boom generation (like me) who postponed having babies until their thirties are looking at their experience in a different way than their mothers did. They are looking at the experience from the perspective of having had careers. Also we are seeing motherhood not as an either/or proposition. You have to reject motherhood if you see it as giving up your brain; but if you see it as a phase of life, it becomes intriguing. I think that's the way our generation is looking at it. And I expect that it will lead to new sorts of novels about the family, novels in which we make sense of this century and our families' odysseys through it, reappraised in the light of this century's coming to an end.

Contemporary Authors Interview

Jean W. Ross / 1987

Contemporary Authors. New Revision Series. Vol. 26. Edited by Hal May and James Lesniak. (Detroit: The Gale Group, 1989), 189–92. Reprinted with permission of The Gale Group. The interview was conducted on September 30, 1987.

CA: In your new novel, *Serenissima,* set in Venice, Jessica Pruitt goes back in time to have an affair with William Shakespeare, but without giving up her contemporary self. Do you see Jessica as a version of the heroine you've been developing from *Fear of Flying* on, or as a completely separate creation?

Jong: There are obviously similarities amongst my heroines, just as there are similarities between the heroes of most major writers' books. I think you can find, if you look in Saul Bellow's books, that there's a pretty straight line from *Dangling Man* to *The Dean's December.* There are similarities because of the consciousness of the creator, and the heroes in Bellow's books or in Isaac Bashevis Singer's books or in Philip Roth's books are always some version of the consciousness of the authors. I think it's probably true of my heroines in that they tend to be very bright and bookish, and they tend to be eager to reconcile the demands of the body with the demands of the mind. The whore/Madonna split persists in our culture, and persists in a way that is very deleterious to women. My heroines are always looking for wholeness and integration in a society where women are not allowed to be bodies and brains both. Certainly that was Isadora, certainly that is Fanny, certainly that is Jessica, and it's true of me.

What's interesting are the differences. Isadora is the smart Jewish kid on the couch, as I think John Updike said. She's a female Holden Caulfield or Henry Miller. Jessica is the WASP aristocrat, very well educated, literarily educated, the girl who starts out to be a Shakespearean actress and somehow winds up in Hollywood, wondering how she got there. If I had to tell you who my favorite heroine was, I would say Fanny, still, because she has the most joie de vivre, and because she is the most heroic. She is the heroine I wish I totally were, and interestingly enough, she is the heroine I am coming to be in my life. She is fearless. She truly knows that her life is guided by a higher power. She surrenders to her fate, and her fate never disappoints her. Insofar as I learn to be more that way myself, my life gets happier and happier. I think Fanny is pointing the way for me. When I wrote her, I was not quite there yet, but my life has imitated my books at times. My books point to ways I want to go in my life.

CA: In a talk with Karen Burke published in *Interview,* you described *Serenissima*'s progression from notes in a journal to "What if?" to book. Tell me about the research. You must have had to immerse yourself not only in Shakespeare, but in Venetian history and Jewish history as well.

Jong: I read everything I could lay my hands on about the history of the ghetto of Venice and the Jews of Venice, which I found was a great education, and which I adored. It taught me a lot about my own heritage. It taught me why Jewish mothers wanted their sons to be doctors: doctors were the only ones who could leave the ghetto at night without wearing a red hat; those mothers wanted their sons to be free. I read lots and lots of Elizabethan stuff that I had read in graduate school and much that I had not. I read many biographies of Shakespeare. I read biographies of the Earl of Southampton, Christopher Marlowe, Queen Elizabeth I; studies of Elizabethan England and street life in Elizabethan England, studies of daily life in sixteenth-century Venice. I listened constantly to John Gielgud's recording of the sonnets to get the sound of Elizabethan English in my ears. I listened to the Royal Shakespeare Company's recordings of *The Merchant of Venice* and other of the Italian plays of Shakespeare. I listened to Monteverdi at times during the writing.

I wrote much of the book in Venice, in a friend's sixteenth-century house, in fact in the room described in the last chapter of *Serenissima,* the room that looks out on the little canal and the French Embassy, the room in which Jessica wakes up. Every time I would get stuck on the story, I would fly back to Venice and let the stones dictate it to me.

The book was written in a kind of hallucinatory state, as was *Fanny,* a state in which I was searching back to past lives or searching ahead to future lives. It was a book that owed its inspiration to *Orlando* in the sense that I tried to abolish linear time and say that time is a fiction we invent to please ourselves. I don't believe time really exists, and I'm not saying that as hyperbole—I literally believe that times does not exist in the unconscious. I believe that Einsteinian physics proves that time is circular and that we can drop into it at any moment. We live at any moment in our lives in past, present, and future, remembering a childhood memory; whether it's biting into a madeleine or watching our own child having her first horseback lesson, we're constantly in our own childhoods simultaneously in the present and in the future. Every time I walk my daughter to school, I am remembering myself as a nine-year-old going to school, and I am experiencing her life and my life and simultaneously future lives.

I have tried as a novelist to mirror in *Serenissima* that doubleness and tripleness of vision with which we see the world. Virginia Woolf said it appalled her that contemporary novelists were not trying to show time as we actually experience it. They were sticking to the nineteenth-century way of writing novels. Back in the '20s and '30s she wondered why people were not breaking out of the parameters of that old novel form. She tried to in *Orlando* and in *The Waves* and, I think, succeeded very well. It's interesting that most British and American novelists have abandoned all experimentation with linear time, and I wonder why. Both Virginia Woolf and James Joyce were interested in such experimentation. Certainly it's a very rich field for exploration, and I think I may deal more and more with it in my new novel as well.

CA: You had art training and artists in your family as well as a background and interest in literature. Was the choice between painting and writing a difficult one to make?

Jong: Not at all. There were so many talented painters in my family that I just wanted out of the competition. I abandoned painting when I was eighteen or nineteen and turned to poetry. I had always written, but I had gone to art school throughout my teenage years and had attended the High School of Music and Art and was a pretty good painter. I think I retain a terrifically visual sense of the world. I think you can see the traces of the painting in my poetry.

CA: Yes. I've thought there was a connection between the painting and the imagery of the poetry.

Jong: I think it's there from *Fruits & Vegetables* to *Ordinary Miracles*, and it's certainly there in all my novels. My apprehension of the physical world is very visual. It's not rare, you know, for poets to be painters—E. E. Cummings, Alexander Pope, many poets have been painters throughout the history of English literature. In my case, I think the visual sense is very much there in my books. The *Fruits & Vegetables* poems certainly show it, and also the later poems.

I also think there's a frustrated travel writer in me longing to get out. You could almost make a compendium of travel writings out of my various novels. There are large sections in all five of them that deal with a sense of place: Wiltshire and Oxfordshire in *Fanny,* Connecticut in *Parachutes & Kisses,*

Vienna and Heidelberg in *Fear of Flying,* Venice in *Serenissima,* California and New York in *How To Save Your Own Life.* There's a great visual connection there, and I see it looking back on my own work. The painter in me is not dead, but she took another form.

CA: In "A Note from the Author" in *Ordinary Miracles,* you said that the poem is "as much a container of energy as the unsplit atom. Speaking the poem aloud should activate the energy in much the same way as splitting the atom activates nuclear force." Is speaking the poem aloud, hearing it as you make it, a central part of the writing?

Jong: After I've written a first draft of a poem, I read it aloud to myself as one of my ways of reworking it. I like giving public readings of my work, and I've just recorded all of *Serenissima* on cassettes. When I read a poem aloud to an audience, I feel I'm re-experiencing the creation of the poem. I am very aural, and the sound of a poem is very important to me. There are whole sections of my prose works also that scan in iambic meter. If you read aloud, as I often do when I go to universities, the section of *Fanny* in which Fanny is describing her pregnancy, you will find that it could be set as blank verse. I'm very aware of the rhythms of the writing. I think in *Serenissima* I succeeded better than in any other book in mingling the poet and the novelist completely. The rhythms of the language are of great importance to me.

CA: Do you think of yourself as a poet and a novelist equally?

Jong: I think of myself as a poet who stumbled into the habit of writing novels. But they use different muscles, really.

CA: *Fear of Flying* came out in 1973 and fell in perfectly with the burgeoning women's liberation movement. At the last count I saw—long ago—it had sold more than six million copies. Does it continue to attract new readers?

Jong: Yes. Teenagers all over the world read me. That book sold six million in the U.S. in the paperback version, and about ten million total around the world. This was not just a book, but a phenomenon, a force. It sold 600,000 copies in Italy alone and about the same in Japan. And these are little book markets. It really was an extraordinary best-seller, and it's been a kind of curse for me. It made me a household name in much of the world—including China and Russia, where the books aren't published!—and also typecast me in a way that I've been trying to get free of ever since. I'm enormously grateful to it, and yet very eager to be seen as a woman of letters and not just Erica "Zipless" Jong.

CA: Karen FitzGerald, writing for *Ms.,* said, "As a member of a generation fed on the melodramatic and farfetched plots of blockbuster miniseries
and evening soaps, I find this is all pretty tame stuff and I wonder what all
the fuss was about back in 1973." How do you feel about *Fear of Flying* in
that sense, looking back on it almost fifteen years later?

Jong: I forced myself to read the first three chapters not long ago. (It's
very hard for me to reread my books, because I rework them so endlessly
and read them aloud to myself and edit and revise so much that when I'm
done, I don't want to see the damn things again.) I think that judgment is
wrong. Reading those few chapters again recently, I was struck by their incredible chutzpah, by the fearlessness of a woman absolutely putting down
the contents of her brain. It was *not* the sex that was so fearless; it was her
telling the truth about men. It's what Muriel Rukeyser said in one of her
poems: if one woman were to tell the truth about her life, the world would
split open. That's what was radical about *Fear of Flying.* It was a woman
giving a no-holds-barred description of what was going on in her mind with
relation to husbands, lovers, fathers, mothers; and it still is shocking, even to
me. When I read it a few days ago, I thought, What a ballsy kid I was. How
did I *dare?* One of the reasons, I think, is that I didn't realize how cruel the
world was. I was very naive. I was fresh out of graduate school and I believed
that the word could change the world. I believed that books were instruments
of social change. I still do. And I wrote as if it was going to be overheard,
seen through a keyhole. I try always to write that way. I try never to think of
the marketplace or the audience, because I think the only value of being a
writer is to tell the truth. I think we live in a society where there's a mass
conspiracy for hypocrisy, where no one tells the truth. Politicians don't. People in corporations *can't*—they'll lose their jobs. Most people are bound to
the system in one way or another, so they self-censor because they're afraid
for their jobs, for their marriages, for their children. If writers don't tell the
truth, no one does.

CA: As reported by *Publishers Weekly,* you said at a National Book Critics
panel discussion entitled "A Decade of Change in American Letters" that
you saw a "greater emotional openness" and "more openness to writing by
women." Maybe the word *has* helped to change the world. Don't you feel
that *Fear of Flying* played a role in greater openness?

Jong: I think it made a tremendous difference. I think it opened doors for
women writers, and it opened doors for men writers. It opened doors for

people writing movies. I believe we accept a level of intimacy in writing now that we never accepted before. It's still very hard to write honestly and gutsily about your life. It doesn't get easier. What happens is that you develop a new form; you have the woman's confessional novel. And it's possible to do it honestly or to do it in a canned way. The most important thing about a book is whether or not it has the gift of life. Does it seem real? Does it seem like life, not literature? What was good about *Fear of Flying,* I think, was that it seemed like life, not like a book. That was why all the criticism it got, which was primarily that it was confessional, was almost a compliment.

CA: Will we see Isadora White Wing again?

Jong: She's fighting her way back through my unconscious, wrestling me to the ground. She's creeping into the book I'm writing now, as a minor character. She will not be ignored. I want no part of her—she's trouble—but she's going to get in there somehow. She's very difficult for me, because every time I publish an Isadora book, I get holy hell from everybody. It's a real gauntlet I have to run. But she is determined to come back, and I think she is stronger than I am.

CA: *Fanny* was a brave undertaking, using the form of the eighteenth-century picaresque novel. What were the toughest challenges?

Jong: The question was, could I get the language? Could I create a language that wasn't Fielding or Swift or Smollett, that had its own sound and evoked the eighteenth century and the balance and antithesis of the sentences. Those writers were all trained on Latin, so their sentences were Latinate. We've abandoned that in the last two hundred and fifty years. We write Hemingway sentences now. I had to go back to that rhythm of language, of a generation trained on the classics, on Horace and Catullus, and find a sentence that sounded eighteenth-century and yet was not a turn-off for the modern reader, that was fun to read and pulled you along. That was a terrific challenge. If I had done it in a dry-as-dust academic way, who would have read it but eighteenth-century scholars?

The form of the novel was clear. It was a picaresque, and an eighteenth-century picaresque has all its parameters given to you: the hero is an orphan who goes through the trials and tribulations of the Road of Life and tests herself or himself and winds up an heir to a great country house. The form is given. But I was both using the form and spoofing the form, and I was using the form in order to comment on the plight of women then and now. It was great fun. I never had more fun writing any book.

CA: Did the nonfiction book *Witches* grow directly from your research for the witches segment in *Fanny?*

Jong: Absolutely. I was left with all this fascination with that world, and I also had come, during the process of writing *Fanny,* to be a pagan. I had come to be a mother goddesss worshipper. And I had become a mother. I had become interested in matriarchal religion, and it had become absolutely clear to me that what was known as witchcraft in a pejorative sense was probably midwifery, white magic, herbal lore, and very healing pagan arts that were carried along in the countryside by women and passed from mother to daughter underneath a patriarchal culture. I still believe that—I believe it more than I did when I wrote *Witches*—and I wanted to write a book that would rehabilitate the witch. That book has had a kind of cult following. It's been reprinted, and it sells out every new printing. Every Halloween they repromote it. Although it was never promoted in a kind of best-seller fashion because it was published by an art-books publisher, and there were people who didn't even know it existed, it keeps on going. And I get very interesting mail about it, including letters from people who want to ban it as anti-Christian. Last year a school library in the Northeast took it off the shelves, and the Freedom to Read Committee of PEN took up the cause.

CA: You've become at least an unofficial spokesperson for women's concerns. How would you assess the progress of the current feminist movement, and what are your main worries for us?

Jong: I think we have an incomplete revolution. We have made things better for women in certain superficial ways, but we haven't changed the culture at its root. We have women editors-in-chief in publishing houses, we have women in movie studios—we have women in the communications industry with more clout than they ever had when I was in college or graduate school, or when I was starting out as a writer. We don't have women running Exxon, we don't have women enough in the Senate, and we are not near having a woman president in America. The real power is still the big bad boys. Even where women have entered the culture in middle management, and in upper management in the communications industry, we have women mimicking the male model in the boardroom—in other words, pretending that they don't have breasts and uteruses, dressing like men, behaving and acting on the male model. I think this is a mistake. What we need is women breast-feeding in the corporations. This will make people scream and say, "That's what we always suspected they wanted—breast-feeding in the boardroom!" But I mean it as a metaphor for feminizing our culture. For women to copy all that is the worst of the white male culture is no liberation. Interestingly enough, our culture is a de facto matriarchy and becoming more so, and one in which women and children are being penalized and impoverished by the white male culture. The nuclear family no longer exists in any great numbers. There are great numbers of single mothers raising children, and these mothers and children are sliding into poverty at an alarming rate. We have to go back to feminism and be more radical in the sense of looking at the roots of our culture and changing things there. I don't think that's being done.

CA: Don't you think many younger women are complacent about it all because they didn't have to fight for much of it?

Jong: They are complacent, but women get more radical with age. And until you're thirty-five and you have two babies and a husband who just left you for a twenty-five-year-old and is not paying child support, you're not truly radical *yet.* At that point, you get radical fast. That is going to happen to the Yuppie generation. They haven't hit it yet; they haven't hit the tough stuff.

CA: Now you're putting your art background to use in the novel in progress, according to the interview with Karen Burke. Can you talk about it?

Jong: The new novel is in a state of creative chaos at the moment. It is about an artist, the artist I might have become had I become an artist. But that's all I can say, because the more I talk about a book, the less I'm able to write it. Somehow, one defeats the other.

Erica Jong

Steve Kemper / 1990

From *The Hartford [Connecticut] Courant* (May 6, 1990). Reprinted with permission of Steve Kemper.

Steve Kemper: You've said that *Any Woman's Blues* was so hard to do that you aren't interested in writing another novel.

Erica Jong: I've always felt that way at the point of completing a novel—completely emptied out and exhausted. But I'm sure I'm going to write many more novels. I don't know that they will take quite the same form as the novels of the past.

SK: You experimented a little with this one.

EJ: The early drafts were far more experimental—very Nabokovian and deconstructionist and postmodernist. I cut the novel drastically because my storyteller's instinct told me, "Don't be so clever that you make the book a puzzle. People come to your books to save their lives. Don't turn off those readers who depend on you for the next stage of their journey."

SK: What's the lesson you're trying to give them here?

EJ: That the fate promised by our mothers—that if you didn't have a man you'd be dead and in despair—is *not* a fate worse than death, that you can find happiness if you like yourself, that it's better to be alone than in a bad relationship.

SK: Do you really think the main issues for women in the '80s were addiction to sex and problems with handling success?

EJ: Absolutely. As women get more freedom to go outside the home and earn a living, they discovered paradoxically that their problems were multiplied, not halved. They won the right to be eternally exhausted. And they found themselves atoning for doing things mommy and grandma didn't do by having abusive relationships with men who weren't worthy of them. I think that's why there's been this outpouring of identification with this book. I haven't seen that since *Fear of Flying*.

SK: The sex in the book seems different from that in the other Isadora books, and you wrote an essay in *Ms.*—

EJ: How do you think the sex is different?

SK: In *Fear of Flying* it was more of a happy experiment. Here it's more of a torment.

EJ: Sex is very dark in this book a lot of the time, yes. I think that the book is a mirror of the times. In the '60s and '70s, people saw sexual liberation as a panacea that was going to change the world—if we could have sexual liberation, that would bring political liberation and liberation of the soul. We discovered that sex could be liberation or bondage, depending on how we use it. Leila is in servitude to Dart and wants desperately to be free. She'd rather be celibate than be in servitude to someone who abuses her. I think that's where a lot of people found themselves, post-sexual revolution, so they identify with that very strongly.

SK: Leila is very self-obsessed, don't you think?

EJ: Well, she's a searcher, a quester. All of my heroines are. I don't see that as narcissistic, because I don't see that you can save the world unless you work on your own problems. It seems to me we need both.

SK: It's romantic melodrama in some ways. Leila often crumples to the floor, pounds her head on it, considers suicide, weeps a lot, and waits for her black knight. Were you using those conventions consciously?

EJ: I was just writing about the women I knew. I was also aware of the humor of it. I see these fabulous women who run a business, take charge of their lives, and boy are they idiotic where men are concerned. And I have been myself. Not now [she married for the fourth time last year], but I went through a period of incredible belated boy-craziness.

SK: Your books are often called autobiographical, and it sounds like you drew on yourself a lot for this one.

EJ: One always does, but people think that since you draw on your own emotional states, every incident or character in the book is true, and that's not true. I'm not into S&M, but if those chapters seem so real that people think all I do is kinky sex with black leather, so be it. I've lived with this for so long that I think it's funny at this point.

SK: You've complained in the past about being known mostly for *Fear of Flying* despite all the books since then. It sounds like you think this book will change that.

EJ: *Fear of Flying* was my first novel. It intersected with the times in a way that made it very famous. It sold 10 million copies. I think it reached the average person who doesn't read novels, and that is very rare. It seems to me that *Any Women's Blues* has a chance of doing that. It's been on every best-seller list across the country for the last month, and it's going on the [New York] *Times* list as of next Sunday [March 18] And it's still gaining force. That tells you it's a word-of-mouth book, so that leads me to believe it's another *Fear of Flying* in terms of hitting a nerve.

SK: The reviews I've seen haven't been very good; it sounds like the public's opinion differs from the reviewers'.

EJ: Always with my books—except for *Fanny*, which was treated as liter-ary masterpiece from the time it arrived on the scene. But all my novels are in print. My books have always gotten pretty rotten reviews when they've come out. I think that's an indication of being a pioneer. I used to go around gnashing my teeth for weeks, but now I have a bad day and then move on.

Interview with Erica Jong

Charlotte Templin / 1990

Printed with permission of Charlotte Templin. The interview was conducted by telephone in April and July of 1990.

Charlotte Templin: What is the story of the publication of *Fear of Flying*?

Erica Jong: When the book first went out to my publisher—Holt, at that time—I was a young poet who had published two volumes of poetry: *Fruits & Vegetables* and *Half Lives*, '71 and '73, respectively. I was a graduate student at Columbia, and I was teaching poetry at the 92nd Street Y in New York. I was thought of as a very literary young poet and in general as a literary creature around the New York poetry scene. *Fear of Flying*, when it first was seen in galleys, was therefore considered just as a literary first novel about a Barnard girl who wanted to be a poet. At Holt—although they loved the book—they never dreamed that it would become a worldwide bestseller. It was acquired for relatively little money, so all the self-fulfilling prophecies of publishing that go into effect when a book is acquired for a lot of money and predicted to be a "big book" did not go into effect. Those are just the ground rules. My advance on the hardcover was $15,000—the most money I had seen at the time. The book would normally have been published in such a small edition that it would most likely have been an invisible publication but for one fact: a woman editor at NAL [New American Library]—Elaine Koster—read the book in galleys, or in manuscript, and said, "This book is the story of my life."

CT: It sounds like a moment of serendipity.

EJ: Had we not been at a period in history when there were women editors in power, this wouldn't have happened. The book would have been published probably in an edition of 6,000 copies and vanished, I think. Elaine read it and said, "This book is the story of my life; it's the most honest book ever written by a woman"; and she forced the editor at Holt to print 30,000 hardback copies. That was part of the deal she made with him in negotiating the rights to the paperback. And she printed 100 copies of the galley—the advance reading copy—in addition to the rather small number of galleys that were going out. I know about all this, of course, because I was there and also

158

because I'm a mad book collector. That first galley with the green paper covers has become something of a collector's item, a bibliographical rarity. Elaine really believed in the book and gave it the added push.

CT: What were the responses of the first reviewers?

EJ: The initial reviews were mixed. In the *New York Times* I think Christopher Lehmann-Haupt reviewed it in conjunction with Jane Howard's *A Different Woman*, a nonfiction book, so that it was a joint review trying to yoke together a fiction and nonfiction book, sort of not understanding really what was new about *Fear of Flying*, but it wasn't negative, nor was it really very positive. Then there was a review in the *New York Times Book Review* around the time of publication written by a young man who had come on to me at a poetry reading and been rebuffed. I would ask, "How on *earth* does the *New York Times Book Review* find these enemies to review my books?" But they always do. They always find an interested party, often an interested party with a negative viewpoint.

CT: But the success of the book really did not depend on the reviewers.

EJ: No. Meanwhile the book had acquired a kind of word-of-mouth celebrity. It was disappearing from editors' desks. People kept stealing it to take it home, which is always the sign of a hot book. Editors, publicists, and other writers were dog-earing it and passing it along saying, "This is really something new; you've got to read this." So the "official" early response was lukewarm, but the underground response was hot. Somewhere along the line, about three months after publication, John Updike published a very important lead review in the *New Yorker* called "Jong Love," which positioned the book in I think an accurate way, saying, "This book is really more like *Catcher in the Rye* or *Portnoy's Complaint* than it is like all these trendy feminist novels; it's a *Bildungsroman* about a Jewish kid in New York lying on the analyst's couch revealing everything that's gone on inside her head, but the difference is, it's a woman's point of view." The Updike review turned things around critically, but by then the book was sold out. It kept hitting the bottom of the bestseller list and then going out of print for months and months. At that time the *New York Times* bestseller list only went to number ten, and it would get on at number eleven or barely cling on at number ten, and then go out of stock; they never printed enough. My editor, also the publisher and head of house, was fired by the conglomerate, and nobody was hired to take his place. I mean this is a horror story of publishing, really. For the first year I was developing an ulcer about all this stuff because there was nothing I could do to influence it.

CT: This is an amazing story.

EJ: Somewhere along the spring of that year I got a fabulous fan letter from none other than Henry Miller in Pacific Palisades, saying "Your book is incredible. Your book is the female *Tropic of Cancer*. It was pressed into my hands by a friend. I never read my contemporaries, but I read this. I think you're amazing. Let me do anything I can for you." And he began sending the book out to all the foreign publishers and translators he had all over the world, which was an incredible act of generosity and kindness and really began a great friendship between us. He published his response to *Fear of Flying* on the op ed page of the *New York Times*, and I published a brief piece about him opposite it. The Updike and Miller pieces really came too late to help the hardcover in a sense, but meanwhile a kind of grassroots thing was happening with the book. People were sharing it with their friends, saying, "This book is the story of my life. This is different, this is special, this is honest, this is funny." When I give college readings, people come up to me with tattered copies of the book—dog-eared, underlined—and they say, "This book was given to me by my aunt, by my mother, by my best friend, who said, 'You've got to read it.' I in turn gave it to this person and this person."

CT: When did the paperback come out?

EJ: In November of '74 NAL published the paperback. It was really the book everybody had heard of, but nobody could get a copy of. NAL promoted it very aggressively, which of course Holt had not. By then they had Updike's and Miller's reviews in hand. They knew that the book had a kind of vigorous life in it, despite the mixed opening reviews, and I had in my corner Koster, a woman of my generation, who felt this book was her life story. That made a great difference, as you can imagine.

CT: So the mass media didn't really have anything to do with the book's initial success?

EJ: The book sort of took off and sold three million copies in the first year without benefit of any media, because the media didn't want me until the book was number one on the bestseller list, about January of 1975. At that point, when the book was number one, they *all* wanted me on television, but before that, I was an unknown to them. In January of 1975 I did the *Today*

Show with Barbara Walters; I did *60 Minutes* with Henry [Miller] and Mike
Wallace and a couple of other shows, but there was no tour. They couldn't
have booked me on enough shows to make it worthwhile. The first year I
think the sales were about three million copies, but it just kept going like
wildfire, very much by word of mouth, woman to woman, man to woman,
woman to man, eventually selling six and one half million in the U.S. alone
and twelve and one half million around the world. As a point of comparison,
Catcher in the Rye has only three million in print as of today.

CT: And then very soon, your fame—your celebrity—precipitated a series
of attacks.

EJ: First we had a literary first novel that nobody wanted to promote because it was about a Barnard girl who wanted to be a writer, and supposedly
nobody would be interested; then we had a number one bestseller. At that
point everybody turned around and said, "She just wrote it to make money;
she *calculated* a sexy bestseller." There was a *whole wave of attacks*. By the
way, I have seen this happen with other writers. I saw it with Alex Haley's
Roots. First he had a book that was considered literary; then it became number one and gave birth to a big mini-series, and everybody turned about and
attacked him and said he had calculated it. Other African American writers
came out of the woodwork to accuse him of plagiarism. Envy took its toll.
It's a kind of cycle of American success: set you up, knock you down.

CT: You think it's a particularly American story.

EJ: It is particularly an American story. We pay such homage to the famous and we feel so humiliated by the homage that we pay that as soon as
we get a chance, we turn on them. I mean "we" loosely because I try not to
do that in my response to people, but the press tends to do that.

CT: How do you explain this phenomenon? The media make money from
it, I suppose.

EJ: My theory is this: they operate like a narcissistic personality, seeing
black or white, but no shades of gray. They're primarily interested in selling
newspapers or raising ratings, and they believe that only *adversarial* journalism sells. Black or white makes headlines and shades of gray do not.

CT: And then there is the need for a new and startling story every day.

EJ: Exactly. There is a constant need for a shocking news peg, so you're
assailed as being a hypocrite. She was a poet but now she's sold out, and

she's a pornographer. Nothing has changed; the book is the same, you are the same, but the news pegs need to shift.

CT: I want to ask you about the TV appearances you made after the book became well known. Were you one of the first literary celebrities to do the talk shows?

EJ: I don't know if I was one of the first, but I do remember that at the time I did it there were still a lot of writers who refused to. The feeling in the literary world was that you didn't *do* that—that it was sort of gauche, declassé. Remember that I was a snob myself. I came out of graduate school and out of the inbred poetry world. I had great inner conflicts about bestsellerdom myself. I was torn about doing TV, but when I saw how unfairly my work was treated in print media, I realized that I could be a good advocate of my work on television. When people saw me on television, they saw that I was a perfectly reasonable person, articulate and with a sense of humor, and they had a better take on who I was than if they just read the printed attacks. The printed attacks made me seem like some kind of valkyrie/gorgon/monster. People would meet me and say: "But you're so short" or "You're so *nice*," so I understood that the Erica Jong in the press was so far from who I was that I really *had* to go on television and be myself since I was very able to do it with ease and humor. I was so misinterpreted in the beginning—seen as a "mammoth pudenda" by Paul Theroux [in a review in the *New Statesman*]—that almost nothing I could do could make it worse, it seemed to me. It was *not* a situation in which you could keep silent. I envy writers like Pyncheon and Roth who can hide out and not advocate their own work, and I suppose if I had reviews like theirs I would do the same and write more books and probably be less interrupted by public life—which I truly *hate* being interrupted by. But since it fell to me to be a pioneer for women's sexuality, I really had no choice but to speak out.

CT: Can we go back to the point at which the media blitz began? In December of 1974 *Fear of Flying* came out in paperback, and that was a crucial moment.

EJ: That is absolutely the moment at which it all changes, December of '74. Because up until then the people at New American Library couldn't book me on anything because nobody knew or cared about this young poet, and then it all just shifted. It was like some kind of enormous object rolling down hill. I had no idea what was happening to me. Had I been able to manage it with the hindsight I have now, I would have done many things differently, but I had absolutely no idea what was going on. It is quite an astonishing experience for person to have.

CT: I just can't imagine suddenly being a celebrity. It must be incredible.

EJ: It has its funny aspects too, you know. Some of them still happen to me. I have a letter sitting on the dining room table downstairs from a Russian spy who is in a penitentiary, who has been locked away—he says by the CIA, or else he's a madman—since 1970, and he appealed to me to plead his case and get him out. There are letters like that that come into my mailbox addressed to Erica Jong in Western Connecticut, and the postman brings them—or the postwoman brings them. Sometimes there's stuff about people wanting your soiled underwear; long, unreadable manuscripts; people with obvious sexual dysfunctions and disorders. It's quite astonishing. You can be drowned by it for a period of time, and if you're a sensitive person you can really be thrown because some of these things are cries from the heart. You have to learn to deal with it. That part is really tough—to be reasonably kind and yet not exploited. And it's really hard if you don't have ice water in your veins, and you have a natural curiosity about people.

CT: My take on your reputation now is that you have a bifurcated image; on the one hand you have—and have had through the years—a reputation as a literary artist, but, on the other hand, there is an image of you as a mere pop artist, or even a kind of quasi-pornographer.

EJ: I think that is true, but I think the work is there. There are these six novels and seven books of poetry, a book on witches, and a book on Henry Miller. There's even a children's book. And I have written hundreds of literary essays in newspapers, magazines, literary quarterlies. It takes a lot for these to be overlooked, and they are overlooked. For example, how can somebody review *Any Woman's Blues* and fail to mention *Fanny Hackabout-Jones*, or *Fear of Flying*, or my books of poetry. *Fanny* had a front-page review in the *New York Times*. It is considered a very important book that reclaims the picaresque tradition for women. I don't want to trumpet my own work, but how can they review *Any Woman's Blues* and fail to look at the *body* of work? There has to be a strong animus for them to do that. Look at Norman Mailer, who is in some ways a very parallel figure to me. Like me, he's an activist, he stands for authors' rights, he was president of P.E.N. And when one of his books comes out, he is treated with respect, even if it is grudging at times. The other thing is that it seems to me that when men, important male writers, issue a book—when Kurt Vonnegut has a book or

Updike has a book or Mailer has a book—reviewers don't stoop in a certain way as they do with a woman. When Helen Vendler reviewed Seamus Heaney recently in the *New Yorker*, she said in her review, "Seamus Heaney is my colleague at Harvard." Well, I think that is honorable; that is disclosure of a personal relationship. People have personal feelings, but how do they act this out in public? The men have a men's club. Yes, they know each other, and women like Helen Vendler reviewing Seamus Heaney adhere to the male value, which is, "I will disclose that this person is my colleague, but I will bend over backwards to give an objective review." With women writers, they do just the *opposite*, utterly confident that no one will call them on it. A better example even than my raging reviews is Alfred Kazin attacking his former wife, Ann Birstein. They would never let a woman do that. So this is misogyny in action. There is a literary club, there are unspoken rules. Women don't benefit by them. And men writers don't get treated that well either. They are subject to envy and all kinds of unfairness, but the added element of misogyny is not there. They do protect each other.

CT: Virginia Woolf said in *A Room of One's Own* that male authors have to bear the indifference of the world, but women authors have to bear the hostility of the world.

EJ: It hasn't changed that much since her time, unfortunately. Where the male reviewers are concerned, the mean ones—that doesn't mean that there aren't some very generous ones, who have been generous to me in particular, like Miller and Burgess and Updike—there is a great deal of misogyny at play, but it is even worse in the case of the female reviewer. That's what I call the "harem syndrome." In these reviews a woman is acting out her token status, and she absorbs the dominant patriarchal negative view of women and exhibits it even more hatefully. She is really the "house nigger" in her reviewing, and so she will be even crueler to the woman who manifests humor, sexuality, lustiness—who blows the whistle on the men's club. This has been going on for the last twenty years in my reviews. And you will see it, oddly enough, from the point of view of the radical feminists, as well as from the point of view of the more conservative women, except in each case it takes a different form. The radical feminists used to get after me because I slept with men and wore lipstick and high heels, and I was not a good PC lesbian in overalls, which somehow I am supposed to be. Now they hate me because I am pro-free speech and against censorship. I also believe women and men have to find strategies to live together in equality. If I were a separatist, how

I could represent the lives of the majority of women whose main conflict is that they must live with men and children and also somehow fulfill themselves? Separatism is easy compared to the life of the average woman. I sympathize very much with gay rights, and I sympathize very much with lesbian rights, but I think the problems of a woman who lives in a separated culture are very different from the problems of a woman who lives with men and with children and yet has to find her own identity. This is the struggle that I chronicle in all my books. I often dream of going off to a women's colony and being a monastic, but, in fact, I don't write about that. There's too little conflict there.

CT: But there are also feminists who respond positively to your work. Some feminist academics claim your work for feminism, noting in your work comedy, irony, "criticism of life"—in other words, literary quality. It's related to who they are and the position from which they read your books. There was a feminist community involved in the reviewing of *Fear of Flying*, but they have sort of dropped out. I don't find the feminist community among the reviewers of your latest novel, *Any Woman's Blues*.

EJ: Well, look at what has *happened* between then and now. Early on you had people like Molly Haskell, Elizabeth Janeway, Hannah Greene, Lois Gould, Betty Friedan, Judy Blume, Norma Klein. Then feminism became established in the universities, and it was as a separatist brand of feminism, a very ideological brand of feminism, and those feminists had no use for my books because ideologically, my books were not "pure." My books did not toe the party line. They were full of the real ambivalence of life. I strongly believe that books which toe only one ideological party line will never survive—except in the history of agitprop. There is only one way to write truly about the human heart, and that is to be unsparingly honesty about what the human heart feels. If you are writing on behalf of a particular brand of feminism or communism or whatever, your books will soon be as dead as all those '30s novels that nobody reads now—except scholars of radical literature of the '30s. I think you can *only* write out of your feelings and never out of a political point of view, however much you may be a strong *intuitive* feminist. So there is absolutely no way I can please that faction. I can't write a book that Robin Morgan is going to say is ideologically correct, probably because it wouldn't be an enduring book.

CT: Can you comment on how the phrase "zipless fuck" has been taken up? Why did the phrase catch on and what has happened to it since it first appeared?

EJ: When I coined the phrase, it was a moment in history when women were discovering that they had the right to sex for pleasure only, that they didn't have to know the name of the person, that they could affirm their own potential sexually. There had not yet been a book that told them that. All the 19th-century books about women who reached out for sexual fulfillment condemned them to death—the Anna Karenina/Emma Bovary syndrome. In the 20th century, astonishingly enough, the same paradigm often holds. Look at the novels of a writer like Mary McCarthy; the sexual woman in every one of her books usually dies. Look at the ending of *A Charmed Life*; look at *The Group*. The most sexual woman in *The Group* is the first to die—in fact they all gather at her funeral. That archetype remained in force for well into the 20th century, even with feminist writers like Mary McCarthy. So *Fear of Flying* came along and said, "Here is a woman who reaches out for sexuality"—the fact is she screws up and finds a guy who is impotent and can't even do it, which is comic to me. But "here is a woman who reaches out for her sexual fulfillment and winds up in a bathtub being reborn." The archetype of the book is radical and "zipless fuck" embodies that archetype. It says, "You can have pleasure; sex is not so serious." And so it was a catch phrase that was needed at that moment in history. Having caught on, it went through a whole transformation into a pejorative. That's my analysis of it. What women won in the '70s was the right to their own pleasure, their own bodies, and *Fear of Flying* was the book that gave the voice to that quest, and so it fulfilled something in the culture—it struck a nerve. That phrase evoked the struggle for women's sexuality. So it entered the language.

CT: You have certainly managed to provoke a lot of negative reactions.

EJ: Well, I have pushed a lot of buttons—the uppity woman button, for one, the sexual woman button for another. And then the Jewish woman button. The most distressing surprise to me was the prevalence of anti-Semitism in literary culture. I think there is a kind of denigration of the Jewish Princess or wealthy New York Jewish woman. It's as if Jewish is identified with spoiled, overblown, tasteless, self-indulgent. There's a whole cluster of qualities that accrue to the Jewess, as one might satirically style her, as a literary archetype.

CT: What are the strategies by which a writer copes with a public reception of the type you have received? How does one manage not to react with bitterness?

EJ: I start each new book with a great load of despair. I have to go through

a psychological process even to get *started*. I have to say to myself, "Read
not the times but the eternities." I remind myself that Henry [Miller] couldn't
get his masterpiece, *The Colossus of Maroussi*, published. The only publisher
that would take it was Colt of San Francisco, a tiny press, and it's a great
novel. I stop reading newspapers when I write. I opt out of social life. And it
does get harder with each book. I'm proud of the fact that I wrote *Any Woman's Blues* with the same nakedness that I wrote *Fear of Flying*, as if no eyes
would ever see it. I wrote nakedly with the wind of inspiration at my back.
Then, of course, I did a lot of cutting and revising. My original impulse is
always to be as honest as possible. It's the only way to write, I think. After I
had gained fame, I had to create strategies in the self to go on writing in this
way. I have often wondered how these strategies are similar to those of male
writers and how they are dissimilar. What are the strategies others use? Go
to Italy, go to France, become an expatriate, live in Big Sur [like Miller],
don't go to New York cocktail parties. I want to go on; I want to mine this
talent before I die, so I can't think too much about the reception of my work.
In a way it's not my business. My business is to be as true as I can be to my
gift. *Any* Woman's Blues was rejected by many publishers because *Serenissima* hadn't sold as well as the rest of my books and because the S/M sections
scared people. (I was writing about S/M before it was chic.) Perhaps the title
of *Serenissima* baffled non-Italian speakers. Perhaps it was too precious for
a mass audience. But my main problem is how do I remain a survivor and
write honestly? I say, "I am writing this for me." I wrote all of *Any Woman's
Blues* without a contract. There is a story by I. B. Singer in which a writer is
condemned to hell. His punishment is to have to throw every page he writes
into the fiery pit. In many ways, women writers work under conditions like
these. It makes us spiritually strong—but how will the *next* generation of
women find our work so they can write out of a *female* tradition? Unfortunately, Woolf's *A Room of One's Own* is still as true today as it was in 1928.
We lack a women's tradition, yet we deliberately *destroy* our women pio-
neers. The great loss is to the coming generations of women who will think
themselves historyless, as before. In this sense, the women who have attacked
my work are the dupes of the patriarchy. Why, oh why do they think they are
striking a blow for freedom by attacking their sisters?

CT: Your third novel, *Fanny*, was highly praised. Do you think the feminist
message was more palatable by 1980 when *Fanny* was published?

EJ: No, palatable because it was in petticoats. It is a very radical book, but

I discovered that if you put people in costumes, it was more palatable. It is what the Soviet novelists did throughout the pre-glastnost period; they wrote about early Soviet history in order to disguise their material. Sometimes they wrote about the Roman Empire. But because I put everybody in eighteenth-century costumes and wigs, I was able to say very radical things and get away with it, and also the book was so obviously literary. I was doing this whole ventriloquist act throughout and writing in an 18th-century idiom. That made it more palatable, I think.

CT: What happened to the negotiations for the movie *Fanny*?

EJ: Fay Weldon wrote a script for *Fanny*, a brilliant script, which I helped to outline with her, along with the director. We became acquaintances through that and like each other a lot, and then we could never raise the money. We put together a production company, and we could not raise the money to make the movie. The rights reverted to me, and as you know, I'm now developing the book as a musical. The movie script, alas, is shelved. The movie rights may someday be acquired by somebody, and I'll look Fay up. So that's where it is.

CT: You have also written many magazine articles. Do editors suggest the subjects of articles?

EJ: Yes, they do. Editors of glossy magazines always call up and ask well-known writers, will you write about this or that. In the beginning when you first start to publish, you're flattered that they want you. I have done a lot of occasional journalism on that basis. I would say in the last two years I've stopped because I find the topics very trivial, and I don't want to bother with writing about "Is there sex after 40?" But I guess in the first two decades of my career I would in my optimistic way write for these glossy magazines thinking I could write something intelligent, and sometimes it would squeak through. Some of the magazines are better than others. *Elle*, for example, has a rather literary staff. And at the moment they are a very good place. If I wrote a piece about Virginia Woolf, they would publish it. This changes as the editors change. But in general I'm sort of bored to death with the slick magazines for women. They seem like advertising media pure and simple, and I don't write for them much anymore. But that's quite a recent decision. At any rate, in the early part of my career they would call me up and they would say, "Would you do this?" and I would do it and try to make it as intelligent as I could, given their parameters.

CT: Tell me about your work with the Authors Guild. I know that you are president of the Guild.

EJ: The Authors Guild is the oldest (it was founded in 1912) and probably the most distinguished professional organization of authors. We have about 7,000 members. It is not a cultural organization but a professional one. Our mandate is to protect the rights of authors, in other words to negotiate with publishers for a minimum contractual boilerplate. We go to Washington and lobby for fair tax treatment of authors. We did win the battle for fair tax treatment of authors two years ago under Bob Massie's presidency—Robert Massie, the historian. The new tax bill was going to make it impossible for us to average our research costs over the several years of writing a book, and they were going to make us only take deductions in the year the book was published. Many of us went to Washington—James Michener, Arthur Miller, Herman Wouk, a lot of people the senators and congress people knew—and explained that an author may take six years to write a book, so it makes no sense to tax the entire profit in one year. We won that battle.

We are at an absolute crisis point in history because we now have fewer and fewer major publishers. The contractual boilerplates in authors' contracts have gotten worse and worse and worse. We are in a situation where the average author has absolutely no bargaining power against the conglomerates. In fact the average author's editor has no bargaining power, so however close the relationship between author and editor, it is overridden by the relationship with the conglomerate, which can put these caveats about contractual boilerplate into action. And we are in the moment when we really have to act or we will lose all our rights. I think it is an enormously exciting time. I have been involved with the Authors Guild Council now since the '70s, but I always found it a very sleepy organization with the membership not really inclined to act. In the last two and three years, because of Bob Massie and a lot of younger writers joining the council—Susan Cheever, Jay McInerney, Mary Pope Osborne, the children's book writer, and others who are younger and activist—we really understand that we have to protect the rights of professional authors.

CT: And you hold an elective office?

EJ: I think I was elected because of my activist stand. Bob Massie had a very activist stand, and I think they were looking for someone to succeed him—he served two terms—who was equally activist. I hope that I can achieve all the things they want me to achieve. It's a tough time, but it is a critical time.

CT: Have you won any literary prizes?

EJ: There are a number of prizes. One is the Bess Hokin Prize, of *Poetry Magazine*, which Sylvia Plath also won. I won it in the early '70s. There was the [Alice Faye di Castagnolia] award of The Poetry Society of America. There was the Boarstone Mountain Award, also in the early '70s. Then something remarkable happened. I publish *Fear of Flying* and become the Madonna of my literary generation, and nobody reviews my poetry any more or gives it awards [laughter].

CT: Can you give me a thumbnail sketch of the success of the novels in terms of sales?

EJ: It's hard in a way because we're just now assembling this data. *How to Save Your Own Life* was a bestseller and probably around the world sold upwards of two and one half million copies. Ken, my husband, is tabulating all this on spread sheets. We'll know the figures eventually for each book, but he's not finished with this gigantic task. *Fanny* was a bestseller in all three editions in the states and was a bestseller in many other countries where it appeared. *Parachutes & Kisses* was a bestseller. They've all done remarkably well except *Serenissima*. The worldwide figures on *Serenissima* are about 500 or 600 thousand, which is considered a flop—which is sad, ridiculous, but there it is. I think *Serenissima* was poorly titled. And yet, it's been a very beloved book by a lot of people. If any other novelist had published these books that followed *Fear of Flying*, they would be considered quite successful. The first novel, which now stands at about twelve and one half million worldwide, is just being translated into Russian and Polish and Czech—now that Eastern Europe is opening up. When you have a first book like that, nothing you do afterwards is even seen as a success, numerically speaking. So that's my albatross. Sort of an interesting albatross. I mean it is what it is; it's been a blessing and it's been a curse.

That Mispronounced Poet: An Interview with Erica Jong

Charlotte Templin / 1991

From *The Boston Review* (March/April 1992), 5–8, 23, 29. Reprinted with permission of Charlotte Templin and *The Boston Review.* The interview was conducted on September 20, 1991, at Jong's home in New York City.

Charlotte Templin: I want to talk with you about your *Becoming Light: New and Selected Poems* [HarperCollins]. Given the difficulties that poetry is faced with today, you must be pleased to have this handsome volume—with the beautiful Mapplethorpe photograph on the dust jacket—coming out this fall.

Erica Jong: Indeed I am—because the difficulties for poetry are very real. In the last twenty years since I have been publishing—since 1971—poets have had a tougher and tougher time because general interest publishers mostly no longer *do* poetry. Harper does, Norton does, Knopf does, but most publishers don't. Morrow doesn't, Putnam doesn't, Simon and Shuster doesn't. All of the publishers who still do poetry generally do poetry because the poet is interesting for some other reason. Either they're movie stars like Ally Sheedy or Charlie Sheen, and publishers think they can market the books to kids, or the poets (like me, like Louise Erdrich) also write novels. Another example is Diane Ackerman. Her selected poems, *The Jaguar of Sweet Laughter*, is very interesting—but she wrote a best-selling nonfiction book for Random House, and she's a travel writer and a naturalist, and she's written a book on flying. So they take pity on us and do our poetry. The advance is tiny. One doesn't care. They don't advertise. They print as few copies as they can possibly get away with, but you feel very grateful to them for doing it at all. But whether anyone will ever see it in a bookstore is another matter. Poetry doesn't get any space at all in what is laughingly called "the real world." If you're a poet, you really have to start your own small press or ally yourself with a small press and print broadsides of your own work. And it has gotten worse. Twenty years ago, when my first book was published, there were *many* New York publishers who did poetry. Now we have to contend with the power of the conglomerates. Also unfortunately,

171

the news media and the magazines seem to conspire—of course they're owned by the same companies, conglomerates, usually—in pronouncing poetry not important. They actually ignore it.

CT: Poetry doesn't get reviewed much. The *New York Times Book Review* doesn't review poetry. Their very format excludes it—it's neither fiction nor nonfiction.

Jong: They don't review it, and if they do, they tend to review it very late and also in round-ups in which three books which don't have any connection are violently yoked together. I've written some of those reviews, and one feels such a despair as a reviewer having to make the connections between books that *have* no connection. You call your editor and say, "How can I put Eleanor Ross Taylor, Louise Clifton, and Maya Angelou all in the same review. And they say, "Oh, we're sorry; it's just space." Or else they'll do three black woman poets together, which I find offensive, or three women poets, which I also find offensive. I think the world of poetry is filled with self-fulfilling prophecies. People act as if poetry won't make it, and then of course it doesn't. I honestly think that if many people read poetry, they would find that it was quite life-changing, but they can't even find it. It's not in the bookstores; it's not in the review media.

CT: But there is the other world of poetry—the small presses and poetry reviews.

Jong: In that world poets read each other, and for the most part they hate each other cordially. The economic rewards are so minuscule, and the few grants and endowments are so small that it's quite a vicious world. I said to a friend of mine who is songwriter, "Why are songwriters so nice to each other?" and he said, "Because we're all so rich." I don't know if that's really true, but I think there is much more generosity among people who are well-taken-care-of financially. Not always, but often.

CT: By this measure, poets should rightfully be the nastiest of all.

Jong: They should, exactly [laughter], and often they are.

CT: The new poems in *Becoming Light* suggest that you have found a place of peace or a new way of being in the world.

Jong: I think this process of finding a kind of contemplative place was beginning in the metaphysical poems in *At the Edge of the Body*. That book deals very much with my practice of yoga and my experience of meditation—a process which is continuing. I came to a place in my life where I understood that there were really only two subjects in poetry—love and death—and that if you didn't confront your own mortality, you couldn't grow as a poet. My poetry has been very preoccupied with those things ever since I entered mid-life and certainly after I had a child. The relationship with my daughter has been, I would say, the most life-transforming experience I have had. But it has also pushed me to accept my own mortality. When you see the chain of flesh before you and after you, you have to accept mortality. But I think there has been a metaphysical dimension to my books from the beginning. The poets I loved as a college student—Blake, Keats—were most interested in those issues, and as I've gotten older, it's been a greater and greater preoccupation. Lately I've been rereading Aldous Huxley's work, in part because I'm struggling with a novel about the future; I've been reading Huxley's *Perennial Philosophy*. I also find this metaphysical dimension in Miller. Certainly it's in *Colossus at Maroussi*. I think if we don't come to a place where we give up preoccupation with the flesh and find the part in ourselves that is *beyond* time, we never truly grow up. We see a kind of infantilism in the people who are constantly fixing their faces, lifting their faces; we see it in the men who are obsessed with working out. I have a friend who was killed at the age of fifty. I have a poem about his death in *Becoming Light*.

CT: "The Color of Snow."

Jong: He died in perfect physical condition, skiing down a glacier in Canada, and the first thing his daughter said when she heard about it—and the first thing I said—was "David never wanted to grow old." I think our difficulty with confronting mortality is an important issue in our culture. In the next ten years it will become increasingly important because we all have aging parents. *Final Exit* [the Hemlock Society book] is now number one on the bestseller list. We need rituals for dying, ways of dealing with the AIDS crisis, and this is what the poet can deal with best.

CT: I sometimes think you have a Romantic conception of the poet —the poet as someone in touch with the divine.

Jong: I do really believe in what Whitman calls the divine *litteratus*—or the unacknowledged legislator of the human race. I do think of writing as a calling and not a trade. I recognize that it is *also* a trade. You can be a very good writer and also an entertainer in the way that Ken Follett is, and you can entertain on the very highest level. But the writer is also a shaman to the tribe.

CT: It has been said that every poet has only one poem. I think though that you have several: the love poem, the slave/prisoner poem (or the witch bewitching herself), the mother and/or daughter poem. Or are all these the same poem?

Jong: Your question interests me very much. It's wonderful when a reader looks at your work and sees categories because, of course, you never think of your own work in categories. I think the slave/prisoner poem is a very important part of my work, and it takes many forms. It seems to me the central issue of my life has been freedom: how do I get free from being the middle child—how do I get free from my older sister who was such a bully and a tyrant, but whom I adored. How do I get free from my mother? Then later in my life, how do I get free from this relationship in which I'm trapped? How do I get free from this sexual thrall to this man who's mistreating me? It is a very potent paradigm in my work; I think you're right. The witch who bewitches herself is also interesting and clearly there is a preoccupation with sorcery throughout my work. The subject of mother and daughter is fascinating to me because I always seem to have foreknown that I would work out my problems with my mother by being the mother of a daughter. There are prophetic things in the early books, which say "my daughter" fully ten years before Molly was conceived. There's this kind of foreknowledge in my life, and in a way, I've dealt in my relationship with Molly with the anger and trapped feeling that I had about my mother, and my relationship with my mother is utterly transformed now. There's no anger. My mother—who is now in her eightieth year and not terribly well—was sick this summer and while I was sitting with her in the hospital, we had conversations we never could have had before.

CT: Could you talk about "Lullabye to a Dybbuk," the title poem for the section of the new poems?

Jong: "Lullabye for a Dybbuk" nearly was the title of the whole book. It's a poem about letting go of the sexual demons that controlled my life at a certain point and letting go of the demon of anger and finding a calm place, finding the inner garden. I had to reach a certain point of calm in my own life. There was a turning point, and I've written about it through Leila's experience in *Any Woman's Blues*, and I've written about it through some of the new poems. The turning point in my life, as in Leila's, and for the narrator in these poems, was when I began to enjoy my own solitude. I would go up to the country and sit alone and read and walk and write. Having just come out of an abusive relationship, not so unlike the relationship in *Any Women's Blues*—although that one is an exaggerated version of it —I decided that if I never had another relationship with a man it wouldn't matter because I had found something inside myself that was so profoundly fulfilling that I could live by myself forever. It was a profound turning point, and even now, I am remarried, but, more than ever, I look forward to time alone. I think solitude is the gate to that place of calm.

CT: I think I recognize some of the experience behind the new poems as the same experience behind *Any Woman's Blues*. Do you sometimes treat the same experience comically in one medium and seriously in another?

Jong: Often.

CT: How does that work?

Jong: Often the poems precede the fiction. The poems that you are reading in *Becoming Light* (in the "Lullabye for a Dybbuk" section of new poems) are the poems that preceded my breaking through on *Any Woman's Blues*. It happens first in poetry—the poetry points the way. I submerge myself into the material in the poetry, and then I find a different form in the fiction. I can't really just crank out books in the way some writers can. It takes me about three years, and the next novel takes me to the next stage of my life. I envy those writers who are able to write more easily. I often wish I would invent a pseudonym like Amanda Cross and write in another genre when I'm not ready to write a big novel under my own name. For me a novel is a climbing up to another plateau, spiritually, and describing that climb and that plateau and pointing to the next.

CT: And what is the function of the poetry that comes before the novel?

Jong: The poetry is my way of exploring my own spiritual journey, and, I hope, the spiritual journey of the reader. It's my way of coming to terms with my own stages of evolution. I don't write poetry all the time. I write it in bursts, and then I may not write for two years. Poetry is not always given to me.

CT: Well, I've heard other poets say that, but some of them are not able to write in other forms in that blank space in between poetry.

Jong: I think that most poets wish that they could do something else— nonfiction, criticism. More and more poets are writing novels. It's a good thing because the language is always better when a poet is writing. It's staggering how many poets have become novelists—Graves, Joyce, Lawrence . . .

CT: Margaret Atwood, of course.

Jong: She's a very gifted writer. Joyce Carol Oates—poet and novelist; Robert Penn Warren—poet, novelist, also a rare critic.

CT: You are known as a writer who gave the subject of a woman's body a place in poetry (and the novel). But as a pioneer you have gotten a lot of flak.

Jong: People are squeamish and embarrassed about female anatomy. It's sad; it's misogyny in action.

CT: Yes, it's sad. Women's bodies are unmentionable.

Jong: Unmentionable, yes. Even by women themselves.

CT: And not a fit subject for literature.

Jong: Yes, unless idealized in a particular way by the yearning male. *Then* they become a fit subject. But if confronted by woman in a realistic way, not a fit subject. One of the feelings I used to have, particularly as a young writer, as a young poet, was that they had stolen our subject matter. Even our subject matter was not our own.

CT: A woman's body.

Jong: They were allowed to write about it, but we weren't.

CT: And where does that leave the women poet? It invites her to become an imitation male poet.

Jong: Which I was, early on. If you look at the early poems—some of which I have chosen to save, a lot of which I have thrown out—you will see that often they are written in a male voice. It's as if I am trying to create a composite of a male voice or a neuter voice because I believe the gender of the poet is male or because I am trying to please a prospective, non-existent, or projected editor. As a young poet I put myself into a male persona—unconsciously—because I believed that if I spoke as a woman *no one* would be interested! This is very telling. It bespeaks my generation. I took a modern poetry course at Barnard—a feminist college—and we didn't study a single woman poet. And we never asked why. A few years later, Barnard women *would* ask why. But I think it is shocking that my class didn't. Then ten years went by, and suddenly you could articulate the problem. In my early poems I was very influenced by my literary education. I wrote a whole mock epic, for example, and a mock 18th-century novel 20 years before I wrote *Fanny*.

CT: There is a poem in rhymed couplets among the early poems in your book: "To X. (With Ephemeral Kisses)."

Jong: That woman's point of view was very much derived from Dorothy Parker and Edna St. Vincent Millay—who deserve a revival. It was the brittle flapper of the twenties looking at life from a satirical female point of view. In my teens, when I was Molly's age, I was reading Parker and Millay. They were not considered kosher poets by the literary establishment, but I *died* for those poets. I read them over and over. Why? Because they wrote about a woman's subject matter and wrote wittily about it.

CT: To some degree they have been rehabilitated, at least in feminist circles.

Jong: To some degree. Not enough, I fear. Millay was one of the most successful poets who ever lived, and she's hardly taught today.

CT: She was very much dumped on by the New Critics.

Jong: She wrote as good Shakespearean sonnets as anybody. There's a lovely story in Margaret Mead's *Blackberry Winter* about her wanting to be a poet and about her admiration for Millay. Millay was an enormously influential poet in the '20s and '30s. It is truly frightening how many women poets have been buried.

CT: A few have survived as the chosen female poets in a male-dominated literary tradition.

Jong: Gertrude Stein, Marianne Moore, Elizabeth Bishop.

CT: Definitely Elizabeth Bishop.

Jong: I see a certain similarity in the chosen. They are women who have abjured their own sexuality in their writing and possibly also in their lives. They have chosen to write about non-female subjects, subjects that seem neutral—neutered or neutral. Or else they are aggressively lesbian in their stance—like Gertrude Stein. A man need not deal with his sexual feelings or possibly his revulsion against them. They have placed themselves outside the heterosexual. That in itself makes men more comfortable. Marianne Moore with her tricorns and her wispy white hair. But if a woman is shoving her uterus in their face—like Anne Sexton—*woe* to her critical reception. Men can't focus on sexuality *and* literature at the same time. The male inability to deal with sexuality and literature they then project onto women as a handicap for women. Now with Diane Middlebrook's book—and Sexton is safely dead a decade and a half—she has gone through purgatory. Even at the very end of her life with *The Awful Rowing Toward God* and the selected poems, which Diane Middlebrook edited, the reviews were horrific. You would not have believed it—in the last days of her life—I'm not speaking of her early books like *To Bedlam and Part Way Back*, before she became a literary figure, but she was very attacked, and attacked—I would say—*ad mulieram*, for her uterus—her persona—and then she fell into this kind of purgatory and nobody *literary* read her work though she continued to have fans among general readers. Now with Diane Middlebrook's biography and the controversy surrounding it—which I think is good for Anne's poetry—she'll be read and discussed again.

CT: Your novels have been widely reviewed, but this is not true of your poetry.

Jong: That simply has to do with the fact that poetry gets hind tit in the world. It would be true of *any* poet. With me there's another problem, which is that I'm not allowed to have two identities. I've not only had successful novels, but in *Fear of Flying* I wrote a novel which became part of the culture, part of people's youth. Sometimes people will come up to me and say, "I remember where I was when I read *Fear of Flying*. I was traveling through Europe; I had just met this Greek boy, and I was wondering whether or not to sleep with him, and then I read your book, and I did." And the unspoken (or sometimes spoken) coda is "And here you still are, embarrassing me." It's as if they want me to vanish because I intersected with their youth in a certain way. Not only am I not allowed to be a poet and a novelist, but I wrote a book that was sort of like *Catcher in the Rye* or *Lord of the Flies* in becoming part of everybody's initiation into life for a certain generation, and they'll never forgive me for it [laughter]. I have to go on from there in my own personal estimation of myself, but it's clear that I'll never be publicly forgiven. I could go to New Hampshire like Salinger and write manuscripts which are never published. Some people do that after writing a book like *Fear of Flying*—and they don't give interviews. They hide away, because it's really impossible to live with that monkey on your back. But that's my fate, and the thing that has saved me is my sense of humor about the world's standards. I think the world's standards are totally cockeyed, and I remain a shit disturber. If the world thinks it's right, it must be wrong because the world functions on hypocrisy and the buying and selling of people as commodities. So I've managed to survive my peculiar early success, but sometimes I have profound depressions about it.

CT: Well, we know that you have gotten a lot of media attention—it could even be said that in some sense you have been made a commodity—so perhaps you have every right to be pessimistic or to see the worst side of our media culture, our commercialized culture. First the media made you a star, and then, in typical fashion, they turned on you. Has the media attention also had a negative effect on how you are received as a poet?

Jong: Oh, absolutely. One is not allowed to be a poet and also known to a wide public. It's OK if you are white-haired and have one foot in the grave, as Frost was when he read a poem at Kennedy's inauguration. But until the age of 40 he was virtually unknown in this country; his first book was published in England. The fame the elderly Frost had is an OK kind of fame for a poet, but the kind of fame I've had is absolutely *verboten*.

CT: It's impossible to be a poet and a celebrity.

Jong: In America and England. Not in other cultures. Neruda was a diplomat and world-famous. The South American take on it is different. Neruda was a political leader, a leading Communist intellectual. I'm sure he was someone who could have filled a stadium. His *Twenty Poems of Love and a Song of Despair* was the best-selling poetry book of our time in Spanish. In South American culture, the poet may be visible and still be a poet. But our particular Anglo Saxon/American notion of the poet says that the poet must hide under a rock. I find it extremely ironic that our poet laureate—who is a very good poet—is Joseph Brodsky, who writes in Russian! Can't we find a poet laureate who writes in American English? We have such a funny hairshirt syndrome about what it means to be a poet in the Anglo Saxon world. We want our poets to suffer obscurity, poverty and neglect to make themselves worthy. The Canadians are rather better because they have gone through a convulsion of Canadian identity, and so they have turned to people like Robertson Davies and Margaret Atwood and Mordecai Richler and said: "Lead us to find our national identity." The Canadian writers who are our opposite numbers have been blessed by this state of affairs.

CT: Your poetry has sold well for poetry. How big do sales have to be to be considered good for poetry?

Jong: I have one book of poems that sold twenty or thirty thousand copies because it was a Book-of-the-Month Club alternate. On the heels of *Fear of Flying*, the Book-of-the-Month Club and the Quality Paperback Service dared to take on a book of poetry. Now they wouldn't, but the business has changed drastically for the worse as far as *belles lettres* is concerned, and certainly it has changed drastically for poetry because now a book that sells fifteen thousand copies, or even twenty or thirty, is a marginal book, whether a novel or a book of poems. All such books are being chopped. It's a shame but there's less and less room for even good-selling poetry, let alone best-selling poetry. The number-crunchers in the conglomerates don't want any books that don't make money. I think it's an abrogation of responsibility on the part of New York publishers, and that's the really bad thing that has happened as a result of consolidation and putting accountants at the helm instead of editors.

CT: Could we talk about the early days of your career? You got off to a strong start. Your first published in your twenties; you won prizes and published books with major publishers. Can you comment on those days?

Jong: Well, I remember publishing in the *Beloit Poetry Journal*, in *Poetry* magazine, and in *Epoch*, a quarterly published at Cornell. I published my first poem in a glossy magazine in *Mademoiselle*—like Plath. I won the Bess Hokin Prize of *Poetry* magazine—like Plath. And I had that quiet sort of reputation a young poet has. I read at the 92nd Street Y and taught poetry workshops there. I had a CAPS grant and a National Endowment grant. I remember going around to the parks to read my poems to try to turn the populace on to poetry. Four poets would go down; we would set up shaky sound equipment. We all had long hair, granny glasses, that sort of thing—and we would read poems to these perfectly indifferent people eating their lunches out of brown paper bags, and we would make speeches about how poetry was the most important thing in the world. It seems very sweet and touching now. I remember reading at Dr. Generosity's, a jazz club on the east side, with Yehudi Amihcai, the Israeli poet, and with others. I was a graduate student in eighteenth-century lit at Columbia and a teacher and poet. My career was progressing well in that I had published a first book, which was quite noticed and well-regarded, and I won some prizes; then I published a second book, which was possibly a miracle, and then I had this literary first novel about a Barnard girl who wanted to be a poet, and everybody who read it early on said, "It will sell about three thousand copies," and it was called *Fear of Flying*. And then my life changed.

CT: Everything changed.
Jong: And the retrospective estimation of my work also changed.

CT: So then you were found to be a commercial poet?
Jong: I battled for a year or more for people to take my novel seriously either commercially or critically. *Fear of Flying* kept going out of stock.

Then it was taken up by a woman editor at NAL who heavily involved herself in the marketing of the book, first sending out the galley proofs to people. Then the book began getting stolen from publishers' desks—the sign of a hot book. When the novel finally came out in paperback and sold those millions upon millions of copies, the estimation of the book changed and the estimation of me changed. I went from being this kosher younger poet to being this bawdy, uninhibited person, a figure that embodied all the gripes and grievances people had about the women's movement. I became the target and the embodiment. I remember once reading, "If the Erica Jongs of this world had their way, women would leave their husbands from California to Maine."

CT: You became feminism's symbol and then its scapegoat—which was perhaps inevitable or, at least, understandable.

Jong: It's understandable and, in retrospect, it's crystal-clear what happened. At the time, to the person living through it, it was like being in a washing machine with the wash, being tossed and catapulted around. It was certainly distressing.

CT: And, of course, that impinged on your career as a poet.

Jong: I went on writing poetry because I *had* to, but from the time that *Fear of Flying* became this great *succès de scandale*, and then sort of settled into its place as a novel about growing up, it has never been possible for me to rejoin the poetry world. *Loveroot* sold very well, but never again after *Fear of Flying* was I reviewed as a poet, with my poetry treated as poetry. Always, my life was reviewed—or the presumed scandalousness of my life was reviewed.

CT: There are often—perhaps always—extra-literary factors that affect the reception of a writer's work. That's something the critical community hasn't acknowledged. I'm sure it's always been that way; it's just a fact, but it seems in some cases in particular to have had very unfortunate consequences.

Jong: It makes the work unread by the people who would most understand and enjoy it. I can't tell you the number of times people have come up to me and said, "I had a resistance against reading your work because of what I read *about* it, and then I began to read it and it changed my life."

CT: A reader of the new volume is struck by how close you feel to some poets of the past—Keats, Neruda, Anne Sexton. Can you comment on this?

Jong: Keats was one of my first loves, and I think that what I loved about

Keats and still love about Keats is his amazing "rift of ore," to use one of his terms. He's an immensely touching figure both as a poet and a letter writer, and he's someone with whom I felt a major identification as a student and young poet. I continue to feel it today. I see a similarity between Keats and Neruda: Neruda is also a poet of visual images. Neruda takes French surrealism and appropriates it for America and makes it earthy and not so terribly French and intellectual. He takes all the lessons of the surrealists of the twentieth century and brings them to the New World. And I love him for that. I identify with his visual quality and with his pagan earthiness. I come from a family of painters; I started out to be a painter, and I think if you read my poetry you will see that there is something very painterly about it.

CT: Yes, beginning with *Fruits & Vegetables*.

Jong: They are the poems of a painter manqué, in some ways. They are sometimes still lifes, sometimes animated objects. Both Keats and Neruda are connected with that, and Sexton too. There's a great sensuality of the eye and of the mouth.

CT: What is poetry for?

Jong: Poetry for me is a way of coming to terms with our mortality and our essential humanness. For me, it's more allied with ritual and myth— religious ritual—than it is allied with social commentary. I see the poet in a shamanic role, as I've said. I think the poet is the one who says the incantation over the newborn baby, who cuts the umbilical cord, who says the incantation over the dead person, who wraps the corpse in swaddling clothes and who has the words that console and make clear to the hearers how we fit in this great line of life. The poet is the mediator between birth and death. The poet says the truth that you don't want to hear, the truth that you have to puzzle over. The poet is the divine fool. I don't see the poet as much as a social commentator as some do although inevitably many of the poems that I love *contain* social commentaries, as Neruda's poems do. Maybe because I also write fiction and essays, I have other forums for social critique.

CT: Would you like to teach again?

Jong: I'd like to teach, not even on the college level, but on the high school or primary school level, before kids get closed and self-conscious. I'd like to see a poetry revival. I think we kill creativity in our world. This is something that people who follow the Steiner or Montessori theory of education have observed for decades. We kill kids' creativity; we kill adults' creativity. We don't allow access to primary process; we don't allow access to the side of the self that dreams, creates, invents. I would like to go back to that self. Our crushing of poetry in the world is very much correlated with our stress on aggression, on war, on competition. Poets are the antennae of the race, as Pound said. Unfortunately poetry is so badly taught and people are so frightened of it that they don't realize that poetry is available to all of us and that it can save the dreamer in us all.

Better the Devil You Know: Talking about de Sade, Dworkin, and Miller with Erica Jong
Susie Bright / 1993

From Susie Bright's *Sexwise: America's Favorite X-rated Intellectual Does Dan Quayle, Catherine McKinnon, Stephen King, Camille Paglia, Nicholson Baker, Madonna, The Black Panthers and the GOP* (Pittsburgh: Cleis Press, 1995), 96–101. Originally published in the *San Francisco Review of Books* (May/June 1993). Reprinted with permission of Susie Bright. Bright is the author or editor of over twenty books, including *How to Write a Dirty Story, Full Exposure: Opening up to Sex and Creativity,* and *Best American Erotica.* Her web site is www.SUSIEBRIGHT.COM

Erica Jong's *The Devil at Large* concerns her literary relationship, affection for, and analysis of the prolific and notoriously censored Henry Miller. Miller first contacted Jong when he read her novel *Fear of Flying,* which he thought was marvelous. He wasn't the only one. I remember reading Jong's description of the "zipless fuck" and realizing that this was the dawn of the modern women's erotic novel.

Miller had something in common with Jong in terms of commanding simultaneous public disdain and admiration. I've had a bit part in that same scenario for the past few years, so I was eager to meet another woman who has made her name as an explicitly erotic and feminist author.

SB: I heard that you were on a panel in New York called "Is Sex Politically Correct?" What did you think of that title? What was the panel all about?

EJ: The panel was my invention. The title was my husband's. I've been incredibly dismayed over the last few years to find feminism increasingly identified with antisexuality, which is really an East Coast phenomenon more than a West Coast phenomenon—

SB: Why do you think that is?

EJ: It has to do with the baleful influence of Andrea Dworkin and Catharine MacKinnon, or their popularization. Andrea's a friend of mine and I have great empathy for her as a person. But feminism is seen by the East

Coast media as taking an antisex position. Maybe you're not aware of that here.

SB: Oh, of course we are, but when I travel to the East Coast the force of that opinion is bigger. On the West Coast, it's been a real tug of war, and I even believe that the pro-sex position has carried the day. But in terms of who gets published and who you find represented in the daily papers, it's the Dworkin-MacKinnon position that gets named as "feminist."

EJ: I'm very opposed to that because I feel that they are a tiny minority. Most feminists understand that the First Amendment is our tool. Most feminists would never have joined forces with the Meese commission, as they did. I think that was an incredibly naïve act, a crazy alliance of the evangelical right wing with the forces of Dworkin-MacKinnon. What could they have been thinking? Had they never read the history of censorship? Didn't they know that censorship is always used politically and that it is always used against dissidents? The first dissidents it's used against are sexual dissidents. You look at the Weimar Republic, you look at the rise of National Socialism, you look at censorship going back to Zola and D. H. Lawrence, and it is always about putting down the sexual dissident. So I think Andrea was hopelessly naïve.

SB: She hasn't changed her mind about it; she's not saying, "I was naïve."

EJ: Andrea and I just had a dialogue at the New School, as a matter of fact. It was called "Women on Women." What's interesting about our relationship is that we've agreed to disagree.

SB: That's amazing.

EJ: We have agreed to disagree in the name of sisterhood. We talked about the problem of violence against women in our culture and its relation to pornography, and we still don't agree. But the dialogue was respectful, smart; we dealt with her as a banned writer because she has been a banned writer, we dealt with me as a banned writer, we dealt with women working together, feminists of different stripes finding common ground, which I think is terribly important—

SB: If this is true, your dialogue is precedent-breaking. All the conversations between the radical sex and antiporn factions have been along the lines of the antiporn activists insisting, "You are a bad person, oppressing and demeaning women." And the equivalent reply of the radical sex wing has been to say, "You're a frigid cow." It's become stuck at that, as if we had nothing in common in terms of women's enpowerment. Instead, the debate has been so degrading—

EJ: Terribly degrading.

SB: . . . that when you tell me you've been able to have any kind of respectful discussion—

EJ: Well, there's a history with Andrea. I got very interested when I read her book *Intercourse,* which basically posits that all intercourse is rape. It's a brilliantly written book. I don't agree that all intercourse is rape, but I'm interested in her as a writer. The *Washington Post* called me up and wanted me to do an article on a writer who I felt had been banned, some subject that had not been written up, and I said, "I want to do a profile of Andrea Dworkin." So I wrote a profile of Andrea saying that I disagreed with her about certain things, but that I was even more appalled at the horrible way that she was trashed. And the *Washington Post* didn't run the piece.

So the article went begging. Eventually Andrea said, "Send it to *Ms.,*" and they took it. Since then, because I defended Andrea's right to publish, we became friends. We agreed to disagree about some of the things that we disagree about. I don't believe that pornography causes violence against women. But her points about the way women are treated in society, I agree with totally.

SB: Well, I defend her right to publish. Does that mean we could be friends, too?

EJ: She's a very bright woman.

SB: I know. That's obvious. I've read everything she's published. And I respect that she has the guts to go to the ends of an argument that most people stay liberal about. So much mealy-mouthed complaining about men is annoying. I always say, if you want a complete gender-based analysis of what's wrong with the world, read *Intercourse.*

EJ: I agree with you, and I think that's immensely salutary.

SB: She gets trashed for being like a dyke—

EJ: Fat, wearing overalls—

SB: She gets trashed for being butch, for looking like a bulldagger, and that's why the press is so horrified by what she has to say. Lots of people say horrifying, banal, oppressive, disgusting things, but they fit their gender role more suitably.

EJ: She doesn't conform.

SB: Yeah, exactly.

EJ: She doesn't conform, she has big boobs, she doesn't wear a bra. You know what she's really trashed for, it's the same thing Henry Miller was trashed for: she refuses not to be an anarchist. She maintains her anarchy even in dress. I'm enough of a '60s person to say I think that's fabulous. And the way she's been treated by the press shows me how superficial it is, how women are forced into a very narrow range of physical expression—so narrow, you're not allowed to look over thirty-five. You can walk around and way, "Yes, I'm fifty," as long as you don't look fifty, right?

The problem is, I think, that she's also a danger to the First Amendment. I don't think the ACLU is wrong to censure her for that.

SB: My biggest beef with Dworkin isn't that she assaults freedom of speech, but that she doesn't acknowledge her own fantasies. Why doesn't she come out of the closet as the reincarnation of the Marquis de Sade! When her novel *Ice and Fire* was released I said, "My god, this is the complete retelling of *Justine,* it's the modern day *Justine.* I'm gonna go get *Justine,* I'm gonna compare page for page—"

EJ: Did you write about it?

SB: Yes I did, it was just remarkable to me. If Andrea Dworkin wanted to write pornography, she could just blow everybody else out of the water. If she would take the sexual power that she fights against so much, and move it into her own erotic identify, she'd be unstoppable. My problem with Dworkin is a closet-case problem. So many women like her are overwhelmed by men's sexual aggression, brutality, violence, yet they refuse to acknowledge that women have that same dynamic in themselves—

EJ: You're absolutely right.

SB: . . . and that it's in all of us, and some women have it more than others who are more docile, more conventional. Dworkin is certainly not that.

EJ: It's unanalyzed. Totally unanalyzed. I think that's brilliant, and I think that *is* Andrea, but you know she had a pivotal experience during the '60s, during the protest against the Women's House of Detention in New York, when she was put in prison as a protester—

SB: You mean where she was strip-searched, and—
EJ: And raped.

SB: Yes, it's sickening.

EJ: And that has marked her entire identity about abuse of women. It's become her political theme. I wonder if it wouldn't have marked mine or yours as well.

SB: Look, the whole act of rape is the idea of crossing someone else's boundaries and doing what you will with them, with no compassion or feeling about they want. It's like, "I declare war on you, I don't care about you." That's what a rape is, but it also has different individual effects on people, depending on where they're coming from sexually. For a butch woman, which Andrea is, getting violated in that way takes on a meaning that it doesn't have for other kinds of women.

EJ: Why are you saying she's a butch woman? She lives with a man.

SB: I know. That doesn't—

EJ: He's a lovely man, by the way—

SB: I know. I don't care. To me, it's a butch-femme world. A lot of straight women are very butch to me.

EJ: Mmhm.

SB: It doesn't matter who she goes to bed with. But with a butch woman, it's really important not to make her feel like a girl, to make her effeminate. You cannot girly-ize her. When I fuck a butch, I can't insist that she respond like a girl with a capital G, or she will shut down. I can't get inside her no matter how much she wants to be fucked, no matter how much she wants to spread her legs for me.

EJ: Yeah . . .

SB: I have to respect her butch identity. When a woman like that gets assaulted by a man, there is not only the assault on the body—the lack of consent, and the general brutality of it—it's also that her sexual identity has been humiliated in a very profound kind of way.

EJ: That's fascinating.

SB: Obviously this is only my pop psychology speculation [*laughter*] about Dworkin, but it's the only way I can understand how she—

EJ: I'd love to see a dialogue between you and her. Wouldn't that be fascinating?

SB: She's the only other person I know who, as a tourist, goes to another country and looks for the pornography. When she went to Israel, she talked about looking for Holocaust pornography, that she saw it everywhere she went. I said that's just what *I* would be doing, but of course, we come to different conclusions about the same material.

EJ: What do you think of *Faut-il Brûler Sade? (Must One Burn Sade?)*

SB: I was thinking about it when I was reading your book on Henry Miller, because some hardcore people would accuse you of doing the exact same thing.

EJ: I was very aware of that.

SB: Her book was less defensive than yours because she wasn't faced with the same kind of fundamentalist feminist outcry.

EJ: For feminists to say, "You can't read Henry"—I mean, not even Kate Millett would say that. People popularize Kate by saying, "Let's burn Henry," which I think is an insane response to a book. Kate came to this event at the New School which Andrea and I attended, and she said, "I said years ago that I thought that Henry was a great writer. And everybody picked up on *Sexual Politics* and popularized the wrong thing about it."

The Story of O is another extraordinary book. I reread it once a year. It's such a turn-on to me. And I've tried to analyze why I find it so profoundly erotic. It's really a book about surrender.

SB: Maybe your answer is in that one word.

EJ: Surrender is the secret of everything. The secret of poetry, the secret of life, the secret of sex. You never learn anything unless you surrender yourself to it. People say to me, *"O is a sexist book,"* but I don't see it that way. I see it as a book about surrender—sexual surrender and every other kind of surrender.

My new book, *Fear of Fifty,* has a whole chapter of my erotic fantasies, about my sexual fantasies at different stages of my life . . . I don't care about the critics anymore. I have reached the point, hitting my fiftieth birthday, where everything terrible has been said about me, right? I can't lose. I'm no longer afraid. Can they say something worse than "She's a mammoth pudenda," which Paul Theroux said in the *New Statesman?*

SB: It's the worst insult, and yet, from the subversive point of view, it's wonderful. I mean, I would love to be called a massive pudenda.

EJ: That's why I quote it—

SB: "I control everything with my massive pudenda—"

EJ: I am the mother goddess.

SB: Yes!

Flying without Fear: Erica Jong's Feminist Fire Is Still Crackling

Viveka Vogel / 1994

From *Scanorama* (November 1994), 10–16. Reprinted with permission of Viveka Vogel.

Erica Jong has done it again. Her most ambitious book yet, *Fear of Fifty—A Midlife Memoir,* was published this autumn.

The irrepressible feminist started the new work on her own 50th birthday last year. "It is about everything," she says. "It's [my] generation told through my life." Above all, *Fear of Fifty* is the autobiography of an extraordinary woman: four marriages, Jewishness, poetry and novels, joys of motherhood and, most notoriously, female sexuality and its role in her creative life.

"My first novel was *Fear of Flying* and I hope that, by now, I have taught both myself and other women to fly," she says. "So I think the title *Fear of Fifty* is very appropriate. I write about the fact that society hates, truly hates, older women; . . . that the industrial world wants to put women back in the home; that women are, as always, an economic barometer of how things are in society; that social cutbacks usually hit women and children the hardest; and that things are worse than ever for women in the Third World."

Jong's new book is also an examination of what she calls the Whiplash Generation: "Raised to be Doris Day, traversing our twenties yearning to be Gloria Steinem, then doomed to raise our midlife daughters in the age of Nancy Reagan and Princess Di. Now, it's Hillary Rodham Clinton, thank goddess. But sexism, like athlete's foot, still flourishes in dark, moist places."

She says that by the time her first book of poems, *Fruits & Vegetables,* came out in 1971, the second wave of feminism had already begun. "Women were in again—and sex was in again," she says. "But not for long."

". . . I hate the American way of sex. One decade we pretend to fuck everyone, the next decade we pretend to be celibate. Never do we balance sex and celibacy . . . Never do we acknowledge that life itself is a mixture of sweets and bitters.

"Greedy for more and more life, we seldom appreciate what we have.

Many of my friends have become mothers in their forties and their babies are beautiful and smart. We have extended the limits of life, yet we dare to rage at growing old. It seems damned ungrateful. But then we baby-boomers are a damned ungrateful bunch. Nobody gave us limits. So we are good at squandering and complaining, bad at gratitude."

Among the classic Jongian aphorisms is the simple assertion: "Women are not gentlemen." An important theme in *Fear of Fifty* is the way that women, in particular, have seldom passed up an opportunity to take sides against her. "The diminution of women by women is taught everywhere," she says. "Women are not born knowing how to trash other women; they are carefully taught. They are taught there is only room for one token, one teacher's pet, one capo whose job it will be to show the nonexistence of discrimination." At the same time, "Women don't protect each other's pleasures. They have so few of their own, they want other women to suffer, too."

Jong recalls the hatred that came on the heels of *Fear of Flying*. "Women journalists who confessed deep identification in private would attack it in public, often using the very confidences they had extracted from me," she says. "The sense of betrayal was extreme. I felt more silenced by this than I ever did my male critics."

"When my last book was published, some middle-aged reviewer called me a middle-aged writer. She stopped short of calling me a middle-aged Jewish woman writer, though she was one herself. I thought a lot about the use of the epithet 'middle-aged' and why it bothered me so."

Jong wonders, as do some of her critics, whether she might be writing the same book over and over again: a book about women's right to play different roles, to be both body and intellect, to be taken seriously. "But, you know, no matter how many books I write, I will always be associated with *Fear of Flying,*" she says. "There's nothing wrong with that, but it would be fun if I got a little more attention for my poetry collections, or for my [last] book, about Henry Miller, *The Devil at Large.*" Miller and Jong became friends during the last years of his life; he once said to her that she was his female counterpart—a compliment she clearly treasures.

Fear of Flying, written in 1973, made Jong an overnight celebrity and became a milestone in feminist literature. It affirmed the idea of a woman's sexuality being as strong as a man's. The book has sold 10 million copies in over 20 languages. "I came along at the right time and was able to formulate myself in such a way that people could identify with what I said," she says.

Fear of Flying transformed its author into the champion of all women fighting for their right to sexual freedom and self-expression, and the sudden blaze of success and celebrity was almost too much for her to handle, an experience addressed in *How to Save Your Own Life* a few years later.

Today, Jong suggests, the feminist movement has reached a crossroads. "We need to take a new step forward, we need a new time when new thoughts can be assimilated," she says. "I believe that a great revolution will be required. Women aren't the only gender going through a transformation of roles; men have been asked to change everything about their lives, too. They are being asked to take care of babies and share responsibilities their mothers never prepared them for."

She defines a feminist as "a woman who has taken control of herself and who wishes other women would do the same," and considers it unfortunate that women with power seem to deny their femininity and become surrogate men: "Think of Margaret Thatcher. The third sex!" The Clintons, she says, have shown great understanding of women's position in America. "But the next election could spoil everything and bring us back to the reactionary period that Ronald Reagan represented, and that was torture for American women," she says.

Jong has always been a disciplined worker: her books include six best-selling novels, several prizewinning books of poetry, a book about witchcraft and one on children's experience of divorce.

She has also managed to fit four husbands into her life—and, of course, into her novels—plus a number of time-consuming and painful affairs, one of which is dissected in *Any Woman's Blues* (1991). Here, the author describes an obsession with a beautiful, manipulative, leather-clad man who gives her exquisite sex but little else.

Jong is unrepentant. "Think of all the great feminists who ran off with bad boys," she says. "The truth is that many very gifted women fall for total bastards. Look at some of history's most satirical and sarcastic women: George Sand, Mary Shelley, Mary Wollstonecraft." She adds: "Nice women are drawn to rule-breaking men because our female-goodness training is so absolute that we deeply need to find the suppressed part of ourselves: rebellion. We can't always break free alone—we need a man to cut the ribbon with us, if not for us."

Married for the fourth time, to Ken Burrows, Jong says: "I'll never divorce him—how can I, he's a divorce lawyer—but I may just shoot him! This is the way two people know they're mated."

Interview with Erica Jong

Charlotte Templin / 2001

Printed with permission of Charlotte Templin. The interview was conducted by mail from September 1999 to October 2001.

Charlotte Templin: One of the things I love about the novel *Inventing Memory* is the immigration story. It's the quintessential American story. Did you do research?

Erica Jong: I always do lots of research. It's a habit from graduate school I can't shake. I read lots of memoirs, many novels from the first generation of Eastern European Jewish American writers (i.e., Michael Gold, *Jews Without Money*). I used the database at YIVO (Institute for Jewish Research) to find unpublished memoirs and letters. I looked at YIVO's extensive photo archive of Eastern European schtetls and their inhabitants. I immersed myself in this material until I felt the pulse. But also I had my grandparents' stories in my cars. Since I grew up with them, I realized I had great riches on which to base the novel, but finding the form was a struggle. I also interviewed a cousin from the Mirsky side of my family, Sarah Sellin, who was born in Russia 90-something years ago and has a wonderful memory. She actually remembered leaving Russia by train though she was only five at the time.

CT: Which of the characters in *Inventing Memory* do you feel closest to? You seem to have a special affection for the first Sarah or Old Sarah—or perhaps you just inspired such affection in me.

EJ: I do love her best of the four heroines. I suspect it's because she's such an innocent—in a way like Fanny. She hasn't been made cynical yet. (Often in my novels, my heroines are consumed with the battle between cynicism and innocence, which they want to preserve even as the world attempts to beat it out of them). Old Sarah has many sources: my maternal grandfather, the painter Mirsky: the mother of a dear friend who claimed to be a follower of Emma Goldman; my own imaginative recreation of myself in other historical times. Every novel is a what-if. What if I had been born in my grandparents' generation rather than my own? How would I have fared?

CT: One of the things you explore is the attitude of those who left their homes and parents behind in the old country. I've tried to imagine what it

193

would be like to turn one's back on everything one knows. Old Sarah retains her strong feelings for her mother.

EJ: The immigrant generation idealized parents in the Old Country in part because they *were* so far away. Whether Jewish, Italian or Irish, they loved to wallow in crocodile tears about their little Mamas left at home. Songs were written to exploit this sentimental yearning. Of course it's easier to love a controlling, assertive mother from afar than from up close!

CT: What were the challenges of doing a multi-generational novel? Were you thinking of any novels as "models"?

EJ: I knew I did not want an omniscient narrative because I wanted to get inside each character's mind. Most generational novels are third person and I wanted the intimacy of first person. From the very start I imagined old Sarah telling her story into a tape recorder for a child or grandchild or great grandchild. But I wanted the other voices to be equally intimate and distinctive. It took me a while to come up with letters, interviews, other archival materials. I like this sort of reconstruction of a life. It's the ultimate postmodern narrative. The archive becomes a novel. But it's tricky. You don't want the reader to give up in frustration. You must shape the imaginary archive, make it accessible.

CT: I know you wrote about tracing your roots in *Parachutes & Kisses*. How is this novel different?

EJ: *Parachutes & Kisses* started out to be the story of my grandfather leaving Russia. I wasn't ready to write it yet, so I veered off into another story. *Inventing Memory* is the Russia to America story I had wanted to write, but, of course, I flipped genders for the protagonist.

CT: I take it your focus in the novel on women made that necessary. Was that hard to do?

EJ: I've wondered a lot about switching genders of a protagonist because it changes everything. Old Sarah is not really my grandfather but a new character. The best thing about writing is what happens without your conscious knowledge, the surprises created by imagination, in some ways I think gender doesn't matter at all (we are all mortal, we all fight against mortality) and in other ways it changes everything.

CT: I love the Jewish proverbs in the novel. Did you do research on that element of the novel. (I'm imagining your readers all over America repeating them, as I have. I love "You can't ride two horses with one behind.")

EJ: Some of them came from my family like the one you mention. The others were collected from books, interviews, and in some cases—yes!—invented by me. I love aphorisms as you know from my other books and I love inventing folk proverbs.

CT: The Holocaust section is very interesting. I don't recall anything like that in your previous fiction. Was it hard to write?

EJ: Very hard to write because one feels one has no right to write about the Holocaust. There are so many great Holocaust memoirs (Primo Levi is the greatest in my opinion). And even the poorly written ones have a kind of brave authenticity. But you cannot talk about the 20th century without mentioning the Holocaust or having some characters marked by it. And *Inventing Memory* is a novel about the 20th century. The Holocaust had to be there, just as the Blacklist had to be there.

CT: Memory is at the heart of the novel, but you suggest that memory is not a simple matter—certainly not for Jews.

EJ: Memory is at the heart of Jewishness as it must be for a people who endured despite the fact that they had no country for thousands of years. Memory is what gave us a country, a country of the heart. What the Jewish people have contributed to civilization is exactly this: memory as a moral compass, belief in unseen territories, belief in spirit. This was transmitted to early Christianity, which lost it in becoming a temporal power. Many people wonder if Jews can keep their special status as guardians of conscience, memory, law above land, while having their own country. This is the struggle in Israel today. We tend to hold the Jews to a higher standard than other people because of the spiritual and philosophical gifts Jews have given the world. Is this fair? Can countries preserve themselves territory and still be spiritual? That is the challenge for Israel today.

CT: The women in the novel are stronger than the men. Was that true of your portrayal from the inception of the novel?

EJ: I have known some strong men in my life—my maternal grandfather for example, my husband, Ken—but for some reason I believe it's my mission to create strong women characters. Perhaps I yearned for them as a young reader. Perhaps my unconscious really dictates to me in ways I'm unaware of.

CT: *Inventing Memory* contains a lot of narrative innovation: notes from fictional editor, journals. How does one decide how to tell a story?

EJ: For me this is the hardest part of writing fiction—finding the voices, finding the form. I find my way only by writing. All the thinking in the world cannot do it. I must take pen to paper. After about one hundred pages, I start to see the light. Until then, I'm desperate, sure the book will never work. I knew I wanted an archival novel—as if the reader went into a library and found the traces of her own history. But it was a mixed-up puzzle and she had to put it together.

CT: I like the famous people that turn up in the novel (as I loved the portrayals of Swift and others in *Fanny*). But this time the historical references are more serious. Do they anchor the story in reality?

EJ: *Inventing Memory* was meant to be a novel of the 20th century, told through the lives of women. The historical characters do anchor the century. Often they are also role models: Edith Wharton, Emma Goldman.

CT: What can the novel do that other forms of literature can't do?

EJ: The novel can mirror daily life in a way that other forms can not. Its very sprawlingness enables it to mirror the messiness of life. Poetry is much more distilled and deals with life in a mystic way. It's harder to get daily life in all its squalor into poems. I love *Don Juan* by Byron because it combines fiction and poetry. Wish I'd written it.

CT: I read recently that Jane Smiley tries to teach her writing students that readers need to be given some work to do. Is it hard to strike a balance between making a work readable and giving the reader work to do?

EJ: You want the reader to turn the page and be absorbed, but you also want the reader to learn something. At the same time you don't want to be obviously didactic. This makes for a difficult juggling act.

CT: I was drawn to your work because of the humor. Can you talk about how humor happens? Or how a joke happens?

EJ: Humor comes from speaking the unspeakable. It comes from liberty. Perhaps that's why women humorists are few. You have to expect to be misunderstood, possibly pilloried for mocking sacred cows.

CT: What writers do you think are funny?
EJ: Woody Allen, Philip Roth, Fay Weldon.

CT: Could you say what makes these creators of comedy stand out for you?
EJ: I admire Woody Allen for making a movie a year, rain or shine, box

office or not. His vision grows darker as he ages, but he sees through hypocrisy better than anyone. That's what I delight in with these three—they can penetrate the hypocrisy of our culture.

CT: Do you have any ideas about the source of your humor?

EJ: Like all humorists I'm a bit manic depressive. I deal with black depression through laughter.

CT: Of course the comic mode celebrates human resilience and endurance. It is based on the possibility of hope, some would say. Is this how you see the comic, or is something left out?

EJ: You are more likely to survive if you see life's frustrations as comic than if they sap all your strength and make you cry, "Oh woe is me." Laughter is a survival tool.

CT: Why do novelists choose painters for protagonists?

EJ: You want an objective correlative for writing but you can't always write about writers. The painter also works alone, is self-starting, self-judging. In my case, I started to *be* a painter and many members of my family painted. So the smells of studios and the passions of painters were familiar to me.

CT: What's important about your relation to painters and painting?

EJ: My early training in painting makes me a good observer. Color is important in my books. I tend to think in images.

CT: I suppose that is what one would expect of a poet and painter manqué. Were there some strong images that started *Inventing Memory* for you?

EJ: The whole book started for me with the image of the baby smothered during a pogrom. That's really where I started.

CT: You made the comment in an early interview that self-consciousness is the enemy of art. Is it harder to avoid self-consciousness as you get older?

EJ: YES! Doris Lessing said somewhere "a reputation is a death mask." People think they know your limitations and that can be discouraging. You want to break limitations—or why write?

CT: Does writing become easier as time passes?

EJ: Actual writing becomes harder as time passes. You know all your own quirks and flaws, the self-consciousness is greater, and it's less comforting to know that books change the world only in the most indirect ways. All this makes writing harder and harder.

CT: Does maturity help the writer bare the soul—defeat those inside and outside sources of censorship?

EJ: Maturity can only help in this sense: you say to yourself, "It's only a damned book!"

CT: Which of your works gave you the most trouble to write?

EJ: *Any Woman's Blues* was excruciating because I had to confront my own addictive behavior.

CT: Have you ever tried writing short stories?

EJ: I've tried writing short stories, but they either turn into poems or novels.

CT: I understand there are some writers who never reread their works (the late John Cheever, Mavis Gallant). How do you feel about rereading your works?

EJ: Sometimes I reread my work and think I am absolutely brilliant, but it doesn't seem like I wrote it.

CT: Is Fanny still your favorite character, as you have told past interviewers?

EJ: I still like Fanny but I like Sarah too.

CT: The two of them have something in common. They are probably your strongest women characters. And they are both very funny.

EJ: I like to imagine women who are not crushed by the things that would crush most people.

CT: You have written about fame in an article in *Mirabella* (August 1999). As you look back on a life as a famous person, would you say fame has been a good thing?

EJ: It gives you access—as I say in *Mirabella*—but it is also a trap. You are seen as the sum total of all the erroneous things written about you!

CT: Have you made your peace with reviewers? Do you read reviews of your work?

EJ: I try never to read reviews, but people quote them to me. Espccially the mean ones.

CT: What do you think of the state of book reviewing today?

EJ: The state of book reviewing today is appalling. Most reviewers never even read the book. They don't have to; they already know what they think of the writer.

CT: Why do you write articles? What are the satisfactions?

EJ: I write articles to avoid writing novels, to have the satisfaction of finishing something short when I am struck between books and terrified of plunging in. I write nonfiction because, despite my feeling that poetry and fiction matter more and last longer, I do feel involved with my world and do feel I can change people's minds by clear and rational argument. I studied eighteenth-century English lit in graduate school, and I was always drawn to Swift's satirical writing. I also adored Byron and George Bernard Shaw as a young writer—so I must confess to a polemical streak. Also I always had the ideal of the woman of letters in mind—antique and outmoded though it may be. Many of my favorite writers wrote in various forms and saw nothing odd about it. Today we mistrust the generalist, applaud only the specialist—but it wasn't always so. Pope translated Homer, also wrote contemporary satires and songs. Swift wrote prose and poetry. In our day Anthony Burgess wrote novels, operas, films, poems, composed music, wrote nonfiction on Shakespeare, on language and a host of other subjects. Mary McCarthy wrote fiction and nonfiction and criticism. So did Robertson Davies—who started as a actor. Updike writes in many forms. So do Margaret Atwood, Gunther Grass, many others. In America, I feel our over-specialization has diminished us culturally. Many ages—Elizabeth the I's England, Sappho's archaic Greece—celebrated the amateur, the generalist, the politician who could also write poems and compose music. That's an ideal I admire.

CT: The world has changed greatly since you published *Fear of Flying*. Do you feel you have been let off the hook?

EJ: Not really. My reputation is in a time warp even as the freedom I claimed has been claimed by many, many younger writers. I hope that will change eventually.

CT: As a mother yourself, you certainly brought important personal experience to *Inventing Memory*. Has your relationship with your daughter helped you be a better novelist?

EJ: My relationship with Molly has crept into all my writing. It's the most profoundly transformative experience of my life.

CT: I understand that your daughter Molly has also become a novelist [Molly Jong-Fast's novel, *Normal Girl*, was published in 2000 by Villard Books]. How do you feel about that?

EJ: I'm worried for her. It's such a tough gig. Nobody gets the sort of personal attack reserved for women writers. And it's so insecure financially—feast or famine.

CT: As you look back on your career up to this point, what would you say have been the satisfactions? Do you have any regrets?

EJ: My regret is that I've allowed myself to be depressed by the response to my work. I wish I could isolate myself from the trap of caring. There have been books I've given up because of despair. I wish I could be more indifferent to the fate of my books in the world. Self-censorship is any writer's greatest enemy.

CT: Can you say something about your response as a writer. to the September 11 attack on the Trade Center?

EJ: We were all in shock for days. Each of us had a kind of waxworks expression. The real shock was that war had come to our shores. We couldn't believe it. It's as if God had promised us immunity. All those towers pointing to the sky. Would we have built them so tall if we believed we were vulnerable? New Yorkers believe themselves entitled to celestial views if they can afford them. Celestial views don't credit the possibility of terrorism. Last spring there was an earthquake under the East River that shook the apartment tower in which I live. Looking back, it now seems like an omen. There's an insouciance about New Yorkers that measured Europeans adore. It comes from living in a country that has never been ravaged by war and doesn't believe war can cross the Atlantic. On September 11, we lost this insouciance. We will never be the same. We have joined the vulnerable human race.

CT: Do you think Americans will be able to change their attitudes?

EJ: I'm not sure Americans are capable of changing attitudes. Between our worship of the bottom line and our Frank Sinatra-esque I've-gotta-be-me religion of narcissism, we simply fail to understand how easily our security is breached. We expect to win because we've always won. We resist becoming paranoid. But paranoia may be necessary in a world of terrorism. What strikes me increasingly as September 11 recedes is that the al-Qaida terrorists are better chess players than we are. We have to start thinking several chess moves ahead. That's our greatest challenge.

CT: Has the tragedy changed New Yorkers?

EJ: New Yorkers have been positively benevolent to each other. Our normal love-hate relationship to our city has become all love all the time. The city is hugging itself to its own wounded bosom. We are licking each other's wounds rather than rubbing salt in as you'd expect New Yorkers to do. Here is the strangest thing about New York. New Yorkers really love their exuberantly disgusting city. We have taken this direct hit on our island as if it were a direct hit on our hearts. Even as lower Manhattan was cordoned off, forbidden, declared dangerous, many of us could not resist sneaking into the war zone to see the huge craters, the mountains of rubble with our own stinging eyes. It was as if we needed proof that this was not just another disaster movie. It was far worse than television had foretold. Dust still hung in the air and the smell of burning was infernal. The sky was dark. The rescue workers still looked ghostly behind their masks. Their hands and faces were powdered gray with gypsum and asbestos. They were breathing in the poison as they passed buckets of debris to each other, buckets containing pulverized building material, twisted metal, the odd high-heeled shoe. I thought of those writhing figures trapped by molten lava in Pompeii. I thought of the firebombing of Dresden, of Hiroshima and Nagasaki. Here too, people had been vaporized and would never be found. Their relatives would wander from hospital to hospital, from morgue to morgue and finally go home not quite knowing how to grieve. The firefighters and police would stop searching for human remains only when exhaustion felled them. Suddenly it seemed obscene to be one of the lucky ones who was spared. I wanted to crawl into the rubble and start sifting through it myself to prove I was a real New Yorker. I wanted to travel into the rubble and find a survivor or disappear. I wanted to slip my feet into those odd, orphaned shoes. For years I have watched disasters on television without really understanding disaster. Now Vietnam, Rwanda, and Bosnia are under my skin. New York's terrible rubble is a part of me. This dust is mine. As it sifts through my fingers, I know I am going to die.

CT: How might you be different as you sit down at your desk to write your next work?

EJ: It takes a little time to integrate these feelings into the next work—but some of them are inevitably creeping into the novel I'm writing about Sappho. I'm very aware that germ warfare has been used since ancient times, that human destructiveness is far from new, that regimes that oppress women always prefigure other sorts of fascism and cruelty. Like the Taliban, the ancient world was a world of slavery and the oppression of women. The idea of religious freedom is a modern notion, and it is always in danger of being withdrawn by the fanatics. More and more I see how much in our society is worth defending. We have an imperfect society, and I've enjoyed being its satirist and gadfly, but we can never forget that our society was founded on great Enlightenment ideals of liberty, justice and the separation of church and state. These things are well worth defending.

Index

2 3/69